THE SCARECROW AUTHOR BIBLIOGRAPHIES

V.S. NAIPAUL:

a
selective
bibliography
with annotations,
1957-1987

by KELVIN JARVIS

Scarecrow Author Bibliographies, No. 83

The Scarecrow Press, Inc.
Metuchen, N.J., & London
1989

British Library Cataloguing-in-Publication data available

Library of Congress Cataloging-in-Publication Data

Jarvis, Kelvin.
    V. S. Naipaul : a selective bibliography with annotations,
1957-1987 / by Kelvin Jarvis.
        p.   cm. -- (Scarecrow author bibliographies ; no. 83)
    Includes indexes.
    ISBN 0-8108-2190-7
    1. Naipaul, V. S. (Viviadhar Surajprasad), 1932-   --Bibli-
ography. I. Title. II. Series.
Z8610.37.J37   1989
[PR9272.9.N32]
016.823'914--dc20   89-10057

To My Mother, Wife,

and Son

CONTENTS

FOREWORD

All of us, when young, should have a chance to dream.
Mine came in 1958 in Trinidad, where, as an Englishman wed
to a Mid-Westerner, I had just started married life, on the
strength of a job as librarian of San Fernando and South
Trinidad in the Central Library Services of Trinidad and Tobago. In Trinidad, it seemed, the old order had been routed
two years earlier with the electoral victory of Eric Williams'
new People's National Movement. A few months before, a
still youthful Princess Margaret had come to open the first
Parliament of the West Indies Federation (my library had been
hurriedly repainted before Her Royal Highness would see it
as her motorcade passed the top of Harris Promenade). To
the North, Castro was poised to liberate Havana. Across the
Atlantic, Nkrumah was leading Black Africa into independence.
And to the south, Kubitchek was taking a euphoric Brazil
along an audacious path of developmental nationalism, building in the process a complete new capital in the wilderness
of southern Goyaz, to free the country from the baleful influence of its sybaritic ocean coast.

And all this revolutionary change was finding its West
Indian literary expression in the outburst of an exciting new
galaxy of national writers. The popularity rating of the
leaders among library patrons was, as I now recall, Naipaul,
Mittleholzer, Selvon, Reid, Walcott and George Lamming in
that order, even though, at that time (March 1958), only the
very first Naipaul book (Mystic Masseur) had come out. I
count myself singularly fortunate in having gotten to know
Trinidad simultaneously through my own direct experience
and by reading Naipaul.

I returned briefly to England, to cheap lodging in Earl's Court, just in time for Mr. Stone and the Knights Companion, and I read the magnificent House for Mr. Biswas just after my father died. I have never yet returned to Trinidad, but have watched the break-up of Federation, the slow decline and fall of P.N.M., and the bitter tragedy of Grenada from afar: from Franco's Spain, Salazar's Portugal, Medici's Brazil, Thatcher's Britain, and Reagan's America. The rollicking fun of Suffrage of Elvira is no longer so much to my taste, nor is it to Naipaul's. The world seems more and more to resemble rather that of Guerrillas and A Bend in the River. I grow old and nostalgic and preoccupied in planning my retirement to the English countryside. And along comes Naipaul with The Enigma of Arrival....

I plead total bias. But even readers whose approach to Naipaul is more objective, or even perhaps antagonistic, will appreciate and profit from Kelvin Jarvis's meticulous work in this bibliography.

Laurence Hallewell
University of Minnesota

PREFACE

The major West Indian writers of the 1950's produced
a sizeable body of literature which has, in its turn, generated
a growing corpus of critical commentary in the West Indies,
countries of the Commonwealth of English-speaking nations
where West Indian literature is studied, and more recently
in North America where the literature is variously located in
Afro-American, Caribbean or Latin-American studies.

While it is barely possible for one to keep track of
such criticism on West Indian literature as is being produced
in one's area, it now requires the expert bibliographer to
keep the student or enthusiast abreast of what is being written in various parts of the world, said at those proliferating
conferences whose theme is usually the hopelessness of the
Caribbean, or locked up in the reserve collections of various
libraries.

It is in this light that one welcomes Kelvin Jarvis's
comprehensive bibliography on V. S. Naipaul, who is easily
the most controversial of contemporary West Indian writers,
and the one who is most discussed at home and abroad. The
bibliography sensibly groups the essays, interviews and full-
length studies into separate categories, and provides, in addition, helpful abstracts of the content of major articles. The
bibliography is prefaced by an introduction, in which the major trends in Naipaul's criticism are identified.

This bibliography facilitates the researcher in deter-
mining the dominant trends in Naipaul's criticism, e.g., the
notion that writers in the Caribbean are "envious" of Naipaul's talent and success and hence given to harsh criticism
of his work, becomes a questionable one when it is recognized

that critics from India, Islamic countries and North America
have sometimes been saying similar things.

It enables the reader to classify not only the criticism
but the critics, and illustrates the importance of Naipaul as
a writer who, whatever the topic, cannot be ignored.

This bibliography is a rigorous piece of research, which
is most necessary at this time, and will help the researcher,
even as it humbles by its illumination of those vast areas of
Naipaul commentary of whose existence he was ignorant.

Gordon Rohlehr
Professor of West Indian Lit-
    erature
Department of English
University of the West Indies
St. Augustine, Trinidad

INTRODUCTION

The critical responses to V. S. Naipaul's work continue to increase rapidly. This publication aims to control the literature bibliographically and expand its critical coverage, thereby fulfilling a need of the university student and the general reader interested in the study and promotion of Commonwealth Caribbean literature. Systematic documentation of the literature is also necessary to reinforce the work of researchers and curriculum planners. An annotated listing is all the more important, given the range of materials available and the difficulty in locating existing sources on Naipaul. The bibliography attempts also to reflect the versatility of his style and his experimentation with literary forms, as it focuses on the range of reactions to his writings.

EXISTING BIBLIOGRAPHIES

Bibliographies have appeared during the past decade with varying degrees of coverage relating to Naipaul; none are of book length. These publications are listed in section III C of the bibliography.

Since 1975 Commonwealth Caribbean countries have produced national bibliographies, and it is now also possible to trace regional publications from 1977 on a wider geographic scale through the Caricom Bibliography. During this period Carindex: Social Sciences and Humanities also appeared. It has greatly assisted in recording Caribbean literary criticism from the diversity of Caribbean "little magazines," and also remains the single published source for locating newspaper articles in the region, despite the serious publication delays it experiences. Hispanic American Periodicals Index (HAPI)

indexes only a few of the more prominent Caribbean journals.
Caribbean Studies, Caribbean Review, Caribbean Studies:
Accessions Bulletin, and regional newspapers remain some of
the more constant sources for identifying current Caribbean
literary citations. Abstracts of English Studies introduced
a section on Commonwealth literature in 1969. Robert Ney-
meyer and Alvona Alleyne's Bibliography of the English-
Speaking Caribbean (1979) and The MLA International Bibliography (which since 1981 has included a section on English
Caribbean Literature) are all specialized publications that
have provided valuable leads in tracing some of the critical
studies on Naipaul.

A large proportion of unpublished bibliographic sources
for the study of Caribbean literature in English exists in the
area. Much of this undetected material has resulted in some
duplication of research, time, and human resources. S. S.
Bandara's A Survey of Bibliographies of Caribbean Literature
in English (1982) provides a platform for further bibliographic
control of the literature in the field. In a paper addressing
the subject of bibliography of English-language Caribbean
literature, Valerie Bloomfield pointed out in 1979 the need for
union lists on a country or subject basis, since the greatest
problems are experienced in tracing holdings and locating relevant titles. A more elaborate tool to appear is Alma Jordan
and Barbara Comissiong's The English-Speaking Caribbean:
A Bibliography of Bibliographies (1984). This publication
fulfills a need of the type Bloomfield has been advocating.

SCOPE

The guidelines used to determine the inclusion of materials are critical excellence, objectivity, regional bias, thematic study, and literary appreciation. The bibliography
emphasizes American, British, Canadian, and Caribbean
sources. Naipaul wrote a substantial body of reviews for the
New Statesman; from that number only those items he selected for publication in The Overcrowded Barracoon or those
bearing his responses to other Caribbean writers have been
included. Contributions by West Indian scholars and critics
to foreign journals, and papers presented on him from the
published proceedings of Commonwealth conferences are included. When a special issue of a journal is published, the
entire contents of that journal are listed. Fourteen of his

books have been translated and published in sixteen languages; these translations are included in the bibliography. In a Free State has been translated into eleven languages, Guerrillas into ten, and A Bend in the River, eight. No fewer than fifty post-graduate theses have been accepted on V. S. Naipaul between 1966 and 1986 at British and North American universities, and at The University of the West Indies.

Foreign-language reviews and criticism, works that address the West Indies generally with passing references to Naipaul, and brief notices have been excluded. Newspapers as a source for reviews are treated discriminatingly. Edited transcripts of conversations with Naipaul and personal interviews about his life and work are all grouped under interviews.

Many of the theses and critical articles are written from a thematic viewpoint, and except for literary appreciation, the other guidelines are more abstract and harder to define. Therefore, they may be better judged by the reviews and studies reflecting critical excellence and objectivity.

Some of the difficulties encountered relate to the proportion of reviews available. A Bend in the River attracted fifty substantial reviews. The bibliography started as a checklist, thus one of the problems was its conversion to another format. It is not always simple to determine what types of research are in progress in the Caribbean, so the decision to proceed was not automatic. Translations necessitated extensive correspondence with foreign-language publishers, since Index Translationum is incomplete and the details of various other similar sources are inconsistent. To record the writings of any contemporary author of Naipaul's stature, and who is still at work, poses problems further complicated by the impenetrable volume of critical responses to his work from afar. It is uncertain whether some early short stories like "The Mourners" have ever appeared in a periodical before publication in pamphlet format. Naipaul has tended to bridge the creative gaps by revising and republishing several essays and reviews when no publication offered itself. Such changes invariably have made identification of materials difficult. Many valuable reviews have also turned up in small-press publications and in unfamiliar and unindexed periodicals; The Canadian Catholic Review is a case in point.

ARRANGEMENT

Section I gives an overview of Naipaul's work. Section
II, "Works by V. S. Naipaul," is comprised of two parts.
Part A includes all the author's works appearing in book form:
original and subsequent editions, reprints, introductions,
prefaces, and translations. In the case of Penguin paperback
versions, only the first edition of each title is listed, but the
existence of subsequent editions is mentioned. Part B lists
contributions to periodicals, newspapers, and anthologies in
the form of articles and short stories. When articles, short
stories, and essays appear in collected works or journals,
they are cross-indexed and identified by the two-letter symbol (see page xvii) representing the title of the book in which
the item has also appeared. These are listed under "Anthology Contributions, Short Stories, or Articles." Essays,
journals, newspaper articles, reviews, or extracts that do not
appear in collections are listed under "Articles."

Section III, "Works by V. S. Naipaul," is also in two
parts: C and D. Part C lists bibliographies, interviews,
theses and dissertations, and critical studies appearing in
books, journals, and newspapers. It also contains a list of
monographs on Naipaul with full bibliographic details. Entries
for theses and dissertations provide degree obtained, institution, and year of completion. Interviews record the date,
publication source, and name of the interviewer. Part D
consists of selected reviews in English for each of Naipaul's
published books; this selection has been enlarged by the inclusion of some unannotated reviews.

The entire work is arranged chronologically, and is intended to be a guide to the author's critical reputation.
Where dates are identical, alphabetical order dictates the sequence. Each item is numbered consecutively within each
subsection (A through D). A few late additions have been
inserted into the sequence by use of a final "A": e.g., C8A
comes between C8 and C9. Translations are distinguished
from their originals by the use of decimals (e.g., item A2 is
followed by its translations A2.1 through A2.8): such translations are by language, chronologically. Items are indexed
by item number, not page number. When a cited item is re-
printed ("rpt."), this information is given immediately (rather
than separately in its chronological position), using, where ap-
plicable, the two-letter abbreviations on page xvii (e.g., "Rpt.

in FI., OB."). At the end of a citation extracts are identified as follows: "(extract)."

A full list of the sources consulted in the preparation
of this bibliography is contained in Appendix 1. The vast
majority of entries listed have been personally examined. The
form of citation follows that of The Chicago Manual of Style,
13th edition (Chicago and London: University of Chicago
Press, 1982).

From a Caribbean standpoint, Naipaul's work is seen as
a catalyst for comparative study of the literature to which he
has brought institutionalized status beyond the borders of
the Caribbean. Appendix 2, "Universities Holding Commonwealth Literature and Offering Commonwealth Literature
Courses, and Libraries with Commonwealth Literature Collections in The United States, Canada, Europe, and the West
Indies," underlines the growth of that literature. Appendix
3, "Notes on Prizes and Awards," highlights the background
to some of the honors Naipaul has received.

The work concludes with name and title indexes. The
name index is comprised of editors, translators, critics, authors, and other contributors. The title index lists titles of
all the book reviews in the text to which no ascertainable
author, compiler, or editor's name is attached, in addition
to the titles of Naipaul's own articles and short stories.

ACKNOWLEDGMENTS

My remaining task is to acknowledge the help received
in the preparation of this manuscript. I wish to mention the
reference staff at Brock, Guelph, and McMaster universities,
the Buffalo and Eric Public Library, Metro Toronto Public
Library, the National Library of Canada, the University of
London, the overseas international photocopying service of
the British Library, Christiane Keane, librarian of the Commonwealth Institute, London, and library colleagues at the
St. Augustine campus of the University of the West Indies.

My thanks are extended to Dr. Alma Jordan, university
librarian, the University of the West Indies, who invited me
in 1979 to attend the SALALM (Seminar on the Acquisition of
Latin American Library Materials) Conference in Pasadena,
California. There I presented a paper on Naipaul from which

this bibliography has emerged. Both Dr. Jordan and Barbara
Comissiong, deputy librarian, the University of the West
Indies at St. Augustine, have offered much valuable advice.
I wish also to acknowledge all the published sources used in
the bibliography (see Appendix 1), and to state that the lines
quoted from <u>Dissertation Abstracts International</u> are not the
entire abstracts, but portions thereof.

My thanks also go to Dr. Edrick Gift, dean, UWI Faculty of Education, for his encouragement, and to Roy Narine-
singh from the same faculty for his helpful suggestions. Special mention must also be made of Dr. Ken Ramchand, Dr.
Helen Pyne-Timothy, and Dr. Gordon Rohlehr, all of the UWI
Department of English, for their invaluable contributions,
particularly Dr. Rohlehr. Laurence Hallewell, Ibero-American
bibliographer, the University of Minnesota, has been of particular assistance to me from his window overseas in many
significant ways; my sincere appreciation, Laurence. Most
important has been the research grant received from the University of the West Indies at St. Augustine, without which
this bibliography could not have been completed. The responsibility for the final selection and arrangement of the
references remains mine.

K. A. J.
University of the West Indies,
St. Augustine, Trinidad

LIST OF ABBREVIATIONS

AB	Among the Believers
AD	An Area of Darkness
BR	A Bend in the River
CD	A Congo Diary
EA	The Enigma of Arrival
FC	Finding the Centre
FI	A Flag on the Island
FS	In a Free State
GU	Guerrillas
HB	A House for Mr. Biswas
IN	India
LE	The Loss of El Dorado
MiM	The Mimic Men
MM	The Mystic Masseur
MP	The Middle Passage
MS	Miguel Street
MSK	Mister Stone and the Knights Companion
NO	The Naipaul Omnibus
OB	The Overcrowded Barracoon
RP	The Return of Eva Perón
SE	The Suffrage of Elvira
TN	Three Novels

SECTION I: BACKGROUND

V. S. NAIPAUL

V. S. Naipaul is among the best-known Caribbean authors, perhaps most easily recognized as a novelist and socio-
political commentator. The literature by and about Naipaul
has grown extensively over the past twenty-five years and
has appeared in literary periodicals, newspapers, scholarly
journals, and books, and as the subject of symposia and
academic theses. Naipaul has lived in England for many years
where much of his work has been published. His writings are
satirical, pungent, and frequently controversial. Both the
British and Canadian broadcasting corporations have produced
serialized versions of his book A House for Mr. Biswas. Often
he has been accused of imposing pro-Western values on Third
World societies. He has won some of the most coveted literary awards in Britain. The University of the West Indies
in 1975 conferred on him the D.Litt.; he received the Jerusalem Prize in 1983. His recognition in America as a distinguished author is now more firmly established through his
receipt of the Bennett Award in 1980 by The Hudson Review,
and the T. S. Eliot Award for creative writing in 1986.
André Deutsch has already issued a uniform edition of his
writing; few authors are accorded such a privilege in their
lifetime.

Naipaul appeared on the literary stage foremost as a
journalist and freelance broadcaster; he later edited the BBC
literary program, Caribbean Voices, for which the legendary
Henry Swanzy is well remembered. Naipaul has since established himself as literary critic, world traveler, essayist,
short-story writer, reviewer, and exponent on the novel.

A special issue of World Literature Written in English
indicated the growing interest in the area from the United

1

States and Canada; it further stated that "future bibliographers will have to keep a watch on North American publications particularly in the field of Black Studies." Many West Indian observers, including George Lamming, have expressed concern at the conspicuous omission of Caribbean literature from black studies programs in the United States.[1]

As early as 1958 Naipaul was himself not unmindful of his American and British public images and noted that while Americans did not read his books because he was too British, the British did likewise because he was too foreign.[2] Naipaul belongs to the postwar generation of expatriate West Indian writers who

> [c]reated an unusual situation in which the spokesmen for an area were operating not only at a great distance from that area, but for an audience of whom very few were their own countrymen.[3]

The scope of his literary audience was of as much concern to him as the financial returns he received from his writings. He commented painfully that he had written three books in five years and received only three hundred pounds for them.[4] It was the opinion of R. Z. Sheppard that, in spite of Naipaul's collection of awards, it was only after his publication of Guerrillas in 1975 that he became widely known in the United States. John Ayre also believed that beyond New York, Naipaul was virtually unknown in North America.

Ayre thought much of the obscurity could be attributed more to "our infallible aversion to images from the Third World than his writing abilities."[5] While the book received polite acceptance in Britain, Americans saw in it "meaningful extensions of West Indian material in the present-day politics of the Third World."[6] Naipaul continues to play a leading role in advancing the scope and quality of Caribbean writing; he is increasingly coming under closer scrutiny by prominent American reviewers. More attention has been directed at Caribbean literature recently in the United States through his work, which is now widely published there. He has remained in the forefront of contemporary Commonwealth writing and thus has tended to attract and provoke wider attention in British academic circles than in North America. Edward Baugh noted at the 1977 Conference on Commonwealth Literature held in New Delhi that in spite of Naipaul's absence there were

more papers presented on him, and one could not help but
believe that he is perhaps the most successful and widely
read novelist today.

There is also a growing body of literary analysis of
Naipaul's work emanating from Canadian critics and scholars
many of whom write and teach Commonwealth literature at
Canadian universities. Much of that response is not ade-
quately represented in the bibliographies previously mentioned. By 1970 the Ontario Co-operative Programme for Latin America and Caribbean Studies (OCPLALS) began to support the concept of area studies at Canadian universities by
promoting the enrichment of periodical collections and other
categories of material relevant to Latin America and the Caribbean. C. H. Wyke's survey on behalf of the Canadian Association for Commonwealth Literature and Language Studies
(CACLALS) in 1980 indicated that twenty-five Canadian universities offered courses in Commonwealth literature; fifteen
of them in ten provinces provided courses on the literature
of the Caribbean. Thirty-three percent were at the gradu-
ate level.[7] CACLALS is also making valuable contributions
to Commonwealth literature studies through dissemination of
the literature.

In 1982 CACLALS held a conference in Ottawa to mark
twenty-five years of Naipaul's work as a writer, at which
ten papers were presented; those proceedings have not been
published. Another series of papers, done by a group of
academics, was published in the 1983 special issue of Commonwealth, the official journal of La Société d'Etudes des
Pays du Commonwealth. It dealt with an intensive study of
A House for Mr. Biswas. In the following year Modern Fiction Studies honored his work in similar fashion. It was
pointed out that his absence from the Commonwealth Conference in Sweden also failed to detract from his dominance
there.[8]

While the range of his audience widened, his themes of
race, class, color, and colonialism remained unchanged. He
selected sensitive political and geographic areas about which
to write; he became more topical and developed a keen sense
of timing. Accordingly, Naipaul wrote about Africa when
others were avoiding it. The same may be said for Argentina
and, more recently, Iran. In his review of Guerrillas, Baugh
suggested that Naipaul's ability "to speak so broadly and

directly to the Western metropolitan condition" enhanced his international reputation.

Naipaul's literary prominence has given him comparative status among respected English-language writers in this century. However, it is with international figures as those evoked by Updike and Howe that he belongs.[9] Schieder further states that Naipaul has become cosmopolitan, his experiences relating to five continents.[10] This universality is reflected not only in his themes but also in his vision. Naipaul once referred to his work as one big book. Louis James declared that West Indian writing was perhaps the richest and most varied form of writing to have emerged in English since World War II. William Walsh saw much virtue, vitality, and mastery in what he called "a supple and poetic language."[11] Hamner believes that West Indian literature needs to be promoted to maintain its relatively flourishing condition.

Many are of the opinion that A House for Mr. Biswas marked Naipaul's transition to fictional maturity; his moods changed, he became perceptive, very often incisive. Thus the period in which he produced the social comedies prior to this novel is often regarded as his apprenticeship. Naipaul's propensity for travel and his specially long sojourn in England were critical influences on him as an artist. The Biswas novel and In a Free State reflected on his ability not only to perceive and write about his own country and heritage but also helped one to appreciate his obsession with homelessness, identity, and alienation. Naipaul has often incurred the wrath of West Indian and other observers, who view a good deal of his work as distortions of Third World society. There are critics who express concern that Naipaul presents no proper perspective on the historical and contemporary relationships between the Third World and predatory colonial powers,[12] whose activities have contributed in no small measure to Third World predicaments.[13]

It has often been stated that Naipaul's vision seldom moves beyond a paralyzed diagnosis of well-known defects in the moral, social, and political life of the countries he visits. Emerging overwhelmingly from his travel books and essays is a kind of static helplessness, encouraged by all who feel most comfortable with the international status quo. Everywhere one gets the feeling these countries are unlikely to solve their own problems. Gordon Rohlehr, among noted West Indian

scholars, has repeatedly opposed his rigid views and limitations as a writer.[14] In a recent interview Kenneth Ramchand,
another of Naipaul's critics, abhorred his assumptions about
the Caribbean with a passion.[15] Cudjoe has relentlessly supported the West Indian cause while denouncing those critics
who regard Naipaul as the new guru propagating the truth
about colonial reality.[16] What disturbs Eugene Goodheart is
that all Naipaul's alternatives are negative, but "essential
to an understanding of Naipaul's work."[17] He received some
of his earliest and most hostile reactions after he wrote The
Middle Passage and later on An Area of Darkness. Naipaul
once complained of the inadequate response to the writer in
the West Indies. C. D. Narasimhaiah suggested that Naipaul's own malice and Swiftian disgust had abdicated the
right to any response. He further described An Area of
Darkness as a tantalizing mixture of first-rate literary sensibility along with what should belong to pot boilers. In Naipaul he saw a tremendous lack of sympathy, penetration, and
concern for people, in spite of his talent.[18] Martin Amis ob-
served a change in Naipaul's style by the time he had written
India; it had become hardened, public, and responsible. He
also suggested that this was for Naipaul a form of self-
protection; Larson also detected a mellowing in his writing
in A Bend in the River.

In spite of the controversy that surrounds his work,
Naipaul is rarely seen on the defensive. In an interview
given to Mel Gussow he once stated: "Because you are not
left wing, they automatically say that you are right wing."[19]
Angus Richmond refuses to accept the view of Naipaul as a
nonpolitical writer, stating that his political orientation is
"well to the right of the Caribbean."[20] Hamner discusses
fully Naipaul's commitment to duty as a writer.[21] Perhaps
too often the tendency of many of his critics has been to rationalize the cultural, social, and political problems inherent
in Third World societies and to adopt a centrist view of life
in those states. V. S. Pritchett sums up the situation:
"One does not ask a novelist to be absolutely true to life,
in the sense of social or racial record; one asks him to be
true to his design."[22]

Naipaul's treatment of women in his later work is another area of severe limitation in terms of roles and images.
Helen Pyne-Timothy observes that in A Bend in the River
and In a Free State narrative voice is almost totally invested

in the male. In Guerrillas she notes Naipaul makes "the most sustained attempt to interiorize and motivate the personality of a woman, Jane."[23] This view is well supported in López de Villegas's article "Matriarchs and Maneaters."[24] Hemenway, in a subsequent study, looks at the role of sex and politics in Naipaul's work.[25]

The British Book Marketing Council conducted a survey in 1982; Naipaul was among the least popular writers judged by the poll, which centered on twenty major British authors. The survey was made principally to measure book purchases and to determine the areas that needed to be promoted. V. S. Pritchett shared this dubious honor with Naipaul, which may explain the level of interest of those surveyed. It may well have been a distaste for Naipaul's themes of restlessness and impatience with the Third World, his flagrant disregard for some aspects of British life and institutions, or the preference of many British people for the magazine notwithstanding.[26]

Subsequent documentation of criticism on Naipaul's work in other Commonwealth countries, Latin America, and Europe will have to be addressed. The study of Commonwealth literature, more specifically Caribbean literature, is now fairly well established in several British[27] and European universities;[28] the need for further bibliographic control, vigilance, and sustained collection development, therefore, should be addressed.

NOTES

1. Joseph J. Jones. "ACLALS: Conference at Kingston." World Literature Written in English (WLWE) 19 (April 1971): 17

2. "The Regional Barrier." Times Literary Supplement, August 15, 1958: xxxvii.

3. Henry Swanzy. "Caribbean Voices, Prolegomena to a West Indian Culture." Caribbean Quarterly 1 (1949): 28.

4. The Regional Barrier, xxxvii.

5. John Ayre. "India: A Wounded Civilization." Globe and Mail, July 16, 1977: 33.

6. Charles Moritz, Ed. Current Biography 1977 (New York: H. W. Wilson, 1978): 308.

7. C. H. Wyke. "The Validity of Courses in Commonwealth Literature." Chimo, No. 1 (Spring 1980): 12-22.

8. Matt Cohen. "V. S. Naipaul dominated the Commonwealth conference, and he wasn't there." Books in Canada 12 (January 1983): 4-6.

9. Rupert Schieder. "Scrupulous Fidelity." Canadian Forum 50 (November 1979): 26.

10. Ibid.

11. William Walsh. Commonwealth Literature (London: O.U.P., 1973): 39.

12. Edward Said. "Bitter Dispatches from the Third World." The Nation 230 (May 3, 1980): 523.

13. Anthony Boxhill. V. S. Naipaul's Fiction in Quest of the Enemy (Fredericton: York Press, 1983): 82.

14. Selwyn Cudjoe. "Talking about Naipaul." An Interview with Gordon Rohlehr. In: Carib, No. 2 (May 6, 1981): 39-65.

15. _____. "V. S. Naipaul and West Indian Writers; Kenneth Ramchand speaks with Selwyn Cudjoe." Antilia 1 (1981): 9-11.

16. _____. "V. S. Naipaul and the question of identity." In: Voices from Under, edited by William Luis. (Westport, CT: Greenwood, 1984): 89-99.

17. Eugene Goodheart. "Naipaul and the Voices of Negation." In: Salmagundi 54 (Fall 1981): 47.

18. C. D. Narasimhaiah. "Somewhere Something has Snapped." Literary Criterion 6 (1968): 85.

19. Mel Gussow. "Writer without Roots." New York Times Magazine. December 26, 1976: p. 18.

20. Angus Richmond. "Naipaul: The Mimic Man." Race and Class 24 (1982): 125-130.

21. Robert D. Hamner. V. S. Naipaul (New York: Twayne, 1973): 151.

22. V. S. Pritchett. "Climacteric." New Statesman 65 (1963): 831.

23. Helen Pyne-Timothy. "Women and Sexuality in the Later Novels of V. S. Naipaul." WLWE 25 (Autumn 1985): 299.

24. López de Villegas, Consuelo. "Matriarchs and Maneaters: Naipaul's Fictional Women." Revista/Review InterAmerica 7 (Winter 1977/78): 605-614.

25. Robert Hemenway. "Sex and Politics in V. S. Naipaul." Studies in the Novel 14 (Summer 1982): 189-202.

26. "Tightened Belts and a Publicity Push have Brightened Britains's Book Scene." Publishers Weekly (March 26, 1982): 23.

27. Alastair Niven. "Commonwealth Literature Studies in British Universities." Commonwealth Vol. 17 (June 1973): 59-61.

28. Anna Rutherford. "Commonwealth Literature Studies have taken hold of West European Universities." Commonwealth 16 (December 1972): 154.

SECTION II: WORKS BY
V. S. NAIPAUL

A. BOOKS AND TRANSLATIONS: NOVELS, SHORT FICTION AND NONFICTION

NOVELS AND SHORT FICTION

A1.   THE MYSTIC MASSEUR. London: Deutsch, 1957.   215 pp.
MM
New York: Vanguard, 1957.   215 pp.
London: Deutsch, 1959.   224 pp.
London: Deutsch (2nd Russell Impression), 1960.   215 pp.
Harmondsworth, Middlesex: Penguin, 1964.   220 pp.
London: Deutsch (3rd Russell Impression), 1966.   215 pp.
Harmondsworth, Middlesex: Penguin, 1969.   234 pp.   (Six
further reprints to 1981.)
London: Deutsch (Russell Edition), 1969.   215 pp.   Edwards,
Paul and Ramchand, Kenneth.   "Introduction."
Caribbean Writer's Series, no. 3.   London: Heinemann Educa-
tional Books, 1971.
Atlantic Highlands, NJ: Humanities Press, 1975.   Omnibus
edition.   Contents: The Mystic Masseur, pp. 1-171, The
Suffrage of Elvira, pp. 177-355, Miguel Street, pp. 361-
502.   New York: Knopf, 1982.   502 pp.
New York: Vintage Books, 1984.   218 pp.

FRENCH:

A1.1.   Le Masseur Mystique.   Trans. Marie-Lise Marliere.   Paris:
Gallimard, 1965.   224 pp.

SPANISH:

A1.2.   El Curandero mistico.   Trans. Sara Piña.   Buenos Aires:
Compañia General Fabril Editoria, 1965.   213 pp.

A1.3.   El Curandero mistico.   Trans. H. Vázquez.   Barcelona: Seix
Barral, 1983.   256 pp.

HEBREW:

A1.4.   Ha-Ish-mi-Trinidad.   Trans. A. Agmon.   Tel-Aviv: Amichai,
1966.   176 pp.

11

ITALIAN:

A1.5. Il Massaggio Mistico. Trans. Giorgio Monicelli. Milano: Mondadori, 1966. 268 pp.

SWEDISH:

A1.6. Den Mystiske Massören. Trans. Roland Adlerberth. Malmö: Berghs förlag, 1976. 210 pp.

FINNISH:

A1.7. Tays inoppinut hieroja. Trans. Seppo Loponem. Helsinki: Otava, 1978. 235 pp.

POLISH:

A1.8. Masazysta cudotwórca. Trans. Maria Zborowska. Warszawa: "Ksiazka i Wiedza," 1979. 321 pp.

GERMAN:

A1.9. Der mystische Masseur. Trans. Karin Graf. Köln: Kiepenheuer und Witsch, 1984. 252 pp.
Bergisch Gladbach: Gustav Lübbe Verlag, 1987. 280 pp.

A2. THE SUFFRAGE OF ELVIRA. London: Deutsch, 1958. 240 pp. SE
Toronto: Collins, 1958. 240 pp.
London: Deutsch (2nd Russell Impression), 1964. 240 pp.
London: Deutsch, 1969. 240 pp.
Harmondsworth, Middlesex: Penguin, 1969. 207 pp. (Five further reprints to 1980.)
New York: Vintage Books, 1985. 206 pp.

SWEDISH:

A2.1. Röster i Elvira eller Vai i Västindien. Trans. Roland Alderberth. Malmö: Berghs förlag, 1975. 219 pp.

GERMAN:

A2.2. Wahlkamp auf Karibisch; oder, Eine Hand Wäscht die andere. Trans. Werner Peterich. Zug, Switzerland: Edition Sven Erik Bergh im Ingse-Verlag, 1975. 310 pp.
Reinbek bei Hamburg: Rowolt Taschenbuch Verlag, 1986.

POLISH:

A2.3. Wybory w Elwirze. Trans. Maria Zborowska. Warsaw: "Ksiazka i Wiedza." 1977. 255 pp.

DUTCH:

A2.4.   Stemmen in Elvira. Trans. René Kurpershoek. Amsterdam:
        De Arbeiderspers, 1987. 248 pp.

A3.   MIGUEL STREET. London: Deutsch, 1959. 224 pp. MS
        Toronto: Collins, 1959. 222 pp.
        London: Deutsch (2nd Russell Impression), 1960.
        London: World Distributors, 1960. 160 pp.
        New York: Vanguard, 1960. 222 pp.
        London: Deutsch (3rd Russell Impression), 1964.
        London: Four Square, 1966. 158 pp.
        London: Deutsch (2nd Russell Edition), 1966. 222 pp.
        London: Deutsch (3rd Russell Edition), 1970. 222 pp.
        Harmondsworth, Middlesex: Penguin, 1971. 172 pp. (Eight
        further reprints to 1982.)
        Erapu, Laban. "Introduction." Caribbean Writers' Series,
        no. 14. London: Heinemann Educational Books, 1974.
        London: Deutsch (4th Russell Edition), 1976.
        New York: Vintage Books, 1984. 171 pp.

GERMAN:

A3.1.   Blaue Karren in Calypsoland. Trans. Janheinz Jahn. Har-
        renalp: Erdman, 1966. 248 pp.

NORWEGIAN:

A3.2.   Calypso. Trans. Olav H. R. Rue. Oslo: Det Norske Sam-
        laget, 1966. 173 pp.

FRENCH:

A3.3.   Miguel Street. Trans. Pauline Verdun. Collection Du Monde
        Entier. Paris: Gallimard, 1967. 236 pp.

POLISH:

A3.4.   Miguel Street. Trans. Maria Zborowska. Warszawa: "Ksiazka
        i Wiedza," 1974. 261 pp.

FINNISH:

A3.5.   Miguel-kadun väkeä. Trans. Seppo Loponen. Helsinki:
        Otava, 1980. 219 pp.

SPANISH:

A3.6.   Miguel Street. Trans. Francisco Páez de la Cadena. Madrid:
        Debate, 1981. 208 pp.

HEBREW:

A3.7.   Rehov Migel. Trans. Ayala Rahav. Tel-Aviv: Zmora, 1986.
        193 pp.

DUTCH:

A3.8. Miguel Street. Trans. Guido Golüke. Amsterdam: De Ar-
beiderspers, 1984. 181 pp.
Includes "Bogart" (B83, B93), "The Thing without a
Name" (B103), "George and the Pink House" (B96), "His
Chosen Calling" (B98), "Man-Man" (B119), "B Wordsworth"
(B118), "The Coward" (B95), "The Pyrotechnicist" (B102),
"Titus Hoyt, I.A." (B123), "The Maternal Instinct" (B101),
"The Blue Cart" (B92), "Love, Love, Love, Alone" (B100),
"The Mechanical Genius" (B120), "Caution" (B94), "Until the
Soldiers Came" (B104), "Hat" (B83, B97), "How I left Miguel
Street" (B99)

A4. A HOUSE FOR MR. BISWAS. London: Deutsch, 1961. 531
pp. HB
London: Deutsch, 1961. 232 pp.
New York: McGraw-Hill, 1962. 531 pp.
Toronto: Collins, 1962. 531 pp.
London: Deutsch (Russell Edition), 1962. 531 pp.
London: Fontana, 1963. 512 pp.
London: Deutsch (Russell Edition), 1964. 531 pp.
London: Collins, 1966. 521 pp.
London: Deutsch (Russell Edition), 1969. 531 pp.
Harmondsworth, Middlesex: Penguin, 1969. 590 pp. (Ten
further reprints to 1982.)
New York: Knopf, 1983. 481 pp.
London: Deutsch, 1984. 544 pp.
London: Deutsch (3rd edition), 1984. 531 pp.
New York: Vintage Books, 1984. 589 pp.

FRENCH:

A4.1. Une Maison pour Monsieur Biswas. Trans. Louise Servicen.
Collection Du Monde Entier. Paris: Gallimard, 1964.
584 pp.
Une Maison pour Monsieur Biswas. Trans. Louise Servicen.
Preface J. M. G. Le Clezio. Paris: Gallimard, 1985.
588 pp.

ITALIAN:

A4.2. Una Casa per il Signor Biswas. Trans. Vincenzo Mantovani.
Milano: Mondadori, 1964. 690 pp.

SPANISH:

A4.3. Una casa para el señor Biswas. Trans. Floreal Mazía.
Buenos Aires: Compania General Fabril Editora, 1965.
527 pp.
Una casa para Mr. Biswas. Trans. Floreal Mazía. Barcelona:
Seix Barral, 1983. 528 pp.

SWEDISH:

A4.4. Ett Hus åt Mr. Biswas. Trans. Carl Sundell. Stockholm: Bonniers förlag, 1974. 473 pp.

BULGARIAN:

A4.5. Dom za mistŭr Bisvas: Roman. Trans. Aglika Markova. Sofia (Bulgaria): Kultura, 1981. 592 pp.

GERMAN:

A4.6. Ein Haus für Mr. Biswas: Roman. Trans. Karin Graf. Köln: Kiepenheuer and Witsch, 1981. 720 pp. Frankfurt am Main: Fischer-Taschenbuch-Verlag, 1983.

HEBREW:

A4.7. Ba'it Le 'Mar Biswas. Trans. Aaron Amir. Tel-Aviv: Zmora, 1985. 437 pp.

DUTCH:

A4.8. Een huis voor meneer Biswas. Trans. Guido Golüke. Amsterdam: De Arbeiderspers, 1985. 577 pp.

A5. MR. STONE AND THE KNIGHTS COMPANION. London: Deutsch, 1963. 160 pp. MSC Toronto: Collins, 1964. 159 pp. New York: Macmillan, 1964. 159 pp. London: Four Square, 1966. 127 pp. Harmondsworth, Middlesex: Penguin, 1973. 126 pp. (Three further reprints to 1981.) New York: Vintage Books, 1985. 125 pp.

SWEDISH:

A5.1. Mr. Stone och riddarkompaniet. Trans. Roland Adlerberth. Malmö: Bergh, 1979. 177 pp.

FRENCH:

A5.2. Mr. Stone. Trans. Annie Saumont. Paris: Albin Michel, 1985. 200 pp.

A6. A FLAG ON THE ISLAND. London: Deutsch, 1967. 235 pp. FI Toronto: Collins, 1967. 235 pp. New York: Macmillan, 1968. 235 pp. Harmondsworth, Middlesex: Penguin, 1969. 214 pp. (Two further reprints to 1981.)

FRENCH:

A6.1. Un Drapeau sur l'Ile. Trans. Pauline Verdun. Collection
Du Monde Entier. Paris: Gallimard, 1968. 232 pp.
Rpt. 1971.

DUTCH:

A6.2. Een vlag op het eiland. Trans. M. Kock. Amsterdam:
Contact, 1976. 205 pp.
Includes "The Mourners" (B109), "My Aunt Gold Teeth"
(B117), "The Enemy" (B124), "Greenie and Yellow" (B108),
"Perfect Tenants" (B110), "The Raffle" (B116), "The Heart"
(B120), "The Baker's Story" (B121), "A Christmas Story"
(B115), "The Night Watchman's Occurrence Book" (B106), "A
Flag on the Island" (B107).

GERMAN:

A6.3. Meine Tante Goldzahn: Erzählungen. Trans. Karin Graf.
Köln: Kiepenheuer und Witsch, 1981.
Frankfurt am Main: Fischer-Taschenbuch-Verlag, 1983. 94
pp.

A7. THE MIMIC MEN. London: Deutsch, 1967. 300 pp. MiM
Toronto: Collins, 1967. 300 pp.
New York: Macmillan, 1967. 301 pp.
London: Deutsch (Readers Union), 1968. 300 pp.
Harmondsworth, Middlesex: Penguin, 1969. 251 pp. (Six
further reprints to 1981.)
New York: Knopf, 1971. 250 pp.
New York: Vintage Books, 1985. 250 pp.

POLISH:

A7.1. Marionetki. Trans. Maria Zborowska. Warszawa: "Ksiazka
i Wiedza," 1971. 348 pp.

SWEDISH:

A7.2. Imitatörerna. Trans. Roland Adlerberth. Malmö: Berghs
förlag, 1974. 269 pp.

GERMAN:

A7.3. Herr und Sklave. Trans. Ursula von Zedlitz zu Hohenlohe.
Zug. (Switzerland): Edition Sven Erik Bergh im Ingse-
Verlag, 1974. 322 pp.

FINNISH:

A7.4. Vallan hinta. Trans. Paavo Lehtonen: Helsinki: Otava,
1976. 304 pp.

SLOVENE:

A7.5. Posnemovalci. Trans. Joze Fistrovic. Murska Sobota: "Pomurska zalozba," 1976. 337 pp.

DUTCH:

A7.6. De Mimitators. Trans. René Kurpershoek. Amsterdam: De Arbeiderspers, 1985. 289 pp.

SPANISH:

A7.7. Los Simuladores. Trans. Jordi Bertrán Ferrer. Barcelona: Seix Barral, 1983. 276 pp. Bogotá: Planeta Colombiana [1984?].

PORTUGUESE:

A7.8. Os Mímicos. Trans. Paulo Henriques Britto. São Paulo: Companhia de Letras, 1987. 319 pp.

A8. IN A FREE STATE. London: Deutsch, 1971. 256 pp. New York: Knopf, 1971. 256 pp. Harmondsworth, Middlesex: Penguin, 1973. 256 pp. (Six further reprints to 1986.) New York: Vintage Books, 1984. 245 pp.

DUTCH:

A8.1. Een staat van vrijheidij. Trans. W. A. Dorsman-Vos. Amsterdam: Contact, 1971. 256 pp.

DANISH:

A8.2. Fri og uafhaengig. Trans. Merete Ries. København: Gyldendal, 1973. 265 pp.

FINNISH:

A8.3. Vapaassa Maassa. Trans. Sekari Ahback. Helsinki: Otava, 1973. 264 pp.

GERMAN:

A8.4. Sag mir, wer mein Feind ist: drei Novellen. Trans. Ursula Prinzessin von Zedlitz zu Hohenlohe. Stockholm [and] Zug (Switzerland): Sven Erik Bergh in Ingse-Verlag; Düsseldorf [and] Wien: Econ-Verlag, 1973. 293 pp. Reibek-bei-Hamburg: Rowohlt Taschenbuch, 1979. 204 pp.

NORWEGIAN:

A8.5. I en fri stat. Trans. Mona Lange. Oslo: Gyldendal Norsk forlag, 1973. 252 pp.

SWEDISH:

A8.6. Visa Mig Min Fiende. Trans. Roland Adlerberth. Malmö:
       Bergh, 1973. 268 pp.

POLISH:

A8.7. W wolnym Kraju. Trans. Maria Zborowska. Warszawa:
       "Ksiazka i Wiedza," 1974. 306 pp.

SPANISH:

A8.8. En un estado libre. Trans. Ester Donato. Barcelona:
       Destino, 1976. 294 pp.
       En un estado libre. Trans. Ester Donato. Barcelona:
       Destino, 1981. 294 pp.

HEBREW:

A8.9. Be'Medina Chofshit. Trans. Amihood Arbell. Tel-Aviv:
       Zmora, 1978. 228 pp.

FRENCH:

A8.10. Dans un pays libre. Trans. Annie Saumont. Paris: Galli-
       mard, 1981. 245 pp.
       Dis-moi-qui tuer. Trans. Annie Saumont. Collection Les
       Grandes Traductions. Paris: Albin Michel, 1983. 280
       pp.
       Includes "Prologue, from a Journal: The Tramp at Piraeus"
       (B44), "In a Free State" (B112), "One out of Many" (B113),
       "Tell me Who to Kill" (B114), "Epilogue, from a Journal: The
       Circus at Luxor" (B46).

A9.   GUERRILLAS. London: Deutsch, 1975. 253 pp. GU
       New York: Knopf, 1975. 248 pp.
       Toronto: Collins, 1975. 252 pp.
       Harmondsworth, Middlesex: Penguin, 1976. 253 pp. (Four
       further reprints to 1982.)
       New York: Ballantine, 1976.
       New York: Vintage Books, 1980. 292 pp.

DANISH:

A9.1. Guerilla. Trans. Arne Herløv Petersen. København:
       Gyldendal, 1976. 268 pp.
       Guerilla. Trans. Arne Herløv Petersen. Samlerens Bogklub,
       1976. 267 pp.

DUTCH:

A9.2. Guerrilla. Trans. Guido Golüke. Amsterdam: Contact,
       1976. 213 pp.

SWEDISH:

A9.3. Guerilla. Trans. Roland Adlerberth. Malmö: Berghs förlag, 1976. 256 pp.

GERMAN:

A9.4. Guerrillas. Trans. Ursula von Zedlitz zu Hohenlohe. Zug. (Switzerland): Edition Sven Erik Bergh im Ingse-Verlag, 1976. 288 pp.

FINNISH:

A9.5. Gerillat. Trans. Seppo Loponen. Helsinki: Otava, 1977. 296 pp.

NORWEGIAN:

A9.6. Gerilja. Trans. Kjell Risvik. Oslo: G. N. F., 1977. 240 pp.

SPANISH:

A9.7. Guerrillas. Trans. Carmelo Saavedra Arce. Mexico: Lasser Press, Mexicana, 1977. 256 pp.

HEBREW:

A9.8. Aushei Guerilla. Trans. Aaron Amir. Tel-Aviv: Zmora, 1978. 201 pp.

POLISH:

A9.9. Partyzanci. Trans. Maria Zborowska. Warszawa: Czytelnik, 1980. 308 pp.

FRENCH:

A9.10. Guerilleros. Trans. Annie Saumont. Paris: Albin Michel, 1981. 279 pp.
Livres de Poche 5665. Paris: LGF, 1982.

A10. A BEND IN THE RIVER. New York: Knopf, 1979. 278 pp.
BR
London: Deutsch, 1979. 296 pp.
New York: Vintage Books, 1980. 278 pp.
Harmondsworth, Middlesex: Penguin, 1980. 287 pp.

DANISH:

A10.1. Ved en Krumning på Floden. Trans. Christopher Maaløe and Johannes Riis. København: Gyldendal, 1980. 292 pp.

GERMAN:

A10.2. An der Biegung des grossen Flusses. Trans. Karin Graf.

Köln: Kiepenheur und Witsch, 1980. 368 pp.
Frankfurt am Main: Fischer-Taschenbuch-Verlag, 1983.
299 pp. 2. ed., 1985.

NORWEGIAN:

A10.3. Der elva Krummer seg. Trans. Arne Moen. Oslo: Gyldendal Norsk forlag, 1980. 303 pp.

SPANISH:

A10.4. Un recondo en el rio. Trans. Francisco Gurza Irazoqui.
Mexico: Lasser Press Mexicana, 1980. 312 pp.

SWEDISH:

A10.5. Där floden flyter forbi. Trans. Else Lundgren. Stockholm:
Rabén och Sjögren, 1980. 319 pp.

HEBREW:

A10.6. Ikul Ba'Nahar. Trans. Aaron Amir. Tel-Aviv: Zmora,
1981. 240 pp.

JAPANESE:

A10.7. Kurai kawa. Trans. Takeshi Onodera. Tokyo: TBS Britannica, 1981. 390 pp.

FRENCH:

A10.8. A la courbe du fleuve. Trans. Gérard Clarence. Collection
Les Grandes Traductions. Paris: Albin Michel, 1982.
336 pp.
Le Livre de Poche 5879. Paris: LGF, 1984.

A11. THREE NOVELS. New York: Knopf, 1982. 508 pp.
[Omnibus edition]. Contents: The Mystic Masseur, The
Suffrage of Elvira, Miguel Street.

NONFICTION

A12. THE MIDDLE PASSAGE: IMPRESSIONS OF FIVE SOCIETIES--
BRITISH, FRENCH AND DUTCH--IN THE WEST INDIES
AND SOUTH AMERICA. London: Deutsch, 1962. 232 pp.
MP
New York: Macmillan, 1962. 232 pp.
Harmondsworth, Middlesex: Penguin, 1969. 256 pp. (Three
further reprints to 1982.)
New York: Random House, 1981. 232 pp.

A13. AN AREA OF DARKNESS. London: Deutsch, 1964. 281 pp.
AD
Toronto: Collins, 1965. 281 pp.
New York: Macmillan, 1965. 281 pp.
Harmondsworth, Middlesex: Penguin, 1968. 267 pp. (Five
further reprints to 1981.)
New York: Vintage Books, 1981. 282 pp.

FRENCH:

A13.1. L'Inde Sans Espoir. Trans. Janine Michel. Paris: Gallimard, 1968. 286 pp.

SWEDISH:

A13.2. Ett land i mörker. Trans. Roland Adlerberth. Stockholm:
Rabén och Sjögren, 1973. 222 pp.

A14. THE LOSS OF EL DORADO: A HISTORY. London: Deutsch,
1969. 335 pp. LE
New York: Knopf, 1970. 335 pp.
New York: University Place Bookshop, 1970.
Harmondsworth, Middlesex: Penguin, 1973. 394 pp. (Four
reprints to 1982.)
New York: Vintage Books, 1980. 256 pp.
Harmondsworth, Middlesex: Penguin, 1982 (Revised.)

SPANISH:

A14.1. La Perdida de El Dorado. Trans. Julia J. Natino. Caracas:
Monte Avila Editores, 1971. 426 pp.

POLISH:

A14.2. Utrata El Dorato. Trans. Maria Zborowska. Warszawa:
"Ksiazka i Wiedza," 1972. 453 pp.

SWEDISH:

A14.3. Det förlorade El Dorado. Trans. Olle Moberg. Stockholm:
Rabén och Sjögren, 1974. 423 pp.

DUTCH:

A14.4. Het verlies van El Dorado: een geschiedenis (ned) Geertje
Lammers. Niwuwkoop: Heureka, 1978. 235 pp.

A15. THE OVERCROWDED BARRACOON AND OTHER ARTICLES.
London: Deutsch, 1972. 288 pp. OB
New York: Knopf, 1973. 286 pp.
Harmondsworth, Middlesex: Penguin, 1976. 309 pp. (One
further reprint, 1981.)

New York: Vintage Books, 1984. 286 pp.
Includes "London" (B5, C15), "In the Middle of the
Journey" (B13), "Jamshed into Jimmy" (B14), "Cricket"
(B16), "Jasmine" (B20, C15), "Indian Autobiographies" (B22),
"East Indian" (B24), "The Last of the Aryans" (B26), "The-
atrical Natives" (B28), "Mr. Matsuda's Million-Dollar Gamble"
(B30), "A Second Visit; Tragedy: The Missing Sense" (B31),
"Magic and Dependence" (B32), "Columbus and Crusoe"
(B33), "Jacques Soustelle and the Decline of the West" (B34),
"Anguilla: The Shipwrecked 6000" (B37), "St. Kitts: Papa
and the Power Set" (B38), "The Ultimate Colony" (B39),
"New York with Norman Mailer" (B40), "Steinbeck in Mon-
terey" (B42), "Power" (B43), "The Election at Ajmer" (B45),
"The Overcrowded Barracoon" (B49, B127).

A16. INDIA: A WOUNDED CIVILIZATION. London: Deutsch,
      1977. 174 pp. IN
      New York: Vintage Books, 1977. 191 pp.
      New York: Knopf, 1977. 191 pp.
      New York: Vintage Books, 1978. 191 pp.
      New Delhi: Vikas Publishing House, 1977. 174 pp.
      Harmondsworth, Middlesex: Penguin, 1979. 175 pp. (One
      further reprint to 1980.)

      GERMAN:

A16.1. Indien: eine verwundete Kultur. Trans. Susanne Lepsius.
       Zug (Switzerland): Bergh in der Europabuch-AG, 1978.
       Zürich: Neve Bücher, 1978. 191 pp.

       JAPANESE:

A16.2. Indo-Kizutsuita Bunmei. Trans. Akio Kudŏ. Tokyo: Iwa-
       nami Shoten, 1978. 264 pp.

       SWEDISH:

A16.3. Indien, en sårad civilisation. Trans. Svante Löfgren. Mal-
       mö: Berghs forlag, 1978. 191 pp.

A17. A CONGO DIARY. Los Angeles: Sylvester and Orphanos,
      1980. 42 pp. CD (Limited Edition 330 signed copies.)

A18. THE RETURN OF EVA PERON with THE KILLINGS IN
      TRINIDAD. New York: Knopf, 1980. 227 pp. RP
      London: Deutsch, 1980. 228 pp.
      Toronto: Collins, 1980. 228 pp.
      New York: Vintage Books, 1981. 240 pp.
      Harmondsworth, Middlesex: Penguin, 1981. 218 pp.

JAPANESE:

A18.1. Eva Peron no Kikan. Trans. Akio Kudô. Tokyo: TBS
Britannica, 1982. 390 pp.

SPANISH:

A18.2. El Regreso de Eva Perón. Trans. Jordi Bertrán Ferrer.
Barcelona: Seix Barral, 1983. 272 pp.
Bogotá: Planeta Colombiana, 1984. 256 pp.
Includes "Michael X and the Black Power Killings in Trini-
dad" (B58, B59), "The Return of Eva Peron" (B51, B52,
B57, B60, B75), "Conrad's Darkness" (B61, C15), "A New
King for the Congo" (B63).

A19. AMONG THE BELIEVERS: AN ISLAMIC JOURNEY. New
York: Knopf, 1981. 512 pp. AB
London: Deutsch, 1981. 399 pp.
Franklin Center, Pennsylvania: Franklin Library, 1981.
450 pp.
Toronto: Collins, 1981. 399 pp.
New York: Vintage Books, 1982. 448 pp.
Harmondsworth, Middlesex: Penguin, 1982. 399 pp.
Markham, Ontario: Penguin, 1983. 400 pp.

FRENCH:

A19.1. Crépuscule sur l'Islam: Voyage au pays des voyants. Les
Grandes Traductions. Trans. Annie Saumont. Paris: Albin
Michel, 1981. 500 pp.

NORWEGIAN:

A19.2. Blant de troende. En islamsk reise. Trans. Geir Uthaug.
Oslo: Gyldendal Norsk forlag, 1981. 526 pp.

GERMAN:

A19.3. Eine islamische Reise: unter den Gläubigen. Trans. Karin
Graf. Koln: Kiepenheuer and Witsch, 1982. 670 pp.
Frankfurt am Main: Fischer-Tauschenbuch-Verlag, 1984.

JAPANESE:

A19.4. Isuramu Kiko. Trans. Akio Kudô. Tokyo: TBS Britannica,
1983. 352 pp. Vol. I; 340 pp. Vol. II.

SPANISH:

A19.5. Entre los creyentes: Un viaje por tierras del Islam. Trans.
M. Inés Moreno Taulis. Barcelona: Quarto Ediciones, 1984.
456 pp.

A20.   FINDING THE CENTRE: TWO NARRATIVES. New York:
       Knopf, 1984. 176 pp. FC
       London: Collins, 1984. 189 pp.
       London: Deutsch, 1984. 189 pp.
       Harmondsworth, Middlesex: Penguin, 1985. 160 pp.
       New York: Vintage Books, 1986. 176 pp.

       FRENCH:

A20.1. Sacrifices. Trans. Annie Saumont. Paris: Albin Michel,
       1984. 220 pp.
       Includes "Prologue to an Autobiography" (B86), "The
       Crocodiles of Yamoussoukro" (B87).

A21.   THE ENIGMA OF ARRIVAL: A NOVEL IN FIVE SECTIONS.
       New York: Knopf, 1987. 354 pp. EA
       London: Viking, 1987. 318 pp.
       Harmondsworth, Middlesex: Penguin, 1988. 320 pp.

B. ARTICLES, SHORT STORIES AND ANTHOLOGY CONTRIBUTIONS

ARTICLES

B1. "Liza of Lambeth." Q[ueen's] R[oyal] C[ollege] Chronicle 23 (Port of Spain, 1948): 42-43.

B2. "Honesty Needed in West Indian Writing." Sunday Guardian [Trinidad] (October 28, 1956): 29.

B3. "Where the Rum Comes from." New Statesman (January 4, 1958): 20-21.

B4. "Seven Ages of Humour: Young Men Forget." Punch 234 (June 1958): 734-736.

B5. "The Regional Barrier." Times Literary Supplement 2946 (August 15, 1958): xxxvii-xxxviii. Rpt. "London" in OB. Rpt. in Critical Perspectives on V. S. Naipaul, edited by Robert D. Hamner, 5-12. Washington, DC: Three Continents Press, 1977.

B6. "New Novels." New Statesman 56 (December 6, 1958): 826-827.

B7. "New Novels." New Statesman 60 (July 16, 1960): 97-98.

B8. "The Little More." The Times, July 13, 1961, p. 13. Rpt. in Critical Perspectives on V. S. Naipaul, edited by Robert D. Hamner, 13-15. Washington, DC: Three Continents Press, 1977.

B9. "Living Like a Millionaire." Vogue 138 (October 15, 1961): 92-93, 144, 147. Rpt. in MP.

B10. "The Immigrants: Lo! The Poor West Indian." Punch 242 (January 17, 1962): 124-126.

B11. "Trollope in the West Indies." Listener 57 (March 15, 1962): 461.

B12. "Tea with an Author." Bim 9 (January-June 1962): 79-81.

B13. "In the Middle of the Journey." The Illustrated Weekly of India (October 28, 1962). Rpt. in OB.

B14. "Jamshed into Jimmy." New Statesman 65 (January 25, 1963): 129-130. Rpt. in OB.

B15. "India's Cast-Off Revolution." Sunday Times (August 25, 1963): p. 17.

B16. "Sporting Life Beyond a Boundary." Encounter 21 (September 1963): 73-75. Rpt. "Cricket" in OB.

B17. "Speaking of Writing." The Times (January 2, 1964): p. 11.

B18. "Critics and Criticism." Bim (January-June 1964): 74-77.

B19. "Trinidad." Mademoiselle 59 (May 1964): 187-188.

B20. "Words on Their Own." Times Literary Supplement 3249 (June 4, 1964): 472-473. Rpt. "Jasmine" in OB. Rpt. in Critical Perspectives on V. S. Naipaul, edited by Robert D. Hamner, 16-22. Washington, DC: Three Continents Press, 1977.

B21. "Australia Deserta." Spectator (October 16, 1964): 513.

B22. "Indian Autobiographies." New Statesman 71 (January 29, 1965): 156-158.

B23. "They Are Staring at Me." Saturday Evening Post 238 (April 10, 1965): 82-84. Rpt. in AD.

B24. "East Indian, West Indian." Reporter 32: 12 (June 17, 1965): 35-37. Rpt. "East Indian" in OB.

B25. "Images." New Statesman (September 24, 1965): 452-453. Rpt. in Critical Perspectives on V. S. Naipaul, edited by Robert D. Hamner, 26-29. Washington, DC: Three Continents Press, 1977.

B26. "The Last of the Aryans." Encounter 26 (January 1966): 61-66.

B27. "The Writer." New Statesman 72 (March 18, 1966): 381-382. Rpt. in Critical Perspectives on V. S. Naipaul, edited by Robert D. Hamner, 30-33.

B28. "Theatrical Natives." New Statesman 72 (December 2, 1966): 844. Rpt. in OB.

B29.   "Speaking Out; What's Wrong with Being a Snob?" Saturday
        Evening Post 240 (June 3, 1967): 12, 18. Rpt. "What's
        Wrong with Being a Snob?" in Critical Perspectives on V. S.
        Naipaul, edited by Robert D. Hamner, 34-38. Washington,
        DC: Three Continents Press, 1977.

B30.   "Mr. Matsuda's Million Dollar Gamble." Daily Telegraph Mag-
        azine (July 14, 1967): 6-7. Rpt. in OB.

B31.   "Tragedy: The Missing Sense." Daily Telegraph Magazine
        (August 11, 1967):   Rpt. "A Second Visit; Tragedy:
        The Missing Sense" in OB.

B32.   "Magic and Dependence." Daily Telegraph Magazine (August
        18, 1967): 6-7, 11. Rpt. "India: Magic and Dependence"
        in OB.

B33.   "Columbus and Crusoe." Listener 78 (December 28, 1967):
        845-846. Rpt. OB.

B34.   "Jacques Soustelle and the Decline of the West." Daily Tele-
        graph Magazine (January 26, 1968). Rpt. in OB.

B35.   "Out of the Air: In Black Ink." Listener 79 (May 23, 1968):
        666.

B36.   "Biafra's Rights." The Times (November 13, 1968): 11.

B37.   "Anguilla: The Shipwrecked 6000." New York Review of
        Books 12:8 (April 24, 1969): 9-10, 12, 14, 16. Rpt. "An-
        guilla: The Shipwrecked Six Thousand" in OB.

B38.   "St. Kitts: Papa and the Power Set." New York Review of
        Books 12:9 (May 8, 1969): 23-27.

B39.   "Twilight of a Colony." Daily Telegraph Magazine (July 4,
        1969): 6-8, 10. Rpt. "The Ultimate Colony" in OB.

B40.   "Mailer's Dream." Daily Telegraph Magazine (October 10,
        1969): 87-90, 94. Rpt. "New York with Norman Mailer" in
        OB.

B41.   "New Year Predictions." Listener 83 (January 1, 1970): 17.

B42.   "Cannery Row Revisited." Daily Telegraph Magazine (April
        3, 1970): 24-27, 29-30. Rpt. "Steinbeck in Monterey" in OB.

B43.   "Power to the Caribbean People." New York Review of Books
        15 (September 3, 1970): 32-34. Rpt. "Expression; Vidia
        Naipaul Looks Back in Blackness." In Sunday Express [Trini-
        dad], (October 11, 1970): 26 (condensed). Rpt. "Power?" in

OB. Rpt. in The Aftermath of Sovereignty: West Indian Perspectives, edited by David Lowenthal and Lambros Comitas, 363-372. New York: Doubleday, 1973.

B44. "Prologue, from a Journal: The Tramp at Piraeus," in In a Free State by V. S. Naipaul, 7-20. London: Deutsch, 1971.

B45. "The Election in Ajmer." Sunday Times Magazine (August 15-22, 1971): 8, 18. Rpt. in OB.

B46. "The Circus at Luxor: Epilogue to a Novel." New York Review of Books 17 (November 4, 1971): 8, 10, 12. Rpt. "Epilogue, from a Journal: The Circus at Luxor" in FS.

B47. "Escape from the Puritan Ethic." Daily Telegraph Magazine (December 10, 1971): 38.

B48. "Without a Dog's Chance." New York Review of Books 18 (May 18, 1972): 29-31.

B49. "Mauritius: The Overcrowded Barracoon." Sunday Times Magazine (July 16, 1972): 4. Rpt. "The Overcrowded Barracoon" in OB.

B50. "The King Over the Water: Juan Peron." Sunday Times (August 6, 1972): 29-30.

B51. "The Corpse at the Iron Gate." New York Review of Books 19 (August 10, 1972): 3-8. Rpt. in RP (extract).

B52. "Comprehending Borges." New York Review of Books 19 (August 19, 1972): 3-6. Rpt. "Borges and the Bogus Past" in RP (extract).

B53. "It is not easy to be famous in a Small Town." Daily Telegraph (November 17, 1972): 37.

B54. "Prologue: The Dispossessed Conquistador." In The Loss of El Dorado by V. S. Naipaul, 17-21. Harmondsworth, Middlesex: Penguin, 1973.

B55. "Epilogue: The Death of Jacquet." In The Loss of El Dorado by V. S. Naipaul, 371-378. Harmondsworth, Middlesex: Penguin, 1973.

B56. "V. S. Naipaul Tells How Writing Changes a Writer." Tapia 3 (December 2, 1973): 11.

B57. "A Country Dying on Its Feet." New York Review of Books 21 (April 4, 1974): 21-23. Rpt. "Kamikaze in Montevideo" in RP (extract).

B58. "The Killings in Trinidad: Part One." Sunday Times Magazine (May 12, 1974): 16-35.

B59. "The Killings in Trinidad: Part Two." Sunday Times Magazine (May 19, 1974): 24-41. Rpt. in RP.

B60. "Argentina: The Brothels Behind the Graveyard." New York Review of Books 21 (September 19, 1974): 12-16. Rpt. "The Brothels Behind the Graveyard" in RP (extract).

B61. "Conrad's Darkness." New York Review of Books 21 (October 17, 1974): 16-21. Rpt. in Critical Perspectives on V. S. Naipaul, edited by Robert D. Hamner, 54-65. Washington, DC: Three Continents Press, 1977. Rpt. in RP.

B62. "The Reality and the Romance." Sunday Times Magazine (October 27, 1974): 56-66.

B63. "A New King for the Congo." New York Review of Books 22 (June 26, 1975): 19-25. Rpt. in RP.

B64. "Foreword." In The Adventures of Gurudeva and Other Stories by Seepersad Naipaul, 7-22. London: Deutsch, 1976.

B65. "India: A Wounded Civilization." New York Review of Books 23 (April 29, 1976): 18-22, 27-29.

B66. "The Wounds of India." New York Review of Books 23 (May 13, 1976): 8-14.

B67. "Bombay: The Skyscrapers and the Chawls." New York Review of Books 23 (June 10, 1976): 26-29.

B68. "Mother England?" Sunday Times (June 13, 1976): 17.

B69. "India: New Claim on the Land." New York Review of Books 23 (June 24, 1976): 11-18.

B70. "India: A Defect of Vision." New York Review of Books 23 (August 5, 1976): 14-19.

B71. "India: Synthesis and Mimicry." New York Review of Books 23 (September 16, 1976): 14-19.

B72. "India: Paradise Lost." New York Review of Books 23 (October 28, 1976): 10, 12, 14-19.

B73. "Indian Art and Its Illusions." New York Review of Books 26 (March 22, 1979): 6, 8-10, 12, 14.

B74. "The Flight from the Fire." New York Review of Books 26 (May 3, 1979): 28-30. Rpt. in BR.

B75. "Argentina Terror: A Memoir." New York Review of Books 26 (October 11, 1979): 13-16. Rpt. "Terror" in RP (extract).

B76. "Tehran Winter." New York Review of Books (October 8, 1981): 23-29.

B77. "Iran's Walls Speak of Islam and Blood." Globe and Mail (December 1, 1981): 7. Rpt. in AB (extract).

B78. "Straight Man for a Jolly Hanging Judge." Globe and Mail (December 2, 1981): 7. Rpt. in AB (extract).

B79. "Pakistan and the Reality of Islam." Globe and Mail (December 3, 1981): 7.

B80. "I Cannot Disown Trinidad and It Cannot Disown Me." Listener 107 (June 10, 1982): 13-14.

B81. "Introduction." In East Indians in the Caribbean: Colonialism and the Struggle for Identity, Papers presented to symposium on East Indians in the Caribbean. University of the West Indies, June 1971; edited by Bridget Brereton and Winston Dookeran, 1-9. New York: Kraus International, 1982.

B82. "A Note on a Borrowing by Conrad." New York Review of Books (December 16, 1982): 37-38.

B83. "Bogart, Hat and Popo: Prologue to an Autobiography." Part 1 Sunday Times (May 8, 1983): 33-34. Rpt. in FC (extract).

B84. "Family Secrets: Prologue to an Autobiography." Part 2 Sunday Times (May 15, 1983): 33-34. Rpt. in FC (extract).

B85. "Writing 'A House for Mr. Biswas.'" New York Review of Books (November 24, 1983): 22-23. Rpt. "Naipaul Exposes Himself." In Express [Trinidad] (February 2, 1984): 11-12.

B86. "Prologue to an Autobiography." In Finding the Centre by V. S. Naipaul, 15-85. London: Deutsch, 1984.

B86.1. GERMAN: Prolog zu eine Autobiographie. Trans. Karin Graf. Köln: Kiepenheur und Witsch, 1984. 140 pp.

B87. "The Crocodiles of Yamoussoukro." In Finding the Centre by V. S. Naipaul, 89-189. London: Deutsch, 1984.

B87.1. DUTCH: De Krokodillen van Yamoussouko. Trans. Tinke Davids. Amsterdam: De Arbeiderspers, 1985. 116 pp.

B88. "Heavy Manners in Grenada." Sunday Times Colour Magazine (February 12, 1984): 23-31.

B89. "Grenada: An Island Betrayed." Harper's 268 (March 1984): 61-72.

B90. "Among the Republicans." New York Review of Books (October 25, 1984): 5, 8, 10, 12, 14-17.

B91. "India after Indira Gandhi." New York Times (November 3, 1984): 24.

B91.1. "The Enigma of Arrival." New Yorker 62 (Aug. 11, 1986): 26-62.

SHORT STORIES

B92. "The Blue Cart." In Miguel Street by V. S. Naipaul, 118-129. London: Deutsch, 1959.

B93. "Bogart." In Miguel Street by V. S. Naipaul, 9-16. London: Deutsch, 1959.

B94. "Caution." In Miguel Street by V. S. Naipaul, 165-178. London: Deutsch, 1959.

B95. "The Coward." In Miguel Street by V. S. Naipaul, 66-78. London: Deutsch, 1959.

B96. "George and the Pink House." In Miguel Street by V. S. Naipaul, 26-35. London: Deutsch, 1959.

B97. "Hat." In Miguel Street by V. S. Naipaul, 199-214. London: Deutsch, 1959.

B98. "His Chosen Calling." In Miguel Street by V. S. Naipaul, 36-45. London: Deutsch, 1959.

B99. "How I Left Miguel Street." In Miguel Street by V. S. Naipaul, 215-222. London: Deutsch, 1959.

B100. "Love, Love, Love, Alone." In Miguel Street by V. S. Naipaul, 130-146. London: Deutsch, 1959.

B101. "The Maternal Instinct." In Miguel Street by V. S. Naipaul, 107-117. London: Deutsch, 1959.

B102. "The Pyrotechnicist." In Miguel Street by V. S. Naipaul, 79-92. London: Deutsch, 1959.

B103. "The Thing Without a Name." In Miguel Street by V. S. Naipaul, 17-25. London: Deutsch, 1959.

B104. "Until the Soldiers Came." In Miguel Street by V. S. Naipaul, 179-198. London: Deutsch, 1959.

B105. "Caribbean Medley." Vogue 134 (November 15, 1959): 90, 92-93.

B106. "The Night Watchman's Occurrence Book." Saturday Evening Post 236 (September 28, 1963): 72-75. Rpt. in Spectator 213 (November 27, 1964): 719, 721-722. Rpt. in FI.

B107. "A Flag on the Island." In A Flag on the Island by V. S. Naipaul, 147-235. London: Deutsch, 1967.

B108. "Greenie and Yellow." In A Flag on the Island by V. S. Naipaul, 89-101. London: Deutsch, 1967.

B109. "The Mourners." In A Flag on the Island by V. S. Naipaul, 55-61. London: Deutsch, 1967. Rpt. in The Perfect Tenants and Mourners, edited by Francis Curtis, 23-30. Cambridge: Cambridge University Press, 1977.

B110-
B111. "The Perfect Tenants." In A Flag on the Island by V. S. Naipaul, 103-119. London: Deutsch, 1967. Rpt. in The Perfect Tenants and Mourners, edited by Francis Curtis, 1-21. Cambridge: Cambridge University Press, 1977.

B112. "In a Free State." In In a Free State by V. S. Naipaul, 109-245. London: Deutsch, 1971.

B113. "One Out of Many." Atlantic Monthly 227 (April 1971): 71-82. Rpt. in FS.

B114. "Tell Me Who to Kill." In In a Free State by V. S. Naipaul, 63-108. London: Deutsch, 1971.

B114.1. FRENCH: "Dis-moi qui Tuer." Title-story in Dis-moi qui Tuer. Trans. Annie Saumont. Paris: Albin Michel, 1983. See item A8.10.

ANTHOLOGY CONTRIBUTIONS

B115. "A Christmas Story." Encounter 22 (March 3, 1964): 41-52. Rpt. in Stories from the Caribbean: An Anthology, edited by Andrew Salkey, 25-44. London: Elek, 1965. Rpt. in FI. Rpt. in Island Voices: Stories from the West Indies, edited by Andrew Salkey, 52-69. New York: Liveright, 1970. Rpt. in Instructor's Manual for the Berzoi Book of

Short Fiction, edited by Donald H. Richter and Rhoda Sirlin, 126-129. New York: Knopf, 1983.

B116. "The Raffle." In Stories from the Caribbean: An Anthology, edited by Andrew Salkey, 48-51. London: Elek, 1965. Rpt. in FI. Rpt. in Island Voices: Stories from the West Indies, edited by Andrew Salkey, 48-51. New York: Liveright, 1970. Rpt. in Caribbean Stories, edited by Michael Marland, 65-72. London: Longman, 1978.

B117. "My Aunt Gold Teeth." In Stories from the Caribbean: An Anthology, edited by Andrew Salkey, 15-22. London: Elek, 1965. Rpt. in FI. Rpt. in Island Voices: Stories from the West Indies, edited by Andrew Salkey, 40-47. New York: Liveright, 1970. Rpt. in Images: Modern Short Stories, edited by Cecil Gray, 86-94. London: Nelson, 1973. Rpt. in Modern Stories in English, edited by W. H. New and H. J. Resengarton, 285-292. Toronto: Copp-Clark, 1975. Rpt. in Caribbean Stories: Barbados, Guyana, Jamaica, Trinidad and Tobago. Selected and edited with introduction by Bianca Acosta and others, 243-254. La Habana: Casa de Las Americas, 1977.

B118. "B Wordsworth." In Miguel Street by V. S. Naipaul, 56-65. London: Deutsch, 1959. Rpt. in West Indian Narrative, compiled by Kenneth Ramchand, 147-156. London: Nelson, 1966. Rpt. in From the Green Antilles, edited by Barbara Howes, 8-14. New York: Macmillan, 1966. Rpt. in Commonwealth Short Stories, edited by Anna Rutherford and Donald Hannah, 56-65. London: Arnold, 1971. Rpt. in Images: Modern Short Stories, edited by Cecil Gray, 150-157. London: Nelson, 1973. Rpt. in Carray! A Selection of Plays for Caribbean Schools, by James Lee Wah, 97-108. London: Macmillan, 1977. Rpt. in An Anthology of African and Caribbean Writing in English, edited by John J. Figueroa, 154-158. London: Heinemann Educational Books, 1982.

B119. "Man-Man." In Miguel Street by V. S. Naipaul, 46-55. London: Deutsch, 1959. Rpt. in Commonwealth Short Stories, edited by Anna Rutherford and Donald Hannah, 198-206.

B120. "The Mechanical Genius." In Miguel Street by V. S. Naipaul, 147-164. London: Deutsch, 1959. Rpt. in Four Hemispheres, edited by W. H. New, 317-327. Toronto: Copp-Clark, 1971. Rpt. in The Best of Modern Humour, edited by Mordecai Richler, 355-365. Toronto: McClelland and Stewart, 1983.

B121. "The Heart." In Miguel Street by V. S. Naipaul, 121-132. London: Deutsch, 1959. Rpt. in Images: Modern Short Stories, edited by Cecil Gray, 176-184. London: Nelson, 1973.

B122. "The Baker's Story." In A Flag on the Island by V. S.
Naipaul, 133-146. London: Deutsch, 1967. Rpt. in Kenyon
Review 26 (Summer 1964): 469-480. Rpt. in Caribbean
Rhythms: The Emerging English Literature of the West In-
dies, edited by James Livingston, 116-128. New York:
Washington Square Press, 1974. Rpt. in Caribbean Stories,
edited by Michael Marland, 55-64. London: Longman, 1978.
Rpt. in An Anthology of African and Caribbean Writing in
English, edited by John J. Figueroa, 106-112. London:
Heinemann Educational Books, 1982.

B123. "Titus Hoyt, I. A." In Miguel Street by V. S. Naipaul, 93-
106. London: Deutsch, 1959. Rpt. in Literary Glimpses
of the Commonwealth, edited by James B. Bell, 157-172.
Toronto: Wiley, 1977.

B124. "The Enemy." In A Flag on the Island by V. S. Naipaul,
75-87. London: Deutsch, 1967. Rpt. in Vogue 137 (March
1, 1961): 69, 76, 83, 100-101. Rpt. in Caribbean Stories,
edited by Michael Marland, 46-54. London: Longman, 1978.

B125. "A House for Mr. Biswas." In Caribbean Narrative: An
Anthology of West Indian Writing, edited by Oscar Ronald
Dathorne, 174-181. London: Heinemann Educational Books,
1966 (extract).

B126. "The Mystic Masseur." In Caribbean Narrative: An Anthology
of the West Indian Writing, edited by Oscar Ronald Dathorne,
182-189. London: Heinemann Educational Books, 1966 (extract).

B127. "The Overcrowded Barracoon." In Carifesta Forum: An
Anthology of Twenty Caribbean Voices, edited with introduc-
tion by John Hearne, 155-162. Jamaica: Institute of
Jamaica, 1976.

SECTION III: WORKS ABOUT V. S. NAIPAUL

C. BIBLIOGRAPHIES, BOOKS, CRITICAL STUDIES, INTERVIEWS, THESES, AND DISSERTATIONS

BIBLIOGRAPHIES

C1.   New, William H., Compiler. "West Indies." In Critical Writings on Commonwealth Literatures: a selective bibliography to 1970 with a list of theses and dissertations. University Park: Pennsylvania State University Press, 1975, pp. 279-280; 311-312.

The coverage of this item extends to significant general West Indian literature criticism appearing in Caribbean sources up to 1970, and includes theses and dissertations. Documentation of Naipaul's work in Caribbean publications is quite sparse.

C2.   Ravenscroft, Arthur. "V. S. Naipaul: A Select Bibliography." Journal of Commonwealth Literature 10 (August 1975): 34-44.

This bibliography includes a good proportion of British material up to 1972. Mr. Hamner further updated it to 1975 in the following item, C3.

C3.   Hamner, Robert D. "Annotated Bibliography." In Critical Perspectives, edited by Robert D. Hamner. Washington, DC: Three Continents Press, 1977, pp. 264-298.

Hamner's bibliography is equally valuable for the study of Naipaul and his work, but it is mainly the critical articles which he has annotated. It contains a large proportion of material reflecting Naipaul's early career as an extremely prolific reviewer for the New Statesman. Its terminal date is 1975.

C4.   Stanton, Robert J. "V[idiadhar] S[urajprasad] Naipaul." In A Bibliography of Modern English Novelists, Volume 2 by Robert J. Stanton. Troy, New York: Whitson, 1978, pp. 621-664.

It is the only bibliography on Naipaul to exceed forty pages. Includes a record of his book reviewing assignments for the New Statesman, translations and critical articles on his work. Coverage extends to August 1976.

C5. Carnegie, Jeniphier R. "Naipaul, Vidiadhar Surajprasad (1932): Bibliography." In Critics on West Indian Literature; A Selected Bibliography, compiled by Jeniphier R. Carnegie, Cave-Hill: University of the West Indies, 1979, pp. 26-35.
   Caribbean sources are well represented but the articles are not annotated. Coverage extends to January 1978.

C6. Allis, Jeanette B. "Index of Authors." In West Indian Literatures: An Index to Criticism, 1930-1975. Boston: G. K. Hall, 1981, pp. 111-127.
   This work is an important contribution to West Indian literary bibliography. Coverage, however, does not extend beyond 1974 in spite of its terminal date stated as 1975. It is painstakingly cross-indexed in chronological order.

C7. Singh, Sydney. "Bibliography of Critical Writing on the West Indian Novel." World Literature Written in English, Volume 22, (1983): 107-142.
   This is an up-to-date addition to the literature for a study of V. S. Naipaul. The author states that it is geared "for students who wish to undertake studies in West Indian prose literature."

C8. Mann, Harveen Sachdeva. "Primary Works of and Critical Writings on V. S. Naipaul: A Selected Checklist." Modern Fiction Studies, Volume 30, No. 3, (Autumn 1984): 581-591.
   This important list of material is arranged in six categories. The author claims that the checklist endeavors to update "entries that do not find mention in the Hamner and Stanton lists." It excludes newspaper items, encyclopedic articles and "all book reviews."

C8A. Hamner, Robert D. "V. S. Naipaul (1932-)," in Fifty Caribbean Writers: A Bio-Bibliographical Sourcebook, edited by Daryl Cumber Dance, 357-367. Westport, CT: Greenwood Press, 1986.
   Brief bibliography of "Works" and "Studies" preceded by "Biography," "Major Works and Themes," "Critical Reception" and "Honors and Awards."

See also item C138.

BOOKS

C9. Theroux, Paul. V. S. Naipaul: An Introduction to His Work. London: Deutsch; New York: Africana Publishing Corp., 1972. 144 pp.

C10. Hamner, Robert D. V. S. Naipaul. World Authors Series: West Indies, no. 258. New York: Twayne, 1973. 181 pp.

C11. Walsh, William. V. S. Naipaul. Modern Writers Series. Edinburgh: Oliver and Boyd; Toronto: Clark/Irwin, 1973. 94 pp.

C12. Morris, Robert K. Paradoxes of Order: Some Perspectives on the Fiction of V. S. Naipaul. Literary Frontiers Series. Columbia, MO: University of Missouri, 1975. 105 pp.

C13. White, Landeg. V. S. Naipaul: A Critical Introduction. London: Macmillan, 1975. 217 pp.

C14. Thorpe, Michael. V. S. Naipaul. Writers and Their Work, edited by Ian Scott-Kilvert, no. 242. Harlow, Essex: Longman, for the British Council, 1976. 44 pp.

C15. Hamner, Robert D., ed. Critical Perspectives on V. S. Naipaul. Critical Perspectives Series, edited by D. Herdeck and B. Lindfors, no. 2. Washington, DC: Three Continents Press, 1977. 300 pp.

C16. Rao, K. I. Madhusudana. The Complex Fate: Naipaul's View of Human Development. Development Education Series, no. 1. Madras: Christian Literature Society, 1979. 21 pp.

C17. Pitt, Rosemary, ed. Notes on "A House for Mr. Biswas." York Notes, no. 180. Harlow, Essex: Longman, 1982. 64 pp.

C18. Rai, Sudha. V. S. Naipaul: A Study in Expatriate Sensibility. Atlantic Highlands, NJ: Humanities Press, 1982. 192 pp.

C19. Rao, K. I. Madhusudana. Contrary Awareness; A Critical Study of the Novels of V. S. Naipaul. Madras: Centre for Research on New International Economic Order, 1982. 232 pp.

C20. Boxhill, Anthony. V. S. Naipaul's Fiction: In Quest of the Enemy. Fredericton: York Press, 1983. 88 pp.

C21. Thieme, John. "The Mimic Men," A Critical View. Nexus Series, edited by Yolande Cant'u. London: British Council, 1985. 42 pp.

C22. Thorpe, Michael. V. S. Naipaul: "A House for Mr. Biswas," A Critical View. Nexus Series edited by Yolande Cant'u. London: British Council, 1985. 43 pp.

C23. Nightingale, Peggy. A Sense of Place in the New Literatures in English. St. Lucia, Brisbane: University of Queensland Press, 1986. 252 pp.

C24. Nightingale, Peggy. Journey through darkness; the writing of V. S. Naipaul. St. Lucia, Brisbane: University of Queensland Press, 1987. 255 pp.

CRITICAL STUDIES: ARTICLES, PARTS OF BOOKS

C25.   Moore, Gerald. "East Indians and West: The Novels of
        V. S. Naipaul." Black Orpheus 7 (June 1960): 11-15.

C26.   "The Caribbean Mixture: Variations and Fusion in Race and
        Style." Times Literary Supplement 3154 (August 10, 1962):
        578.
           A rather interesting, speculative account. Focuses on
        variations of English spoken in the Caribbean; the miscon-
        ceptions held about the islands influenced partly by the di-
        versity of ethnic conglomerations. Cites some of those dif-
        ferences through the characters both Selvon and Naipaul
        create. Alludes to the inventive tendency of the Scottish
        renaissance being present in West Indian writing and disputes
        the claim of a West Indian school, due to the absence of a
        tradition. Draws constantly on the work of Hearne, Lamming,
        Mittelholzer and Naipaul. Explores the race theme.

C27.   Pritchett, V. S. "Climacteric." New Statesman 65 (1963):
        831-832. Rpt. in Critical Perspectives on V. S. Naipaul,
        edited by Robert D. Hamner, 104-110. Washington, DC:
        Three Continents Press, 1977.
           One of Pritchett's major considerations in this essay is
        the switch which Naipaul makes from the familiar territory
        surrounding A House for Mr. Biswas to Mr. Stone in far-
        off England. This concern stems from the past experiences
        of writers from Commonwealth countries who failed or wavered
        in such an attempt. Argues that in both these books, it is
        not so much the similarities of characters that matter: it is
        the understanding of the distinctions between them. Makes
        the point that Naipaul habitually provides his audience with
        suspended characters, noting Mr. Stone's decision to marry
        and the circumstances surrounding the marriage, a situation
        similar to that of Mr. Biswas. Speculates that Naipaul's im-
        maculate power of observation marshalls all his energy and
        talent instinctively.

C28.   Brathwaite, Edward. "Roots." Bim 10 (July/December,
        1963): 10-21.
           Brathwaite admires the structure of Naipaul's book. Sees
        his writing "as the first significant expression of a minority
        culture in the West Indies."

C29.   Rohlehr, F. G. "Predestination, Frustration and Symbolic
        Darkness in Naipaul's 'A House for Mr. Biswas.'" Caribbean
        Quarterly 10 (March 1964): 3-11.
           Explains that because of the peculiar composition of West
        Indian society, without clearly defined values, emanating
        from slavery and a colonial environment, the West Indian

novelist has had to recreate experiences and develop standards by which to judge these experiences. Defines the purpose of the essay and views A House for Mr. Biswas in its
role as an outstanding artistic achievement. The focus is
principally on its tone, symbolism, structure and Naipaul's
personality. Regards Miguel Street as closely related in
tonal quality to A House for Mr. Biswas, and is therefore
significant for the study of his tone.

C30.   Walcott, Derek. "The Achievement of V. S. Naipaul." Sun-
        day Guardian [Trinidad] (April 12, 1964): 15.

C31.   Cartey, Wilfred. "The Knights Companion--Ganesh, Biswas
        and Stone." New World Quarterly 2 (1965): 93-98.
        In examining The Mystic Masseur, A House for Mr. Biswas
        and Mr. Stone and the Knights Companion, Cartey pays par-
        ticular attention to the development of the main characters:
        Ganesh, Mr. Biswas and Mr. Stone. The political atmosphere
        to which Ramlogan contributes in The Mystic Masseur is more
        fully developed in The Suffrage of Elvira. The obscene
        dialogue used as a device in A House for Mr. Biswas is ex-
        cluded from Mr. Stone and the Knights Companion. Notes
        that the link between Biswas and Stone is the feeling of
        fear. Contends that apart from the comic relief associated
        with his early work, pessimism permeates the body of his
        writing.

C32.   Walsh, William. "Necessary and Accommodated: The Work of
        V. S. Naipaul." Lugano Review 1 (1965): 169-181. Rpt.
        "V. S. Naipaul." In A Manifold Voice: Studies in Common-
        wealth Literature, by William Walsh, 62-85. London: Chatto
        & Windus, 1970. (revised).

C33.   James, C. L. R. "Home Is Where They Want to Be." Sun-
        day Guardian Magazine [Trinidad] (February 14, 1965): 4-
        5.

C34.   James, C. L. R. "The Disorder of Vidia Naipaul." Sunday
        Guardian Magazine [Trinidad] (February 21, 1965): 6.

C35.   Walsh, William. "Meeting Extremes." Journal of Common-
        wealth Literature 1 (September 1965): 169-172.

C36.   Lee, R. H. "The Novels of V. S. Naipaul." Theoria 27
        (1966): 31-46. Rpt. in Critical Perspectives on V. S. Nai-
        paul, edited by Robert D. Hamner, 68-83. Washington,
        DC: Three Continents Press, 1977.
        Draws on An Area of Darkness to highlight the changes
        he discovers between his generation and that of his grand-
        father. Also suggests that Naipaul's main concerns in the
        early novels are to define his own attitudes toward such

changes, as well as those of the society he portrays through a series of constructions, namely characters from which he remains detached or autobiographical. Praises Naipaul's ability to capture the vividness of life which pervades his books while providing cohesion and balance. Lee describes the progression of development in the novels, which is similar to that in Dickens' Pickwick Papers and Hard Times. Focuses also on his fertile imagination and penchant for "grotesquely humorous detail." Regards both Miguel Street and The Suffrage of Elvira as the least impressive of his five novels.

Emerging from A House for Mr. Biswas is that which Lee calls "an almost archetypal symbol," the stability and permanence of a house. The essay draws attention to Naipaul's expanding interest and ability to deal with psychological analysis and close personal relations, an approach which he further develops in Mr. Stone and the Knights Companion.

C37. Nandakumar, Prema. "V. S. Naipaul." In The Glory and the Good: Essays in Literature, by Prema Nandakumar, 267-277. London: Asia Publishing House, 1966.

C38. Ormerod, David. "Theme and Image in V. S. Naipaul's 'A House for Mr. Biswas.'" Texas Studies in Literature and Language 8 (Winter 1967): 589-602. Rpt. "Unaccommodated Man: Naipaul's 'B. Wordsworth' and Biswas" in Critics on Caribbean Literature; Readings in Literary Criticism, edited by Edward Baugh, 87-92. London: Allen and Unwin, 1978.

Cautions that "Naipaul's calculated simplicity should not obscure from us the fact that many of the novel's telling effects are obtained by employing a consistent structure of imagery and near-symbolism." It is a detailed study of Naipaul's use of the house, the middle passage and the vegetation image motifs in A House for Mr. Biswas. Naipaul introduces the house motif at the very beginning of the novel. He renounces "plot and narrative as sources of tension and deliberately declines to invoke in the reader any anxiety as to what happens next." Ormerod portrays a strong autobiographical portrait of Naipaul.

C39. Seymour, A. J. "The novel in the British Caribbean." Bim 11 (January/June, 1967): 239-240.

Traces the political elements in Naipaul's early novels, The Mystic Masseur and The Suffrage of Elvira. It also subscribes to the view that his novels offer "a new set of values into the British Caribbean novel." Also discusses Naipaul's apparent rejection of "Westindianess" and "Indianess."

C40. Rohlehr, Gordon. "Character and Rebellion in A House for Mr. Biswas." New World Quarterly 4:4 (1968): 66-72. Rpt. in Critical Perspectives on V. S. Naipaul, edited by Robert D. Hamner, 84-93. Washington, DC: Three Continents Press, 1977.

Defines rebellion in Biswas by "his state as a cultural, psychological and social orphan," further claiming that his revolt consists of "a childlike rage and grief at violated innocence." Biswas's character epitomizes negatives: he wishes for a sexless, lonely and sterile world, always in his mind is the fear of the future; his character is also immersed in the irony and wit of Trinidad speech. Rohlehr explains that the Tulsis, by regarding Biswas's rebellion as a joke, and him as a clown, neutralize the effect of his wit.

C41. Rohlehr, Gordon. "The Ironic Approach; the Novels of V. S. Naipaul." In The Islands in Between: Essays in West Indian Literature, edited by Louis James, 121-139. London: Oxford University Press, 1968. Rpt. in Modern Black Novelists, edited by Michael G. Cooke, 162-176. Englewood Cliffs: California, 1971. Rpt. in Critical Perspectives, edited by Robert D. Hamner, 178-193. Washington, DC: Three Continents Press, 1977.
Examines Lamming's criticism of Naipaul's first three novels, in which Naipaul presents his views of the West Indian experience, and the nature of his efforts to determine his own position. Also challenges Lamming's assumption that Naipaul uses satire as a form of retreat "and escape from experience," and that the use of irony is not superfluous to West Indian society. Maintains that it is Naipaul's ironic awareness which allows him to air his contempt for West Indian society and the dullness of English life as represented in Mr. Stone and the Knights Companion. Argues that "if one says that the exercise of irony precludes sympathy one is merely defining the limitations of irony." Notes that in The Middle Passage and "A Christmas Story," Naipaul despairs over the colonial process which he rejects outright, and he expresses this despair in ironic terms.

C42. Van Sertima, Ivan. "V. S. Naipaul." In Caribbean Writers; Critical Essays, by Ivan Van Sertima, 39-41. London: New Beacon Books, 1968.

C43. Thorpe, Marjorie. " 'The Mimic Men': A Study in Isolation." New World Quarterly, 4: 4 (1968): 55-59.
Suggests that the problems of isolated minorities exceed merely a restatement of their significance, which the award Naipaul won for The Mimic Men seems to convey. Sees in this book the complications which do arise when people of varying backgrounds and ideologies are lumped together. Focuses on the importance of the "narrator-protagonist's struggle" to determine his proper place by challenging a fragmented society incapable of providing the order he seeks subconsciously. The study reflects on Kripalsingh's dilemma, the French creole "aristocrats' " preoccupation with their heritage. Thorpe notes, on the other side of the spectrum,

that the Africans reluctantly accept and subscribe to the pseudo-established image of "a carefree irresponsible race of self-mocking comedians," that the Asians are participants who share in the distress but are unable to identify with "their fellow subordinates," and that the Mulattos ironically attempt to preserve the "purity" of their group, which serves only to undermine the structure still further.

C 44.   "Slave Colony." The Economist 233, No. 6585 (November 8, 1968): iv.

This account is described as a set of events drawn together by a common theme. The review focuses on two main episodes: the rivalry between the autocratic governor, Picton, and the bureaucratic Commissioner, Fullarton, and the torture of Luisa Calderon and Fullarton's subsequent trial and acquittal in London. Credits Naipaul's skill in creating a vivid account.

C 45.   Ormerod, David. "In a Derelict and: The Novels of V. S. Naipaul." Wisconsin Studies in Contemporary Literature 9 (Winter 1968): 74-90. Rpt. in Critical Perspectives on V. S. Naipaul, edited by Robert D. Hamner, 159-177. Washington, DC: Three Continents Press, 1977.

Talks of a varied leitmotif which forcefully emerges from The Middle Passage. Cites the quandary of the Negro, transported to slavery in the West Indies, and left there to wither in the formulation of a colonial society structured on exploitation, materialism, absence of identity; and the fate of indentured Indians saddled with "a cheating contract" in a far-off land. Reflects on Mr. Stone's helplessness and desolation. In contrast, Ormerod points to A House for Mr. Biswas, in which Biswas displays supreme resilience and struggles for shelter; Mr. Stone concocts a retirement scheme for the employees in Mr. Stone and the Knights Companion; Ganesh shows uncompromising determination to become educated and religious in The Mystic Masseur. Ormerod points out that the symbols of dereliction expressed fictionally in The Mystic Masseur are even present in A House for Mr. Biswas, where the imprisonment is just as real, "the escape is fantasy." Touches on Naipaul's reflection only on Indian communities. The essay concludes with a vivid exposition on Indian indentureship and the social consequences of that settlement in the West Indies, seen through Naipaul's eyes in The Middle Passage.

C 46.   Wyndham, Francis. "Writing Is Magic." Trinidad Guardian (November 15, 1968): 12.

C 47.   Ramchand, Kenneth. "The World of 'A House for Mr. Biswas.'" Caribbean Quarterly 15 (March 1969): 60-72. Rpt. in The West Indian Novel and Its Background by Kenneth Ramchand,

189-204. London: Faber & Faber, 1970. Rpt. "A House
for Mr. Biswas" in An Introduction to the Study of West
Indian Literature by Kenneth Ramchand, 73-90. London:
Nelson, 1976. Rpt. "A House for Mr. Biswas" in Tapia 7,
1977: 5-8.

C 48.   Derrick, A. C. "Naipaul's Technique as a Novelist." The
Journal of Commonwealth Literature 7 (July 1969): 32-44.
Derrick identifies one of the major thematic threads in
Naipaul's novels as the satirical treatment of his characters'
"social limitations," and the confined environment into which
he places them. Also sees failure as a dominant theme in his
work, beginning with Miguel Street. Attributes the rugged-
ness of his mind as the factor most responsible for the aloof-
ness with which he analyzes a character's faults. Dislikes
Naipaul's empty portrayal of the West Indian islands, and his
habit of imposing his values, systems and norms, which are
alien to his characters; these impositions Derrick ascribes to
Naipaul's lack of sympathy. He analyzes the structural differences of each of the first five novels, and the purposes
each of those techniques is intended to serve. Concludes
that Naipaul's most poignant satirical achievements appear in
The Mystic Masseur and A House for Mr. Biswas.

C 49.   Singh, H. B. "V. S. Naipaul: A Spokesman for Neo-
Colonialism." Literature and Ideology 2 (1969): 71-85.

C 50.   Nazareth, Peter. "The Mimic Men" as a Study of Corruption.
East African Journal 7 (1970): 18-22. Originally published
Literature and Society in Modern Africa. Rpt. in An African
View of Literature, by Peter Nazareth, 76-93. Evanstown:
Northwestern University Press, 1974. Rpt. in Critical Perspectives on V. S. Naipaul, edited by Robert D. Hamner,
137-152. Washington, DC: Three Continents Press, 1977.
Stresses in The Mimic Men the theme of corruption both
of the political body and of the individual, which the narrator's instincts reflect as well. The essay also makes some
references to The Suffrage of Elvira, The Middle Passage
and An Area of Darkness. Suggests the political nature of
The Mimic Men makes it relevant to people in ex-colonial
countries experiencing quick political changes. Questions
the manner in which the political link developed between
Singh and Browne; this he regards as a weakness in the
novel. However, credits Naipaul's skills in enhancing the
quality of the book. Concedes it is gloomy, but wonders
whether the scope of his vision on life does not distort his
view of West Indian society. Nazareth is of the opinion that
The Mimic Men projects a focus which the other three books
do not reflect. His conclusion is that Naipaul offers no solution, but sensitizes a reader's awareness of the problems.

C51. Jones, A. D. H. "No Joke." New York Review of Books
      15 (November 19, 1970): 53-54. (response).

C52. Argyle, Barry. "Commentary on V. S. Naipaul's 'A House
      for Mr. Biswas.' A West Indian Epic." Caribbean Quarterly
      16:4 (December 1970): 61-69.
          States that the novel's symbolism is clear and consistent.
      Since the house "is placed early and its shadows appear
      throughout, it dominates the novel as much as it does the
      title." An important assessment of this epic tale.

C53. Warner, Maureen. "Cultural Confrontation, Disintegration and
      Syncretism in 'A House for Mr. Biswas.'" Caribbean Quarter-
      ly 16 (December 1970): 70-79. Rpt. in Critical Perspectives
      on V. S. Naipaul, edited by Robert D. Hamner, 94-103.
      Washington, DC: Three Continents Press, 1977.
          Examines the "cultural clash" which she regards as the
      most dominant theme in A House for Mr. Biswas. Provides a
      lucid account of "Tulsidom," the significance of Hanuman
      House in the evolution of events there, and Biswas's place
      in the extended family. Points to the rigidity and conscious-
      ness of one's place as important ingredients in the structure
      in spite of all appearances of community life. Warner points
      to the more liberal environment to which Biswas is accustomed.
      Draws attention to "religious ambiguity" as one of first in-
      stances of cultural confrontation in the book; another is the
      economic prosperity which the Americans bring during World
      War II. Notes that important issue Naipaul addresses is the
      geographical dislocation of people and the effects of cultural
      contact.

C54. Moore, Gerald. "Discovery." In Modern Black Novelists:
      A Collection of Critical Essays, edited by M. G. Cooke, 147-
      209. Englewood Cliffs, NJ: Prentice-Hall, 1971.

C55. Lacovia, R. M. "Caribbean Literature in English: 1949-
      1970." Black Academy Review 2 (February 1971): 109-125.
          Lacovia explores several themes in relation to Naipaul's
      work on the Caribbean. Suggests that The Loss of El
      Dorado "at best expresses a European concept of history."
      Cites Wilson Harris's view that both the detractors and de-
      fenders of Caribbean history "are wrong in their approach"
      to writing it. Offers some thoughts on Naipaul's belief in
      visual print, while noting "he lacks all comprehension of the
      audile-tactile world."

C56. Maes-Jelinek, Hena. "The Myth of El Dorado in the Carib-
      bean Novel." Journal of Commonwealth Literature 6 (June
      1971): 113-128.

C57. Nettleford, Rex. "Caribbean Perspectives--The Creative

Potential and Life." Caribbean Quarterly 17 (September-
December 1971): 114-127.

Nettleford adopts the view that the changes in Caribbean
life and variants will deepen to the extent that "serious ob-
jections against the pigeonhole analysis of the region can no
longer be dismissed as the indulgencies of insular vanity."
Explores the Rastafarian theme and others in relation to Naipaul's views and those also of Harris and Walcott.

C58.   Wyndham, Francis. "V. S. Naipaul." The Listener 86
       (October 7, 1971): 461-462.
       Looks at the fluctuations of Naipaul's literary fortunes
       and acceptance of his themes from The Mystic Masseur to
       In a Free State. Sees despair creeping into his work after
       An Area of Darkness, which graduates to placelessness in
       In a Free State.

C59.   Calder, Angus. "Darkest Naipaulia." New Statesman 82
       (October 8, 1971): 482-483.
       Questions Naipaul's global vision as expressed in his
       novels. Condenses and comments favorably on each piece,
       particularly his use of the voice technique in "Tell Me Who
       To Kill." Suggests that "In a Free State," Naipaul has more
       scope to expand on his favorite themes of upheaval, cultural
       dislocation of societies and imperialism.

C60.   "An Area of Brilliance." Observer (November 28, 1971): 8.
       Provides some early valuable biographical and literary in-
       sights into Naipaul and his work. Notes that both the theme
       of despair and his work have grown stronger, but "there is
       still no room for sentimental liberalism."

C61.   Willis, David. "A Compassionate Spectator." Sunday Guardian
       [Trinidad] (January 10, 1971): 9.

C62.   Enright, Dennis Joseph. "The Sensibility of V. S. Naipaul:
       Who Is India?" In Man Is an Onion: Reviews and Essays,
       by Dennis Joseph Enright, 204-211. London: Chatto and
       Windus, 1972.
       Reflects on Naipaul's fastidiousness in The Middle Passage,
       his dislike for the noise he finds in Port of Spain, Trinidad.
       In An Area of Darkness he has a problem with public defeca-
       tion in India. Regards both books too full of generalizations.
       Does not think the title of the book on India appropriate,
       reference to the rat-faced Anglo-Indian manager in Bombay
       are such examples. Feels that the richness of his character
       sketches and anecdotes do not blend in with the sadness of
       his conclusion about India. Enright thinks Naipaul's unwilling-
       ness to modify his outlook is one of the reasons which "pre-
       vents him from seeing other people for what they were."
       Writes of Naipaul's light-hearted account of events in Kashmir.

Considers his analysis of the caste system excellent, but dislikes the criticisms levelled at Mahatma Gandhi.

C63.   Lacovia, R. M.   "The Medium Is the Divide."   Black Images
        1 (1972): 3-6.
        A highly analytical and lengthy review on Naipaul's earlier
        works. Like Marshall McLuhan, he shares "an interest in the
        impact of communication technology on culture." Whereas
        McLuhan moved from the audio-tactile to the visual to the
        electronic media, Naipaul focuses his attention in the reverse
        direction. This characteristic of his early novels is regarded
        as one of his weaknesses. Believes his penchant for question-
        ing to be a more serious aspect of his work. An Area of
        Darkness and Middle Passage best exemplify this.

C64.   May, Derwent. "Amis, McCarthy, Naipaul."   Encounter 38
        (1972): 74-78.

C65.   Noel, Jesse A. "Historicity and Homelessness in Naipaul."
        Caribbean Studies 11 (1972): 83-87.
        Regards The Loss of El Dorado as a sequel to The Middle
        Passage in reinforcing Naipaul's belief that Trinidad's history
        is a record of failure. Credits the quality of historical re-
        search, but does not recognize its style of presentation as
        a model which historians should adopt. He sees it as a pre-
        scribed text in prose writing on historical research in Eng-
        lish. Argues that its broad generalizations, "the highly
        subjective inuendo, the deliberate characterization" are not
        applicable to "scientific social studies." Comments favorably
        on his novelistic skills. Links this work to Naipaul's theme
        of homelessness and cites instances of Naipaul's rejection of
        colonial society.

C66-   Ramraj, Victor. "The All-Embracing Christlike Vision: Tone
C67.   and Attitude in 'The Mimic Men.'" In Commonwealth, edited
        by Anna Rutherford, 125-134. Papers delivered at the Con-
        ference of Commonwealth Literature, Aarhus University, Den-
        mark, April 26-30, 1971. Denmark: Aarhus University,
        1972.
        Suggests this novel signals the turning point in his writing
        in terms of regional setting and characterization. Ramraj
        notes too that "the light gay air" of the early trilogy in con-
        trast to "the delicately balanced" tone of A House for Mr.
        Biswas fades. Focuses on the general disagreement among
        reviewers on "their assessment of the quality and character
        of Naipaul's humour" in this trilogy. Ramraj believes in deal-
        ing with tone of a work of art, Naipaul's tone is not particu-
        larly constant, and shifts "often from satire to farce to
        comedy."

C68.   Birbalsingh, F. M. "Mordecai Richler and the Jewish-

Canadian Novel." Journal of Commonwealth Literature 7
(June 1972): 72-82.
Regards Richler's Duddy Kravitz similar in outlook to
Naipaul's Mr. Biswas. Notes among the marked comparisons
that both authors write satirically about their own ethnic
groups, and that they endure vilification and ridicule from
their fellow countrymen. Considers unfair, however, the fact
that Naipaul's work has received very high praise and recognition overseas, while Richler's attracts far less attention.
Maintains that Richler's characters are more richly endowed
than Naipaul's, and that, above all, Richler offers hope to
his protagonists. Naipaul, on the other hand, depicts a negative attitude within his characters, which suppresses their
dimensions.

C69.   Davies, Barrie. "The Personal Sense of a Society-Minority
View: Aspects of the 'East Indian' Novel in the West Indies."
Studies in the Novel 4 (Summer 1972): 284-295.

C70.   Gurr, A. J. "Third World Novels: Naipaul and After."
Journal of Commonwealth Literature 7 (June 1972): 6-13.

C71.   Theroux, Paul. "Perfection, Punctuality and Gloster Cheese:
A Profile of V. S. Naipaul 1972." Daily Telegraph Magazine
(October 27, 1972): 37-38, 40.

C72.   Enright, D. J. "In a Free State." In Readings in Commonwealth Literature, edited by William Walsh, 337-339. Oxford:
Clarendon Press, 1973.
Finds much uneasiness with Naipaul's treatment and judgment of the characters in the stories. Regards "One Out
of Many" as the "least dispiriting," and finds that the title
story, "In a Free State," makes a claim that English bureau-
crats serve Africa--one which "few people are willing to
acknowledge." Regrets that Naipaul uses pitiable, shady
characters in "In a Free State," thus reducing the force of
the piece. Wonders whether Naipaul's squeamishness has dis-
torted his portrayal of people in a real situation.

C73.   Swinden, Patrick. "Time and Motion; Ford, Bennett, V. S.
Naipaul." In Unofficial Selves, by Patrick Swinden, 148-
157. New York: Barnes and Noble, 1973.

C74.   Lane, Travis M. "The Casualties of Freedom: V. S. Naipaul's 'In a Free State.'" World Literature Written in English 12 (April 1973): 106-110.

C75.   Kemoli, Arthur. "The Theme of the Past in Caribbean Literature." World Literature Written in English 12 (November
1973): 304-325.
Traces broken historical links between Africa and the

Caribbean which Kemoli says confront contemporary Caribbean writers searching for authenticity, roots and wholeness. Recreates this dislocation by drawing on Andrew Salkey's A Quality of Violence, V. S. Naipaul's The Middle Passage, as well as the works of Derek Walcott, George Lamming, O. R. Dathorne, Edward Brathwaite, Wilson Harris, Kenneth Ramchand and Gerald Moore. Refutes many of Naipaul's infamous and controversial statements recorded in The Middle Passage and other questionable statements recorded in The Mystic Masseur and The Suffrage of Elvira. Also raps McKay and Walcott for their rejection of "their African past." Supports Lamming's view in Season of Adventure that Afro-Caribbean cultural links are a potent force for future growth.

C76. Gonzalez, Anson. "King of the Hillock--V. S. Naipaul." In Trinidad and Tobago Literature: On Air, by Anson Gonzalez, 53-58. Trinidad and Tobago: National Cultural Council, 1974.

This script, written for radio presentation, requires three voices. Essentially it deals with three of Naipaul's books: The Middle Passage, The Mimic Men and A Flag on the Island. It attacks his controversial statement that "nothing was created in the West Indies." It also questions his presumed superiority, and his love/hate relationship with the West Indies.

C77. Ramchand, Kenneth. "The Theatre of Politics." Twentieth Century Studies 10 (1974): 20-36. Rpt. in Trinidad and Tobago Review 2 (November 1977): 11-15, 18.

Ramchand compares The Mimic Men and George Lamming's Of Age and Innocence. He states that the theme of both books is the creation and operation of a multi-racial political party in a multi-racial society. Notes that "Lamming is constantly striving both to make the broad politico-philosophical statement and to explore it imaginatively in his fictions." Suggests that to understand the role of the metropolis in The Mimic Men is also to signal the serious differences between the authors. Points out that whereas Lamming's book responds to a socio-political status, Naipaul's novel generates a sensibility about man in the world.

C78. Ramchand, Kenneth. "The West Indies." In Literature of the World in English, edited by Bruce King, 192-211. London: Routledge, 1974.

C79. "The Caribbean: Culture or Mimicry." Journal of Interamerican Studies and World Affairs 16 (February 1974): 3-13.

C80. Ramsingh, Ashok. "A Question of Creative Writing vs. Paul Theroux and V. S. Naipaul's Autobiographers - Genesh

Ramsumair and Ralph Singh." Corlit No. 2 (April 1974):
22, 42-45, 48-49, 54.
According to Ramsingh, Naipaul has shown that he possesses "the most exquisite gifts of irony." Takes issue with
Theroux whom he says "does not see the irony nor the satirical effect Naipaul achieves because he does not know the
region." Further states that the essay is concerned with
Naipaul's "purpose and attitude in presenting Ganesh Ramsumair."

C81.   Blodgett, Harriet. "Beyond Trinidad: Five Novels by V. S.
Naipaul." South Atlantic Quarterly 73 (Summer 1974): 388-
403.
The novels discussed are The Mystic Masseur, The Suffrage of Elvira, A House for Mr. Biswas, Mr. Stone and the
Knights Companion, and The Mimic Men. Blodgett focuses
on Naipaul's theme of man's survival in the contemporary
world. Places his work in a global context which she relates
to "literal realism." Hints at A. C. Derrick's displeasure
over Naipaul's switch from compassion in his first novel to
a more destructive satirical style.

C82.   Shenfield, Margaret. "Mr. Biswas and Mr. Polly." English
23 (Autumn 1974): 95-100. See C84, C120, C129.

C83.   Boxhill, Anthony. "The Concept of Spring in V. S. Nai-
paul's 'Mr. Stone and the Knights Companion.'" Ariel 5
(October 1974): 21-28.
Boxhill believes that Naipaul wrote Mr. Stone and the
Knights Companion to provide for his work a wider forum
beyond the West Indian boundaries, rather than merely wish-
ing to shed the image of being a West Indian novelist.
Points to Mr. Stone, Mr. Biswas and Ganesh Ramsumair, as
all creative people whose environments inhibit their talents.
Explores the theme on renewal of life, by referring to Mr.
Stone's fascination with trees and their seasonal changes;
rejuvenation of life symbolized by the black cat; his own marriage late in life as another device; and his final experiment,
the creation of the Knights Companion plan. Whymper is
Public Relations Officer for the firm at which they both work.
He reshapes and implements it for commercial and personal
use, rather than for providing "renewal and springtime into
the lives of old men" which Mr. Stone intends.

C84.   Fido, Martin. "Mr. Biswas and Mr. Polly." Ariel 5 (October 1974): 30-37.
Discusses the many similarities between V. S. Naipaul's
A House for Mr. Biswas and H. G. Wells's The History of
Mr. Polly: The attempts towards higher personal achievement
of culturally deprived people whose efforts are thwarted by
limited education on one hand, yet inhibited by the

restrictiveness of the lower-middle class on the other; and disregard by principal characters for the rituals and traditions of social and family groups. Draws attention to the striking relationship between both antagonists, and assesses the critical importance of that relationship. Some of the predominating features of that relationship noted are the contrast in their handling of words, the status of their marriages, their loss each of one parent during childhood, their dietary problems. Concludes that Wells's theme was deliberately borrowed and adapted to the Trinidad Indian society.

C85.   Boxhill, Anthony. "The Physical and Historical Environment of V. S. Naipaul's 'The Mystic Masseur' and 'The Suffrage of Elvira.'" Journal of Canadian Fiction 3 (1975): 52-55.

Highlights the important features in The Mystic Masseur, particularly the remoteness of Fuente Grove where the novel is set; the role of Ganesh Ramsumair, the main character in the life of the place. Alludes to the link between the village and the sugar plantation, "the principal crop of slavery" as a contributing factor to the inhibiting influence on the lives of its inhabitants.

Reference is made in The Suffrage of Elvira, Naipaul's second novel, to Elvira's location on a once prosperous cocoa plantation. Remoteness features in this novel also; not much is made of Pat Harbans, the "key" character here. Boxhill suggests it is this lack of a central character which may have contributed to the novel's lack of popularity. Politics and superstition feature prominently in the book.

C86.   Niven, Alastair. "V. S. Naipaul's Free Statement." In Commonwealth Literature and the Modern World, edited by Hena Maes-Jelinek, 69-78. Brussels: University of Liege, 1975.

Commenting on the title story, Niven observes "it is clearly about the nature of freedom"; this statement of freedom he expresses some reservation about. Focuses also on "Tell Me Who to Kill" where the concern of language patterns receives attention. The characters throughout the book, he notes, are very unattached. Concludes that all the excursions in the book end without "a psychological resolution or any spiritual fulfillment."

C87.   MacDonald, Bruce. "Symbolic Action in Three of V. S. Naipaul's Novels." Journal of Commonwealth Literature 9 (April 1975): 41-52. Rpt. in Critical Perspectives on V. S. Naipaul, edited by Robert D. Hamner, 242-254. Washington, DC: Three Continents Press, 1977.

Briefly surveys the themes of racial conflict, escape, dissatisfaction, social dislocation and decay, all of which emerge from Naipaul's early novels. Notes also Naipaul's doubt about

the success of even a "new symbolic order." MacDonald
discusses three novels: The Mystic Masseur, A House for
Mr. Biswas and The Mimic Men. Draws attention in The
Mystic Masseur to the introduction of the symbolic action
which Ganesh displays through his spirituality, scholarly
texts and ancestral rituals. Suggests that some knowledge
of Trinidad Hindu community life simplifies one's comprehension of the symbolism expressed in this book. In A House
for Mr. Biswas, where the themes of dislocation and exploitation are also examined, MacDonald relates the planting exercise or destruction of vegetation as "symbolic of the acceptance or destruction of the land." The symbolism of snow,
magical lights and marriage to Sandra all combine to give
The Mimic Men a more universal appeal.

C88.   Harris, Michael. "Naipaul on Campus: Sending Out a Plea
        for Rationality." Tapia 5 (June 20, 1975): 2.

C89.   Boxhill, Anthony. "V. S. Naipaul's Starting Point." Journal
        of Commonwealth Literature 10 (August 1975): 1-9.

C90.   Garebian, Keith. "V. S. Naipaul's Negative Sense of Place."
        The Journal of Commonwealth Literature 10 (August 1975):
        23-35.
            Garebian argues that the original Trinidad landscape was
        one of "primeval force and beauty," but quite alien to the
        early settlers and lacking in "psychic adaption." It is this
        landscape to which Naipaul refers in The Middle Passage as
        one unexplored. Sees a link between Naipaul's thinking on
        art and painting in the West Indies, and the literature of the
        region. Further attributes Naipaul's use of metaphors in his
        writing as contributing significantly to the emergence of the
        West Indian landscape in the literature. Explores the path
        Naipaul follows in the formative years of his career to de-
        velop an "individual literary identity." Also discusses the
        themes of home, identity and exile.

C91.   Thieme, John. "V. S. Naipaul's Third World: A Not So
        Free State." Journal of Commonwealth Literature 10 (August
        1975): 10-22.

C92.   Angrosino, Michael V. "V. S. Naipaul and the Colonial
        Image." Caribbean Quarterly 21 (September 1975): 1-11.
            Looks at the volume of Naipaul's literary output and its
        significance as an art form in relation to its value both to
        the social scientist and the literary critic. Focuses briefly
        on the love-hate relationship which exists between Naipaul
        and some segments of the Caribbean community. Angrosino,
        nevertheless, regards him as "someone who is more than just
        a source of aesthetic delight." Analyses the image of "the
        colonial" as it is developed in Naipaul's journalism and his

historical work. Establishes the fundamental difference between the Indian and the Negro as emanating from the emancipation period: the systematic elimination of Black culture
which placed the slaves at a greater disadvantage. This in
turn explains the fierce resistance to Naipaul's use of satire
in The Mystic Masseur and The Suffrage of Elvira, and his
blatant disregard for "the psychological loss of identity"
nurtured by oppression to which the slaves were subjected.

C93.   Dunwoodie, Peter. "Commitment and Confinement: Two West
        Indian Visions." Caribbean Quarterly 21 (September 1975):
        15-27.
        Contends that even though both the French- and English-
        speaking Caribbean regions emerge from relatively similar
        historical circumstances, the French novels generally reflect
        a sense of optimism, whereas the English novels portray an
        atmosphere of gloom. Draws on V. S. Naipaul's Miguel
        Street and J. Zobel's Rue Cases-Negres to substantiate the
        discussions. In both novels the working class is drawn from
        a cross-section of characters. Dunwoodie interprets the con-
        cept of time in Miguel Street as a type of confinement; in
        the world of Rue Cases-Negres the environment is repre-
        sented as a positive one.

C94.   Harrison, Deborah. "V. S. Naipaul and Colonial Mentality."
        Canadian Forum 55 (December-January 1975/76): 44-47.
        Surveys Naipaul's work up till 1979. Taken as a group,
        she regards The Mystic Masseur, The Suffrage of Elvira
        and The Middle Passage as lacking in depth. Sees The Suf-
        frage of Elvira as too "one-dimensional," the characters hav-
        ing no distinct personality and so could be easily interchanged
        between novels. Thinks Naipaul's critical views in The Mid-
        dle Passage "lacks the greatness of a well-rounded vision."
        The Mimic Men she calls "a sophisticated version" of The
        Suffrage of Elvira. Expresses great satisfaction with An
        Area of Darkness and A House for Mr. Biswas. In The Mys-
        tic Masseur Harrison notes "an overly cold detachment."
        Questions whether the ironic approach is the fittest way to
        analyze the human condition, expressing the view that it
        reduces one's hopes to a relative position. Would prefer to
        see Naipaul prescribe solutions to human problems rather than
        remain detached from them.

C95.   Boxhill, Anthony. "The Paradox of Freedom: V. S. Nai-
        paul's 'In a Free State.'" Critique 18 (1976): 81-91.
        Sees in Miguel Street the analogy of Trinidad to a prison
        because of its colonial past and geographical location; and by
        implication that freedom is attainable through escape to a land
        not so affected. Suggests that In a Free State the world
        at large is the prison and the villain is life and man himself.

Regards Naipaul's shift away from "categoric answers to human problems" as demonstrated in the book, as a sign of his gradual maturity. Boxhill analyzes the significance of each piece, noting the greater freedom the main characters have acquired or that Naipaul has allowed them, and identifies violence as a major theme in the book. He devotes a great deal of attention to the fourth piece, "In a Free State." Set in a recent independent state, he examines the implications of tribal loyalties, political independence, attitudes of politicians and ordinary natives; also considers the use of clothing a very important theme in this essay. Here Boxhill seems to be apologetic for what he fears might be interpreted as unkindness, snobbery or ridicule.

C 96-   Calder, Angus. "World's End: V. S. Naipaul's 'The Mimic
C 97.   Men.'" In The Commonwealth Writers Overseas: Themes of
         Exile and Expatriation, edited by Alastair Niven, 271-282.
         Brussels: Didier, 1976.
             The thesis is that the poet, unlike the essayist, can exploit so many meanings in his work. Calder says that The Mimic Men in spite of a drab analysis and a shabby story, "imposes the order of poetry on the disorder of life." Further notes that "images and motifs recur channelling meaning into each other."

C 98.   Gonzalez, Anson. "On V. S. Naipaul." New Voices 4, Nos.
         7 & 8 (1976): 25-33.
             A detailed examination of Naipaul's critical attitude to West Indian society. Some of the reasons for this stance as identified by Gonzalez include Naipaul's self-estimated superiority, his dislike of and disgust for life in the West Indies at an early age, his abhorrence of Hindu ritual, and the conflict between the dual role in home and school. Draws heavily on The Middle Passage and The Mimic Men to substantiate these absurdities he is wont to impose on the West Indies.

C 99.   Gonzalez, Anson. "Piece Inspired by Reading V. S. Naipaul." New Voices 4 (1976): 35-39.

C 100.   Hayman, Ronald. "The West Indies and British Guiana."
         In The Novel Today, 1967-1975, 58-60. Essex: Longman,
         1976.
             Focuses on three of Naipaul's books: The Mimic Men, In a Free State and Guerrillas. Comments favorably on his techniques as a novelist, and his ability to develop the tone in The Mimic Men. Suggests that he achieves balance in the novel by striking a rhythm through a fluctuation of disappointments within In a Free State. Discusses also Naipaul's control of "the inelegancies of West Indian English," his blending humor and tragic outlook of the frustrations which

confront the inhabitants of that world, peopled with exiles and other characters. Notes the lapse of time in his fiction between both books and the greater intensity of his ironies. Believes his non-fiction may have influenced Naipaul's novelistic development, but concedes that his own integrity in recording his views places limitations on his characters. Hayman gives a brief overview of Guerrillas and concludes that Naipaul, by sharing his sense of homelessness among its three major characters, has increased the depth of his characterization.

C101.   James, Louis. "V. S. Naipaul." In Contemporary Novelists. 2nd ed., edited by James Vinson, 1002-1004. London: St. James Press, 1976.

C102.   Killan, Douglas. "Notes on Adaptation and Variation in the Use of English in Writing by Haliburton, Furphy, Achebe, Narayan and Naipaul." In The Commonwealth Writer Overseas: Themes of Exile and Expatriation, edited by Alastair Niven. 121-135. Brussels: Didier, 1976.
        Draws attention to the previous forums which have discussed reasons why writers from India, Africa and the West Indies have switched to English "as their vehicle of expression." Notes that Naipaul reserves standard English for the narrator, and dialect for principal characters. Concludes that English, regardless of the country in which it is spoken, "should not be judged inferior merely because it deviates from the standards of British English."

C103.   Morris, Robert K. "Substance into Shadow: V. S. Naipaul's 'The Mimic Men.'" In Old Lines, New Forces: Essays on the Contemporary British Novel, 1960-1970, edited by Robert K. Morris, 131-150. London: Assoc. University Press, 1976.

C104.   "Naipaul and the Blacks." The New Voices, Vol. 3, Nos. 7 & 8 (1976): 19-23, 62-64, 87.
        Recaptures the distastefulness of a pamphlet called Mukdar written anonymously by chauvinists presumably of East Indian origin. The tone is venomous and serves only to polarize Negroes and Indians, to ridicule Negroes, to rekindle some of the dormant ideological differences between both races in the society. It attempts to idolize V. S. Naipaul's literary prominence and to disparage any positive contribution or criticism respected black intellectuals make. One of the many false assumptions the paper expresses is the belief that Black anger directed at Naipaul stems from his refusal "to pamper and praise them." It is important for an understanding of the aura that surrounds Naipaul in the Caribbean.

C105.   Winser, Leigh. "Naipaul's Painters and Their Pictures." Critique 18 (1976): 67-80.

C106. Boxhill, Anthony. "The Little Bastard Worlds of V. S. Naipaul's 'The Mimic Men' and 'A Flag on the Island.'" International Fiction Review 3 (January 1976): 12-19.

C107. Mellors, John. "Mimics into Puppets: The Fiction of V. S. Naipaul." London Magazine 15 (February/March 1976): 117-121.

C108. McSweeney, Kerry. "V. S. Naipaul Sensibility and Schemata." Critical Quarterly 18 (Autumn 1976): 73-79.

C109. McSweeney, Kerry. "The Editor's Column." Queen's Quarterly 83 (Winter 1976): 704-708.

C110. Figueroa, John J. "Introduction--V. S. Naipaul: A Panel Discussion." In Revista/Review Interamericana 6 (Winter 1976/77): 554-586.
    Contents: John J. Figueroa, "Introduction--V. S. Naipaul: A Panel Discussion," pp. 554-563; Gerald Guinness, "Naipaul's Four Early Novels," pp. 564-573. Consuelo Lopez de Villegas, "The Paradox of Freedom: Naipaul's later Fiction," pp. 574-579; Bernard Lockwood, "V. S. Naipaul's 'The Middle Passage,'" pp. 580-586.
    Figueroa places Caribbean imaginative writing into an historical context. He lucidly explores some of the controversy surrounding Naipaul. Guinness discusses principally Miguel Street and A House for Mr. Biswas with particular reference to the story "Bogart." Sees it as embryonic in many of the themes and concerns Naipaul expresses in his later work. Lopez de Villegas uses The Mimic Men and In a Free State to demonstrate Naipaul's attitude towards freedom, and suggests it stems from his own self-imposed exile and desire to shed his past. Lockwood, in his assessment of the Middle Passage, re-opens many of the debates on long-standing issues in West Indian society.

C111. Ferres, John H. and Tucker, Martin, eds. "V. S. Naipaul." In Modern Commonwealth Literature, edited by John H. Ferres and Martin Tucker, 390-394. New York: Ungar, 1977.

C112. Hamner, Robert. "Character and Setting." In Critical Perspectives on V. S. Naipaul, edited by Robert D. Hamner, 208-241. Washington, DC: Three Continents Press, 1977.
    This lengthy essay consists of six sections: Local Color, Internal Landscapes, Character and Setting, The Absurd Man, The Little Man, The Hollow Man. Draws attention to the fine details found in Naipaul's fiction with particular reference to "the basic terms of existence" for various strata in the society, discernible in his lighthearted fiction particularly. Touches also on the rarity of panoramic views found in Naipaul's work, which Harbans absorbs in The Suffrage

of Elvira. Further suggests that A House for Mr. Biswas embodies the central principles of the picaresque novel of the earlier work, and a new direction in his writing generally. Feels that the liveliness of his characters, Biswas notwithstanding, and the rigid mould into which he places them, obscure their originality.

C113. Hamner, Robert D. Critical Perspectives on V. S. Naipaul. Washington, DC: Three Continents Press, 1977. 333 pp.
Contents: R. H. Lee, "The Novels of V. S. Naipaul," pp. 68-85; Gordon Rohlehr, "Character and Rebellion in A House for Mr. Biswas, pp. 84-103; V. S. Pritchett, "Climateric," pp. 104-110; Karl Miller, "V. S. Naipaul and the New Order," pp. 111-125; Victor Ramraj, "The All-Embracing Childlike Vision," pp. 127-136; Peter Nazareth, The Mimic Men as a Study of Corruption, pp. 137-152; John Updike, "Fool's Gold," pp. 153-158; David Ormerod, "In a Derelict Land: The Novels of V. S. Naipaul," pp. 159-177; Gordon Rohlehr, "The Ironic Approach," pp. 178-193; A. C. Derrick, "Naipaul's Technique as a Novelist," pp. 194-207; Robert Hamner, "Character and Setting," pp. 208-241; Bruce Mac-Donald, "Symbolic Action," pp. 242-254; Francis Wyndham, "Services Rendered," pp. 255-259.
Hamner's well-documented introduction is ideal, either as preliminary reading, or for more serious study of Naipaul's work. It forms a backdrop to an equally fine collection of writing by and about Naipaul. Part One consists of articles, interviews and book reviews which deal principally with authorship and authors. Part Two treats a range of divergent critical views from Biswas' problems with the Tulsis to sociological change.

C114. Mahood, M. M. "The Dispossessed." In The Colonial Encounter; A Reading of Six Novels, by M. M. Mahood, 142-165. London: Collins, 1977.

C115. MacDonald, Bruce. "The Birth of Mr. Biswas." Journal of Commonwealth Literature 11 (April 1977): 50-54.
Supports a consensus that this book was largely enriched by his father's own writings. The review addresses itself particularly to the article, "They Named Him Mohun," omitted from Gurudeva. In A House for Mr. Biswas, it is "the tone, the characterization of the pundit, and the significance of the Hindu rituals" described, which have been refashioned. Mac-Donald highlights those differences in both versions. V. S. Naipaul's pessimism aside, he manages to convey the view that Biswas's presence in spite of himself "established an identity independent of the empty ritual." Offers several logical reasons for their respective concepts and values of Hindu life in Trinidad. Most importantly it reinforces the "romantic sympathy of the father's art and the more brutal analysis" associated with Naipaul's work.

C116. Kazin, Alfred. "V. S. Naipaul as Thinker." The New York
Times Book Review (May 1, 1977): 7, 20, 22.
Describes the lucid, succinct style of the book, India, as
typically Naipaul. Expresses great admiration and delight
also in his use, "love and mastery" of English. Regards Naipaul as close to the Dickens school, and devoid of any senti-
ment or ideology. Kazin regrets the fact that Naipaul is not
as widely known as some lesser writers. Touches briefly on
some of his social habits: dress, conversation, taste for
good wines. Concludes that he is the most forceful social
commentator among contemporary novelists.

C117. Hearne, John. "The Snow Virgin: An Inquiry into V. S.
Naipaul's 'Mimic Men.'" Caribbean Quarterly 23: 2-3 (June-
September 1977): 31-37.
Praises the quality of the book, but laments "the unre-
mitting integrity of its pessimism." Focuses much attention
on Singh, the narrator. Comments favorably on it as Nai-
paul's work of art, not to be misconstrued for Singh's auto-
biography or an essay in social and political anthropology.
Hints too at the scope for discussion of language use in The
Mimic Men.

C118. Baugh, Edward. "Exiles, Guerrillas and Visions of Eden:
Recent Caribbean Writing." Queen's Quarterly 84 (Summer
1977): 273-286.
Reflects on the interest which Naipaul's work generates
at conferences, and his international image as a writer.
Notes that in spite of his objection to being considered a
West Indian writer, he still draws on the region for some of
his material; cites The Mimic Men and "Tell Me Who to Kill."
Singles out the latter story, as it also deals with West Indian
in London and is written entirely in dialect. Focuses on his
themes of exile and power as treated in Guerrillas. Suggests that he has given comfort to Western societies through
the picture he depicts of "West Indian futility." Baugh talks
about the merits of Guerrillas, Naipaul's style; however,
thinks its weakness lies in the three main characters whom
he regards as transparent.

C119. Black, James, ed. Ariel; A Review of International English
Literature 8 (July 1977): 1-144.
Contents: Victor J. Ramraj, "An Editorial Note," p. 3;
Frank Birbalsingh, "Samuel Selvon and the West Indian Lit-
erary Renaissance," pp. 23-33; Robert D. Hamner, "Myth-
ological Aspects of Derek Walcott's Drama," pp. 35-57; Hena
Maes-Jelinek, "'Inimitable Painting': New Developments in
Wilson Harris's Latest Fiction," pp. 63-80; John Thieme,
"Double Identity in the Novels of Garth St. Omer," pp. 81-
97; Michael Thorpe, "'The Other Side': Wide Sargasso Sea
and Jane Eyre," pp. 99-110; Louis James, "Sun Fire-Painted

Fire: Jean Rhys as a Caribbean Novelist," pp. 111-127; Anthony Boxhill, "Mr. Biswas, Mr. Polly and the Problem of V. S. Naipaul's Sources," pp. 129-141.

C120. Boxhill, Anthony. "Mr. Biswas, Mr. Polly and the Problem of V. S. Naipaul's Sources." Ariel 8 (July 1977): 129-141. Rpt. in Naipaul's Fiction: In Quest of the Enemy, by Anthony Boxhill, 16-24. Fredericton: York Press, 1983. Boxhill develops a very interesting thesis on Naipaul's sources. Notes the distinct similarity between H. G. Wells' Mr. Lewisham in Love and Mr. Lewisham and Titus Hoyt of Miguel Street. Draws parallels in Dickens' Great Expectations and A House for Mr. Biswas. Cites Conrad's influence on Naipaul through In a Free State and A Bend in the River. Naipaul's use of the calypso and West Indian history are also relevant sources mentioned. Concludes that "West Indian society demands a tradition of literature" of its own, this Naipaul is helping to shape.

C121. Ramchand, Kenneth. "Everyman's Spiritual Home Is on Sikkim Street." Tapia 7 (July 13, 1977): 8, 11.

C122. Lopez de Villegas, Consuelo. "Matriarchs and Man-eaters: Naipaul's Fictional Women." Revista/Review InterAmericana 7 (Winter 1977/1978): 605-614.
This study covers Naipaul's fiction to Guerrillas. Lopez de Villegas discloses in this paper that "of Naipaul's creative characters none are women." This theme sets the tone for the entire study. Notes that in Naipaul's early fiction women are portrayed sympathetically, suited to "weak and submissive roles" but who, when given an opportunity, become rebellious. Identifies Sandra, Linda and Jane as some of the major women characters who revolt later on. Cites male characters as conspicuous by their education, while in the female characters like Shama and Leela this quality is absent. In The Mimic Men traces the "vehemence against an ostensible female threat" which Naipaul displays.

C123. Miller, Karl. "V. S. Naipaul and the New Order: A View of 'The Mimic Men.'" In Critics on Caribbean Literature, edited by Edward Baugh, 75-83. New York: St. Martin's Press, 1978.
Suggests that Naipaul's "novels can be said to define the transition from colonialism to independence." Comments on his "swift comic treatments," conservatism, warmth and compassion for the "poor and aspiring." Draws a distinction between Mr. Biswas and Ralph Singh to illustrate "Naipaul's account of colonial freedom in the West Indies." Touches also on the difficult use of the first person in the book. Naipaul is not unscathed either, apart from his eccentricities he "may well have excited suspicions among the West Indian

Left that he is a bit of a Fascist, bearing a cross of Aryan fantasies."

C124. Nandan, Satendra. "The Immigrant Experience in Literature: Trinidad and Fiji." In The Awakened Conscience: Studies in Commonwealth Literature, edited by C. D. Narasimhaiah, 346-357. New Delhi: Sterling, 1978.
Explores the Indian experience in Trinidad and Tobago, principally through Naipaul's A House for Mr. Biswas and The Middle Passage. Suggests that the overriding theme of the Biswas novel conjuring the notion of slavery is a fine example of the "historical experience." Feels that the body of Naipaul's fiction written after that novel could be construed as a failure of the imagination. Draws a contrast between Patrick White and Naipaul, who, Nandan says, for too long "has stared at the void," unlike White who encourages his countrymen "to accept and live out one's humanity." The Fijian experience is expressed through its verse in the absence of the novel in English.

C125. Raghavacharyulu, D. V. K. "Naipaul and Narayan: The Sense of Life." In The Awakened Conscience: Studies in Commonwealth Literature, edited by C. D. Narasimhaiah, 216-225. New Delhi: Sterling, 1978.
Sees Naipaul and Narayan as established exponents of comic fiction. Identifies points of style, technique and aspects of their personality in their work. Explores the differences in their use of the novel. Notes that Naipaul employs it as "a ritual of extinction and exorcism"; Narayan uses it as a ceremony for inauguration and renewal. Recognizes the brilliance of A House for Mr. Biswas, but then points to the treatment of married life in Narayan's The English Teacher as far more tenderly handled.

C126. Ramraj, Victor J. "Diminishing Satire: A Study of V. S. Naipaul and Mordecai Richler." In The Awakened Conscience: Studies in Commonwealth Literature, edited by C. D. Narasimhaiah, 261-274. New Delhi: Sterling, 1978.
A perceptive study of two closely matched Commonwealth writers: Mordecai Richler, a Canadian of Jewish parentage and V. S. Naipaul of Trinidad, East Indian descent. Ramraj points to some very striking comparisons between them. The emphasis in the study centers on the quality, tone and character of their satirical vision in their fiction. Admits there are "unambiguous strictures" in their journalistic essays, but cautions that such views do not necessarily reflect any biased fictional attitudes towards their respective countries. Suggest instead that they have set out to focus on the total experience. Ramraj notes significantly their "apparent disregard for chronology."

C127.   Niven, Alastair. "Crossing the Black Waters: N. C.
         Chandhuri's 'A Passage to England' and V. S. Naipaul's
         'An Area of Darkness.'" Ariel 9 (July 1978): 21-36.

C128.   Stone, Judy. "Naipaul Warns of Apocalypse." Sunday
         Guardian [Trinidad], July 30, 1978: 6.
         Reflects on Naipaul's opinion that India suffers from "in-
         tellectual parasitism," which in turn impedes its development.
         Detects much sympathy and humor in the book. Discusses
         his belief that India still lives too much in the past.

C129.   Carthew, John. "Adapting to Trinidad: Mr. Biswas and
         Mr. Polly Revisited." Journal of Commonwealth Literature
         13 (August 1978): 58-64.
         Draws attention to the collection of short stories by Nai-
         paul's father as the starting point to which V. S. Naipaul
         refers in "Jasmine," touches also on the marked similarities
         in the articles by Margaret Shenfield and Martin Fido which
         discuss characterization, plot and language in V. S. Nai-
         paul's A House for Mr. Biswas and H. G. Wells's The His-
         tory of Mr. Polly. Regards as important the contribution
         of European literature in Naipaul's process of adaptation to
         Trinidad of Mr. Polly, which Shenfield ignores. Sees the
         strikingly divergent attitudes toward their heroes as a sig-
         nificant clue to tracing the differences in the novels. Bis-
         was, he notes, makes correct use of language, whereas Pol-
         ly mutilates his words. According to Carthew this device is
         contrived to keep Mr. Polly in his social place; here Naipaul
         allows Mr. Biswas "to think in the same linguistic mode as
         the authorial narrator."

C130.   Colson, Theodore. "The Theme of Home in the Fiction of
         Canada, the United States and the West Indies." English
         Studies in Canada 4 (Fall 1978): 351-360.

C131.   Naik, M. K. "Two Uses of Irony: V. S. Naipaul's 'The
         Mystic Masseur' and R. K. Narayan's 'The Guide.'" World
         Literature Written in English 17 (November 1978): 644-655.

C132.   Anderson, Linda R. "Ideas of Identity and Freedom in V. S.
         Naipaul and Joseph Conrad." English Studies 59 (December
         1978): 510-517.
         An excellent discussion of the affinity between Naipaul
         and Conrad, which Anderson believes stemmed from "their
         ambiguous relationship with the English tradition." Examines
         the treatment of characters in their novels with particular
         reference to Naipaul's In a Free State and Conrad's Heart of
         Darkness. Concludes that Conrad's vision "can to some ex-
         tent, redeem the world from his characters, Naipaul's vision
         can only confirm his characters' alienation."

C133. Nunez-Harrell, Elizabeth. "Lamming and Naipaul: Some Criteria for Evaluating the Third-World Novel." Contemporary Literature 19 (Winter 1978): 26-47.

Naipaul's contention that West Indian and Afro-American literature are of a protest nature is disputed by Rohlehr who terms it "transitional." Nunez-Harrell maintains that the incidence of slavery and colonization, the introduction of European culture and language "have inextricably tied the past, present and future realities of the Negro" to the metropolitan countries. Consequently the tone of the literature should not be used as the criterion for analyzing its significance. Attention focuses on the "absence of open hostility" and West Indian acceptance of European values in the literature which threatens "the possibility of a West Indian literature." Believes that writers of decolonized countries are greatly affected by nationalism, which bears some relationship to their countries and to their artistic modules--in the case of the West Indies to the comic aura of the literature.

Analyzes several instances in detail to demonstrate the differences in style and attitude between Lamming and Naipaul towards the West Indian. Suggests that the West Indian writer's inheritance of English as the medium of communication and a British literary tradition both pose problems for him. Discussion also centers on his ability to use Standard English which, according to Ramchand, in terms of "form and structure" pose no problems for West Indians, any more than for Britons or Americans. The study also explores the possible use of dialect, but recognizes its inadequacy as a medium for "philosophical thought."

C134. Campbell, Elaine. "A Refinement of Rage: V. S. Naipaul's 'A Bend in the River.'" World Literature Written in English 18 (1979): 394-406.

Attributes one of the main reasons for Naipaul's popularity in the United States after the publication of Guerrillas to American misconceptions of the novel. Notes that, arising from visits to the Congo in 1966 and to Zaire in 1975, Naipaul wrote the novella In a Free State, and later the novel A Bend in the River. Both books reflect the destruction and ruin and the politics of African states.

In the novella his rage is very pronounced, but in the novel he has become conscious of the need for this rage "to be refined away, giving place to comprehension." Campbell touches on the similarity of thought running through Miguel Street and A Bend in the River that living away from "half made" Third World countries is a more acceptable option than remaining in them. She notes that in A Bend in the River Naipaul fully develops the theme of civilization's engulfment by the bush. She focuses on the analogy Naipaul uses in relation to the river and water hyacinths stifling river traffic, a reference to the decline of civilization. Sees Salim as narrator fashioned to reflect the refinement of rage, through a very clear set of devices. The inevitable comparison between Conrad and Naipaul develops, Campbell noting that it is their styles which place them furthest apart. Concludes that Naipaul's rigid assessments could in time "be more therapeutic than the placebos of more optimistic commentators."

C135.   King, Bruce. "V. S. Naipaul." In West Indian Literature, edited by Bruce King, 161-178. London: Macmillan, 1979; Hamden, CT: Archon Books, 1979.

C136.   Nightingale, Margaret. "V. S. Naipaul's Journalism: To Impose a Vision." In Literature in the English Speaking Caribbean, edited by Helen Tiffin and others, 53-65. Canberra: Department of Language and Literature, 1979.
       This study, based on Naipaul's journalistic writings, minutely examines his reactions to the turbulence in postcolonial countries. It focuses on the politics of Africa, India and the Caribbean, specifically Trinidad and Tobago, and Argentina for purposes of this article. Nightingale quotes extensively from his work to reinforce her arguments. She concludes: "he seems to delineate barren relationships and sterile societies with the intention of shattering the complacency which defeats reform before it begins."

C137.   St. Omer, Garth. "The Writer as Colonial: V. S. Naipaul and Miguel Street." Carib 1 (1979): 7-17.
       Looks at the early phase of Naipaul's development as a writer in which St. Omer sees "an evolution towards greater abstraction"; and later a conflict between his "serious new content" and "the persistence of the old entertainment manner." This is an evolution away from "concept of the self as a part of a collectivity, of the world, to a concept of the self as entity and as mirroring the world rather than being part of it." Offers a microscopic view of Miguel Street.

C138.   "V. S. Naipaul." In Caribbean Writers: A Bio-Bibliographical-Critical Encyclopedia, edited by Donald E. Herdeck and others, 155-162. Washington, DC: Three Continents Press, 1979.

C139.   Parrinder, Patrick. "V. S. Naipaul and the Uses of Literacy." Critical Quarterly 21 (Summer 1979): 5-13.

C140.   " 'Guerrillas': A Symposium on V. S. Naipaul's novel." In Journal of Commonwealth Literature 14 (August 1979): 87-131.
       Contents: Peter Murray, "Prefatory note," pp. 88-89; Madhusudana Rao, "Guerrillas: A Fable of Political Innocence and Experience," pp. 90-99; Richard Johnstone, "Politics and V. S. Naipaul," pp. 100-108; Johannes Riis, "Naipaul's

Wood-landers," pp. 108-115; John Thieme, "Apparitions of
Disaster: Brontëan Parallels in 'Wide Sargasso Sea' and
'Guerrillas,'" pp. 116-132.
Murray notes "the novelist and the satirist unite in Naipaul the traveller." Rao traces Naipaul's earlier attempts
at writing the political novel through to Guerrillas; expands
the themes explored in The Mimic Men and In a Free State.
Johnstone concludes "for Naipaul the attraction of politics is
that political action carries with it the illusion of significance."
Riis states that the seriousness of Guerrillas originates "from
a deep and genuine experience of man's miserable plight in
the rapidly disintegrating Western World." Thieme concludes
that "both Guerrillas and Wide Sargasso Sea occupy a mid-
way position" between Harris' "novel of persuasion" and
"dialectic" novel.

C141. Quarry, Wendy. "The Traveller." Montreal Gazette, Sep-
       tember 22, 1979: 42.

C142. Woodcock, George. "Two Great Commonwealth Novelists:
       R. K. Narayan and V. S. Naipaul." Sewanee Review 87
       (Winter 1979): 1-28.

C143. Cooke, John. "A Vision of the Land: V. S. Naipaul's
       Later Novels." Caribbean Quarterly 25 (December 1979):
       31-47. Rpt. in Journal of Caribbean Studies 1 (Spring/
       Autumn 1980): 140-161.
         Claims that critics have expended much energy judging
       The Middle Passage and that so little interest has been taken
       in a search for order in Caribbean society. Such a search
       is quite evident in Naipaul's later works; this, Cooke says,
       is resolved in A Bend in the River in which only "bush"
       exists. Regards his interest in the landscape as a focal point
       in his work. Sees the personal landscape more dominant,
       linking this interest to A House for Mr. Biswas and Mr.
       Stone and the Knights Companion. He has developed a grow-
       ing interest in the historical landscape in his later writing,
       but thinks he still has a problem recognizing any developing
       order emerging from the Caribbean historical landscape. Cites
       "The Circus at Luxor" as one such attempt more fully ex-
       plored in The Mimic Men and in Guerrillas. Concludes that
       apart from Wilson Harris, Naipaul remains the most effective
       interpreter of Third World landscapes.

C144. Cudjoe, Selwyn Reginald. "Revolutionary struggle and the
       novel." Caribbean Quarterly 25 (December 1979): 1-30.
         Suggests that the novel is "the dominant medium for ex-
       ploring and analyzing the new challenges of post-revolutionary
       societies." Draws on Alejo Carpentier's Explosion in the
       Cathedral, Bertene Juminer's Bozambo's Revenge, and V. S.
       Naipaul's Guerrillas to illustrate the case. In dealing with

"the most appropriate artistic form" for describing the colonial experience, Cudjoe cites the earlier ironical and satirical
novels of V. S. Naipaul; prefers, however, Carpentier's
later works because of their "critical realism." Cudjoe
launches a vitriolic attack on Guerrillas which he regards
as one of Naipaul's "worst novels," and labels him "a self-
conscious iconoclast."

C145. Subramani. "The Historical Consciousness in V. S. Naipaul."
       Commonwealth Quarterly 4 (December 1979): 3-22.

C146. Berrian, Brenda F. "V. S. Naipaul's Nihilistic Vision: The
       Dilemma of the Double Outsider." Philadelphia: African
       Studies Association, 1980.
           Sees his themes of fantasy, detachment, insecurity and
       homelessness further strengthened through A Bend in the
       River; here Naipaul explores the theme of "reconstruction
       of the Indian personality in Africa." Claims "Naipaul ex-
       amines his own expatriotism by replacing his European char-
       acters with Indian ones." He also expresses concern with
       their position as "double outsiders." Traces of Conrad's
       darkness are exemplified by "a bend in the river," a steamer
       travelling up an African river and his juxtaposition of light
       and darkness. He uses Salim as the surrogate, and thinks
       Naipaul's own fear of "sinking without a trace into a large
       Indian crowd" helps to explain his very self-exile in Britain.
       Discusses at great length Naipaul's treatment of Africans,
       and condemns his praise for the European view of African
       inferiority.

C147. King, Bruce. "Naipaul, Harris and History." In The New
       English Literatures: Cultural Nationalism in a Changing
       World, edited by Bruce King, 98-117. London: Macmillan,
       1980.

C148. Wilson-Tagoe, Nana. "No Place; V. S. Naipaul's Vision of
       Home in the Caribbean." Caribbean Review 9 (1980): 37-
       41.
           A detailed and perceptive review of Naipaul's work from
       A House for Mr. Biswas to In a Free State. During this
       time he has moved from his themes of displacement and cyni-
       cism about the Caribbean to "a darkening personal vision of
       world placelessness." Argues that the despair generated by
       Naipaul's view of Caribbean society is suspect, since many
       of his conclusions on the Caribbean "are influenced by his
       own private philosophy." Notes that in Guerrillas, Naipaul's
       subsequent work, he questions "all our familiar assumptions
       about place and relationships."

C149. Questel, Victor. "Schooner Flight from Paradise of Trinidad;
       Sailor-Poet Swims Through Ship of Cruel Ancestral Experience."
       Trinidad Guardian (January 3, 1980): 4, 7.

C150. Lopez de Villegas, Consuelo. "Identity and Environment: Naipaul's Architectural Vision." Revista/Review Inter-Americana 10 (Summer 1980): 220-229.

Draws the comparison between Conrad and Naipaul on "a shared feeling of the land," and the neglect inherited from the colonial powers. Relates Joyce's Dublin to Naipaul's Trinidad, deprived of self-achievement, thus making exile "the only means of finding a sense of order." Suggests that in The Mimic Men one of Naipaul's main concerns is "the relationship between environmental necessity and architectural form." This architectural leitmotiv is more fully developed in Guerrillas.

C151. Webb, Peter; Behr, Edward; Kirkland, Robert. "The Master of the Novel." Newsweek 96 (August 18, 1980): 44-48.

Traces graphically the satirical style and critical tenor of Naipaul's writings, his uncompromising stance on issues and countries notwithstanding. Gangadean suggests that in India, Naipaul is unable "to go native" and "switch cultural gears." Flashes upon insights of his personal life, tastes, teaching encounters abroad, the rigid discipline which engulfs his writings, and the comparisons between himself and Conrad. Focuses above all on the vividness of his imagination and his wizardry as a novelist.

C152. Birkerts, Sven. "V. S. Naipaul and Derek Walcott: A Multiplicity of Truths." New Boston Review 5 (August/September 1980): 19-21.

Believes that Naipaul's approach to his concern with the human condition is not the most thoughtful, but his foresight is invaluable. It concentrates on aspects that have not been discussed because so few writers have the experience and language competence to deal with it. Comments highly on his work but dislikes Naipaul's lack of compassion. Thinks his penchant for details is one of the major elements of his style. Suggests that his bitterness is a response to international exploration, born out of colonial avarice and passiveness of a subject people. Notes similarities in the careers of Derek Walcott and Naipaul, their divergent views on Third World issues and other human concerns. Regards Naipaul as the more conspicuous and tells of his leaps onto the international stage after publication of Guerrillas (1975) culminating with The Return of Eva Peron (1980).

C153. Adams, Robert Martin. "V. S. Naipaul." Hudson Review 33 (Autumn 1980): 474-478.

Discusses the recurrent themes in Naipaul's work, primarily on "the anomalies, grotesque and tragic, of half-formed provincial societies." The action of Bend in the River is probably a fuller imaginative achievement than Guerrillas, Adams notes. A House for Mr. Biswas "isn't a flawless piece of work, but it's an extraordinarily warm, grubby and funny fiction." Believes Naipaul's excellence lies not only in his sharp clarity of social vision, but he "may well be one of those rare, lucid minds who write on the dead level."

C154. Kakutani, Michiko. "Naipaul reviews his past from afar." New York Times Biographical Service (December 1980): 1769-1770.
Discusses the darkness which surrounds Naipaul's work. Explores his meaning of the term "bush" which he is so fond of using, as ignorance and obscurity. Kakutani contends that in Naipaul's remarks as in his writing "there is no moralizing, no positing of good and evil." Focuses on Naipaul's half-made societies, "revolutionaries who visit centres of revolution with return air tickets," his intolerance with those who do not accept his work. Suggests his alienation not only brought a distinctive tone of exile to his work, it had a personal influence on him as seen when he wrote A House for Mr. Biswas, namely that his satirical self kept him aloof. Concludes satire turned to contempt and finally to a permanent loneliness.

C155. Woodcock, George. "V. S. Naipaul and the Politics of Fiction." Queen's Quarterly 87 (Winter 1980): 679-692.

C156. David, P. C. "Between Two Stools: Naipaul's 'An Area of Darkness.'" In Alien Voice: Perspectives on Commonwealth Literature, edited by Avadhesh K. Srivastava, foreword B. N. Chaturvedi, 228-234. Lucknow, India: Print House, 1981.

C157. Gurr, Andrew. "A Foot in both Jungles: V. S. Naipaul." In Writers in Exile: The Identity of Home in Modern Literature, by Andrew Gurr, 65-91. Brighton: Harvester Press, 1981.
Gurr not only identifies both exile and homelessness as the major themes in modern Commonwealth writing, but illustrates these themes through the work of three such writers from diverse areas: New Zealand, Kenya, Trinidad and Tobago. Treats Mansfield more in biographical terms with less emphasis on her literary output. The focus on Naipaul is far more critical than that on Mansfield, with particular stress placed on A House for Mr. Biswas. Sees Naipaul's progression to political concerns after this novel as a logical one. However, Gurr appears to have given less attention to Guerrillas and A Bend in the River in relation to the theme of home. The view given of Ngugi is a cultural one. Concludes that of the three writers, Ngugi, Naipaul and Mansfield, Ngugi is the most valuable politically.

C158. Lyn, Gloria. "A Thing Called Art: 'The Mimic Men.'" Carib no. 2 (1981): 66-77.

Points out that one of Naipaul's concerns is that his work is frequently judged from a political standpoint. In addressing this problem Lyn cites The Mimic Men to substantiate her views. She discusses "a theory of criticism which would account for the phenomena of literary experience." Draws on Northrop Frye's opinion that "the writer's life is not the key to the deeper understanding of that work," such as is generally applied to Naipaul. Lyn sees analysis of form and structure of the novel as the base from which to point out and to resolve the main images in the work; and suggests that "one does not get the sense that critics are paying enough attention to form and structure."

C158A. Ojo, Patchechole Poindexter. "Nature in Three Caribbean Novels." Journal of Caribbean Studies 2 (Spring 1981): 85-107. One of the three is Naipaul's Guerrillas.

C159. Raghavacharyulu, D. V. K. "Beyond Exile and Homecoming: A Preliminary Note." In Alien Voice: Perspectives on Commonwealth Literature, edited by Avadhesh K. Srivastava, foreword B. N. Chaturvedi, 31-39. Lucknow, India: Print House, 1981.

C160. Rao, K. I. Madhusudana. "The Complex Fate: Naipaul's View of Human Development." In Alien Voice: Perspectives on Commonwealth Literature, edited by Avadesh K. Srivastava, foreword by B. N. Chaturvedi, 194-209. Lucknow, India: Print House, 1981.

C161. Thieme, John. "V. S. Naipaul and the Hindu Killer." Journal of Writing in English 9 (1981): 70-86.

C162. Doerksen, Nan. "'In a Free State' and 'Nausea.'" World Literature Written in English 20 (Spring 1981): 105-113.
Doerksen remains convinced that the similarities of style, motif, language found in Sartre's Nausea and V. S. Naipaul's In a Free State are too striking to be coincidental; further suggest that the same philosophical theme which Sartre espouses, "man is nothing else but what he makes of himself," rings through in the opening lines of A Bend in the River. Highlights some of the other major themes common to both: "freedom as imprisonment," and abandonment. Notes the journey motif reinforces the placelessness and nihilism which result when "caught between two cultures"; and notes the uselessness of the search for the meaning of existence. The minor motif too is fully discussed in the piece. Naipaul used art as the instrument to demonstrate the significance of history to the existence of man. Doerksen points only to the degree of clarity between Sartre and Naipaul on the "imaging" of various types of humanists. Regards Naipaul's use of the first person narrative, present tense to be a reflection of Sartre's own style.

C163. Boyers, Robert. "V. S. Naipaul." American Scholar 50
       (Summer 1981): 359-367.
          Vividly examines some of the reasons for Naipaul's lack of
       popularity in the United States. In tracing his development
       as a writer, Boyers notes the transition from his satirical
       base to "a kind of political fiction," more closely related to
       Conrad and Stendal. Boyers acknowledges his refinement,
       but not his enlargement of feeling. Discusses in some detail
       the techniques Naipaul has employed in his fiction, analyzing
       in The Mystic Masseur and The Middle Passage the problems
       of Naipaul's relationship with his narrators, Ganesh Ramsumair
       and Ralph Singh. Praises the brilliant use of the first person
       narrator in "One Out of Many" and "Tell Me Who to Kill,"
       pieces from In a Free State. Believes Naipaul's success as a
       writer soars when he establishes a political environment.
       Boyers regards A Bend in the River as his first real political
       novel in the Western tradition; he disagrees with all other
       claims to the contrary.

C164. Boyers, Robert, ed. Salmagundi 54 (Fall 1981): 1-97.
          Contents: Bharati Mukherjee; Robert Boyers, "A Conver-
       sation with V. S. Naipaul," pp. 4-22; Ben Belitt, "The
       Heraldry of Accommodation: A House for Mr. Naipaul," pp.
       23-42; Eugene Goodheart, "Naipaul and the Voices of Nega-
       tion," pp. 44-58; Larry David Nachman, "The Worlds of V. S.
       Naipaul," pp. 59-76; Robert Boyers, "Confronting the Pres-
       ent," pp. 77-97.
          The conversation between Mukherjee, Bowers and Naipaul
       deals essentially with writing and Naipaul's reactions to his
       own work. Belitt presents an incisive analysis and refresh-
       ing interpretation of A House for Mr. Biswas. Goodheart
       concludes in his far-reaching essay on Naipaul that his "so-
       cial vision is deeply marked by the contradictions, if not in-
       coherence, of personality." Nachman explores several of Nai-
       paul's books in the context of European development, and the
       problems of transmission and diffusion of technology in the
       newer societies. Boyers discusses both Naipaul's books on
       India in relation to Bellow's To Jerusalem and Back. Bellow
       he regards as being better able to resist despair, and a "more
       approachable and sympathetic observer." Naipaul's India he
       suggests is the more informative. Praises Naipaul as a
       novelist but charges "the writer appears to savour rather too
       heartily the failure of every enterprise, to rub his hands to-
       gether in a sort of knowing complicity before the spectacle
       of every political humiliation and defeat." Contends this has
       tended to weaken Guerrillas since he has given the impression
       he had a perceived notion of what he wanted to discover.

C165. Rothfork, John. "V. S. Naipaul and the Third World." Re-
       search Studies 49 (September 1981): 183-192.
          Concentrates on analyzing Naipaul's fictional ideas rather

than his style of writing. Draws attention to the development of his themes on self-identity and cultural identity through The Mimic Men. Rothfork discusses at length Naipaul's denouncement of "the futility of politics in the Third World" as he articulates it in Guerrillas and A Bend in the River. He also questions Naipaul's disregard for cultural values in the Third World. Cites the Age of Enlightenment influence and his neo-colonial sentiments as factors instrumental in his support for technology. Suggests that In a Free State, India and The Return of Eva Peron are essential for a thorough understanding of Naipaul's thoughts on the Third World. Concludes that "his philosophy seems to rest on an atheistic existentialism."

C166.   Michener, Charles. "The Dark Visions of V. S. Naipaul." Newsweek 98 (November 16, 1981): 104-105, 108-110, 114-115.
        A detailed and interesting discussion on Naipaul. It portrays many of his inner thoughts, and sketches some aspects of his life. Referring to England, Naipaul suggests it is "the least educated country in Europe. It isn't only Africans who are bow and arrow people, it's so many people here, living at a very high material level who have allowed their minds to go slack." His strong satirical traits Naipaul attributes to his father's "prodigious sense of irony, a way of turning all disaster into comedy." Explores much of the controversy which surrounds Naipaul's writing. Believes that any limitation of his views as "the bearer of bad news" confined only to the Third World is a misrepresentation of Naipaul's vision. Also draws extensively on several of Naipaul's works to underline his concern with the human condition. Michener's summary of Among the Believers further reinforces that urge "to feel history as it is happening among those to whom it is happening." (Published to accompany D423.)

C167.   M. B. "An explanation for Naipaul's attitude." Trinidad Guardian (December 18, 1981): 8.
        Assails Naipaul for making adverse comments about Trinidad, which he calls a primitive island. Reflects the sensitivity and local reactions which Naipaul's criticisms of Trinidad and Tobago generate.

C168.   Rajan, P. K. "Patterns of Cultural Orientation in the Approach to Indian Reality." Journal of Theological Studies 8 (Winter 1981/82): 121-135.

C169.   Jefferson, Douglas; Martin, Graham, eds. The Uses of Fiction: Essays on the Modern Novel in Honour of Arnold Kettle. Milton Keynes: Open University Press, 1982.
        Contents: D. H. Lawrence (Graham Martin), David Storey (David Craig), Lewis Grassic Gibbon (Angus Calder), Joseph

Conrad (Kiernan Ryan), Carson McCullers and Flannery
O'Connor (Cicely Palser Haveley), Wilson Harris and V. S.
Naipaul (Mark Kinkead-Weeks), Nadine Gordimer (Margot
Heinemann), Virginia Woolf (Barbara Hardy), Susan Hill (Ken-
neth Muir). P. N. Firbank, Jeremy Hawthorne, Robert
Weimann and Arthur Ravenscroft have also contributed es-
says to this work.
The festschrift to honor Arnold Kettle, a leading Marxist
critic of the novel consists of nineteen essays including those
on Harris and Naipaul.

C170.   Ramraj, Victor. "Trapdoors into a Bottomless Past: V. S.
Naipaul's Ambivalent Vision of the Indian Experience." In
East Indians in the Caribbean: Colonialism and the Struggle
for Identity. Papers presented to Symposium on East Indians
in the Caribbean, edited by Bridget Brereton and Winston
Dookeran. University of the West Indies, June 1971, 1-9.
New York: Kraus International, 1982.

C171.   Richmond, Angus. "Naipaul: The Mimic Men." Race &
Class 24 (1982): 125-136.
Presents a detailed interpretation of Naipaul's "political
orientation well to the right of the Caribbean norm." Suggests that his non-exposure to Caribbean politics of the
1930s, distance from the labor movement in the West Indies,
and lack of any genuine empathy with Caribbean peoples all
contributed to "this early cultural isolationism in Trinidad."
Argues that Naipaul's use of The Mimic Men to justify the
case for "psychological dependency as a way of life" in the
Caribbean is in fact "rather the characteristic of assimilated
middle-class elements." Naipaul draws heavily on J. A.
Froude's book The English in the West Indies as the backdrop
to The Middle Passage, thus placing it clearly "in the tradition of Carlyle and Froude, full of anti-Negro bias."

C172.   Sederberg, Peter C. "Faulkner, Naipaul and Zola: Violence
and the Novel." In The Artist and Political Vision, edited by
Benjamin R. Barber and J. G. McGarth, 291-315. New
Brunswick, NJ: Transaction, 1982.

C173.   Eyre, M. Banning. "Naipaul at Wesleyan." The South
Carolina Review 14 (Spring 1982): 34-38.
Vividly describes Naipaul's idiosyncracies and wrath in
the classroom at Wesleyan University where he spent a year
teaching. Praises his charm at dinner parties and treasures
his brilliant intellect. Finds Naipaul frequently philosophical,
but equally peevish and intolerant. His verbal attack on
Dinesen's Out of Africa in a lecture, dismissal of Greene and
Hemingway as the "last of the imperialist writers," and his
treatment of students who did not turn in assignments punc-
tually did not endear them to him. Displays a temperament

clearly not suited to teaching: this Naipaul readily concedes. His threat to dismiss his publisher or to punch a
student in the face testifies to his complexity. A penetrating
biographical insight.

C174. Mudrick, Marvin. "The Muslims are Coming! The Muslims
are Coming!" Hudson Review 35 (Spring 1982): 130-138.
The article is heavily critical of Naipaul's attitude toward
people, places and events. Suggests that he dwells too much
on rage and self-pity.

C175. MacDonald, Bruce. "The Artist in Colonial Society: 'The
Mimic Men' and 'The Interpreters.'" Caribbean Quarterly
20 (March/June 1982): 20-31.
Alludes briefly to the continuing debate between Naipaul
and Soyinka on the role of the artist in ex-colonial countries.
Suggests instead that Naipaul's Mimic Men and Soyinka's The
Interpreters can better demonstrate the fight to develop "an
alternative to the colonial mentality," through an individual
conscious decision, rather than by fiery public arguments.
He sees "an irreconcilable conflict in these novels between
aesthetic order and the cultural chaos from which it comes."
Draws extensively on Ralph Singh's role as narrator and
artist in The Mimic Men to illustrate segments of this conflict.
Develops several interesting comparisons between Egbo in
The Interpreters and Singh in Naipaul's book. Concludes
"as with The Mimic Men, the whole structure of Soyinka's
novel reflects the difficulties of the artist in colonial society."

C176. Thieme, John. "Authorial Voice in V. S. Naipaul's 'The Middle Passage.'" Prose Studies 5 (May 1982): 139-150.

C177. Hemenway, Robert. "Sex and Politics in V. S. Naipaul."
Studies in the Novel 14 (Summer 1982): 189-202.
An important analysis of Naipaul's style, his art and politics. Hemenway describes him as "a global citizen, unattached, non-aligned, anti-colonial," which makes his political
attitudes difficult to place. Discusses in detail also "the
complex interplay between politics, vision and technique"
as seen in Naipaul's treatment of women in his fiction; he
uses Guerrillas to illustrate this. Paints a vivid picture
of the main characters: Jane, Roche and Ahmed.

C178. Ramchand, Ken. "From Street to House; Ken Ramchand
introduces a discussion of Naipaul's later fiction." Trinidad
and Tobago Review Literary Supplement 6 (Independence
1982): 11, 14.
In the first of a three-part assessment of V. S. Naipaul's
later fiction, Ramchand places in perspective Naipaul's own
reaction to writing nonfiction: cites examples from Miguel
Street, The Suffrage of Elvira and The Mystic Masseur to

illustrate the technique Naipaul uses to deal with themes of placelessness, self-interest and political fraud in his early work. Touches on his use of the third person "to show, scrupulously, by means of what people do and say." Ramchand sees this narrative technique as "only a deflating device," one which serves "to maintain a strict distance between author and character." Notes that in A House for Mr. Biswas Naipaul uses the narrating mechanism to achieve intimacy instead of distance.

C179. Mordecai, Pamela C. "The West Indian Male Sensibility in Search of Itself: Some Comments on 'Nor Any Country,' 'The Mimic Men' and 'The Secret Ladder.'" World Literature Written in English 21 (Autumn 1982): 629-644.

In the discussion on identity Mordecai looks at the Caribbean woman's role in the literature and the society, and the literary evolution of the society as part of an international momentum. Maintains that proportionately the region has not benefited from their contributions. She questions the "matriarchal" label and suggests it is partly responsible for this situation. The study is centered on Garth St. Omer's Nor Any Country, Wilson Haris' The Secret Ladder and V. S. Naipaul's The Mimic Men. Mordecai also explains why these three books were selected.

C180. Bordewich, Fergus. "Anti-Political Man: V. S. Naipaul Reconsidered." Working Papers Magazine 9 (September/October 1982): 36-42.

C181. Clements, Walter C., Jr. "The Third World in V. S. Naipaul." Worldview 25 (September 1982): 12-17.

C182. Gurr, Andrew. "The Freedom of Exile in Naipaul and Doris Lessing." Ariel 13 (October 1982): 7-18.

Discusses the concept of freedom by drawing on Doris Lessing's The Golden Notebook, and Naipaul's In a Free State and A House for Mr. Biswas. Cites the following as some of Naipaul's key reflections on exile: the paintings in the tomb at Luxor, sketching an ancient vision of Egypt, the activity centered around the desert children, and tourists fighting for sandwiches. Both the examples occur in the Epilogue to In a Free State. Extends this thesis to Mr. Biswas who he says "for once recognizes the constraints on freedom, and forgets his fantasies of escape." Likens Naipaul to Anand and suggests that Naipaul, while becoming free of the demands of home, fully understands what it costs for such freedom. Believes that in both The Golden Notebook and In a Free State "they confront the issue of freedom with honest pain, and make it part of their vision of society."

C183. Neill, Michael. "Guerrillas and Gangs: Franz Fanon and V. S. Naipaul." Ariel 13 (October 1982): 21-62.

C184. Sachs, William L. "V. S. Naipaul and the Plight of the Dispossessed." Christian Century 99 (November 17, 1982): 1167-1169.

C185. Chauhan, P. S. "The Commonwealth of the Imagination: Narayan and Naipaul." In Language and Literature in Multicultural Contexts, edited by Satendra Nandan, foreword by James Maraj, 89-96. Suva, Fiji: University of South Pacific, 1983.
Highlights the dilemmas of the Commonwealth writer by comparing Narayan's The Vendor of Sweets with Naipaul's The Mimic Men, both of which were written in 1967 and dealt with the same theme of the young man's return home from England with a profession.

C186. Goodheart, Eugene. "V. S. Naipaul's Mandarin Sensibility." Partisan Review 50 (1983): 244-256.

C187. Hamner, Robert D. "Aspects of National Character: V. S. Naipaul and Derek Walcott." In Language and Literature in Multicultural Contexts, edited by Satendra Nandan, foreword by James Maraj, 179-188. Suva, Fiji: University of South Pacific, 1983.
Hamner condemns the opening remarks in A Bend in the River. Notes that despite Walcott's more positive outlook compared to Naipaul's, his reception has not entirely been spared the wrath of "sensitive nationalists." Suggests that Naipaul and all his characters are displaced. Concludes that Walcott is less pessimistic than Naipaul because "his voice is tempered with the full might of Caribbean history."

C188. King, John. "A Curiously Colonial Performance: the eccentric vision of V. S. Naipaul and J. L. Borges." Yearbook of English Studies 13 (1983): 228-243.

C189. McSweeney, Kerry. "V. S. Naipaul: Clearsightedness and Sensibility." In Four Contemporary Novelists--Angus Wilson, Brian Moore, John Fowles, V. S. Naipaul, 151-212. Montreal: McGill-Queen's University Press, 1983.
This book introduces four authors through a series of four individual essays. McSweeney stresses, however, that these writers have remained committed to the functions of the novel. The essay on Naipaul is a detailed semi-biographical account which poses some fundamental questions. It points out that not enough attention has been focused on his "technical and formal skills" as a novelist; nor have his views on the novel's function, the state of contemporary fiction, and his own method as a novelist been fully addressed.

C190. Sharma, T. R. S. "Chinua Achebe and V. S. Naipaul: One Version and Two Postures on Post-Colonial Societies." In

The Colonial and Neo-Colonial Encounters in Commonwealth Literature, edited by H. H. Anniah Gowda, 83-93. Mysore: Prasaragana University, 1983.

C191. Singh, Vishnudat. "Naipaul's New Indians." Part One. Trinidad and Tobago Review (Literary Supplement) 6 (Independence 1983): 3, 8.
Draws attention to Naipaul's use of protagonists drawn mainly from East Indians of Trinidad and Tobago origin. Points to Mr. Stone and the Knights Companion as the only exception. The books discussed here are In a Free State and A Bend in the River. Referring to "The Tramp at Piraeus," Singh focuses briefly on The Tramp, someone he regards as Naipaul's "most mobile character." Directs much attention to an in-depth study of the main characters that follow, namely: Santosh from "One Out of Many" and Salim in A Bend in the River. One of the significant points relating to Santosh is Naipaul's departure from his standard norm for selecting someone to fulfill the role of narrator/ protagonist.

C192. Singh, Visnudat. "Naipaul's New Indians." Part Two. Trinidad and Tobago Review 7 (Petit Careme 1983): 17, 23.

C193. Tiffin, Helen. "V. S. Naipaul's 'Outposts of Progress.'" World Literature Written in English 22 (1983): 309-319.
Emphasizes that Naipaul's concern in his work has been to explore "the contemporary repercussions for both colonizer and colonized of imperial colonial history." Admits that the separation of vision influences literary form, a problem that Naipaul encounters early in his career. Cites his satirical attempts in The Mystic Masseur and The Suffrage of Elvira on the one hand, and, on the other, the English setting of Mr. Stone and the Knights Companion, which produces an arid novel. Tiffin notes that In a Free State, Guerrillas and A Bend in the River all attempt to underline man's plight in the post-colonial world. She observes that in A Bend in the River, Naipaul has tended to become more hopeful for man's survival in the post-colonial societies.

C194. Williams, Haydn M. "The Insider and the Outsider: The India of V. S. Naipaul and Nirad Chaudhuri." In Language and Literature in Multicultural Contexts, edited by Satendra Nandan, foreword by James Maraj, 353-361. Suva, Fiji: University of the South Pacific, 1983.
Williams suggests that the main issue in An Area of Darkness is Naipaul's self-discovery, not the despair and pessimism he expresses in the book. He admits it is a story of failure "expressed powerfully and skilfully." Believes his travel writings and related journalism are important for a full appreciation of his fictional work on Africa. Chaudhuri by

contrast is confident that he knows himself. From his autobiography one detects a measure of common sense, calmness,
and learning. His judgment is questioned in relation to
British India and the Indians. Concludes that Naipaul was
unable to handle the paradoxes he encountered within himself and used them as a literary ploy.

C195. Brown, John L. "V. S. Naipaul: A Wager on the Triumph
of Darkness." World Literature Today 57 (Spring 1983):
223-227.
Presents an overview on Naipaul's published books up to
and including Among the Believers, while pulling together
threads of major significance. Observes the close existing
relationship "between Naipaul's travel books and his fiction,"
his sense of history notwithstanding. Regards him as essentially a novelist who has displayed minimal interest in technical
experiments. Sees A Bend in the River as one of his major
achievements in terms of its significance to Conrad's Heart
of Darkness.

C196. Gibbes, Michael. "Hands off Naipaul; Things That Matter."
Challenge (August 10, 1983): 8.
Addresses some of the main issues of contention which
Naipaul has sparked by stating that in the Caribbean "little
of real value is achieved." Gibbes likens him to Dickens,
embodying the conscience of the society. Maintains the view
that the society over time is still one of "a happy-go-lucky,
long-suffering, gullible and uncaring people." Gibbes also
sees it as "oblivious of things like national productivity."
States further that Naipaul's criticism in his view seems justi-
fied in a land where "the vast majority care little for the Humanities and Art and Literature."

C197. Durix, J. P., ed. "V. S. Naipaul." In Commonwealth Essays
and Studies 6 (Autumn 1983): 1-97.
Contents: Bruce King, "Anand's Recherche du Temps
Perdu," pp. 1-18; Anthony Boxhill, "Nothing will Come Out
of Nothing, 'A House for Mr. Biswas,'" pp. 19-29; Pierre
Besses, "Alienation et identité dans 'A House for Mr. Biswas,'" pp. 30-36; Philip Langran, "An Unlucky Child, Superstition and Mr. Biswas," pp. 37-50; Andre Dommergues,
"Les modes de l'espace dans 'A House for Mr. Biswas,'" pp.
51-60; Victor Ramraj, "Sly Compassion: V. S. Naipaul's
Ambivalence in 'A Christmas Story,'" pp. 61-70; John Thieme,
"Surviving 'the Mingling of Peoples': V. S. Naipaul's 'A
Bend in the River,'" pp. 71-82; Michel Lemosse, "The Perception of Time in 'A Bend in the River,'" pp. 83-92; Sud-
hakar R. Jamkhandi, "Travelling with V. S. Naipaul," pp.
93-97.
These essays are selected from a series of studies on Nai-
paul undertaken in Dijon (1981) and Amiens (1982) by the
Société d'Etude des Pays du Commonwealth. The volume

includes a thorough study of A House for Mr. Biswas and other aspects of the author's work; it is intended to update the previous books written on Naipaul and to be used for teaching.

C198.   "Writing 'A House for Mr. Biswas,'" New York Review of Books (November 24, 1983): 22-23. Rpt. "Naipaul Exposes Himself." In Express [Trinidad] (February 2, 1984): 11-12.

Naipaul discusses his youthful ambition to become a writer, recounts some of the frustrations he endures in his early years, his close and emotional attachment to A House for Mr. Biswas. Tells of the skill and the assessment of his own talent necessary in producing such a book. Talks about his father's influence on him, and the shift in emphasis he makes in writing the book from a simple story to one of "a man's search for a house and all that the possession of one's own house implies." Still regards himself as a comic writer.

C199.   Sandall, Roger. " 'Colonia' According to Naipaul." Commentary 76 (December 1983): 77-81. Rpt. "Naipaul's Colonia" in Quadrant 28 (April 1984): 68-72.

C200.   Bhabha, Homi K. "Representation and the Colonial Text: A Critical Exploration of Some Forms of Mimeticism." In The Theory of Learning, edited by Frank Gloversmith, 93-122. Brighton, Sussex: Harvester Press, 1984.

C201.   Cudjoe, Selwyn R. "V. S. Naipaul and the Question of Identity." In Voices from Under, edited by William Luis, 89-99. Westport, CT: Greenwood, 1984.

A very thought-provoking essay which explores the social and cultural identity of Caribbean societies. Cudjoe takes issue with Naipaul's American and European critics whom he states "become the most 'authentic' interpreters of Naipaul's truth." Provides some interesting interpretations of Naipaul's earlier works on the theme of identity. Touches also on his internationalism as a writer and concludes that "the quest of identity in Caribbean people can be found not in the texts of Naipaul but in the songs that express the anguish of its people."

C202.   Kumar, T. Vijay. "Being Nothingness, and the Paradox of Freedom: A Study of V. S. Naipaul's 'One Out of Many.'" Literary Endeavour 4 (1984): 8-14.

C203.   Martin, Murray S. "Order, Disorder, and Rage in the Islands: The Novels of V. S. Naipaul and Albert Wendt." Perspectives on Contemporary Literature 10 (1984): 33-39.

C204.   Ramchand, Kenneth. "Partial Truths: A Critical Account of

V. S. Naipaul's Later Fiction." In Critical Issues in West
Indian Literature, edited by Erika Sollish Smilowitz and
Roberta Quarles Knowles, 65-89. Iowa: Caribbean Books,
1984. Rpt. in Essays on Contemporary Post-Colonial Fiction,
edited by Hedwig Beck and Albert Wertheim, 225-252.
Munich: Max Heuber Verlag, 1986.
    An incisive, lucid account on Naipaul's techniques, style
and development as a novelist. Ramchand draws attention
to the themes in his early works, as well as his manipulation
and presentation of those themes to his audience. Naipaul's
refraining from employing characters in the early novels as
mouth-pieces, and his narrative devices, are discussed at
length. Touches also on the use of Trinidadian setting and
characterization up to and including A House for Mr. Biswas.
Notes that the characters Naipaul uses in the later novels
actually undertake journeys which end abruptly in disillusionment, in contrast with aborted trips which confine the characters in the earlier fiction to their own environment. In a
Free State, Guerrillas and A Bend in the River receive much
attention.

C205. Searle, Chris. "Naipaulacity: A Form of Cultural Imperial-
       ism." Race and Class 26 (1984): 45-62.
           A far-reaching speech dedicated to the memory of J. J.
       Thomas, in his response to J. A. Froude's book, English in
       the West Indies. It is a direct response to opponents of the
       Grenada Revolution and addresses "a legitimisation of the
       people's language" emanating from the revolution. Attacks
       Naipaul on several statements made in his reporting of the
       revolution, but not before paying tribute to The Suffrage
       of Elvira, A House for Mr. Biswas and The Mimic Men.
       Naipaul saw the revolution as a fraudulent, fully socialist
       exercise "built on words, ideas, and slogans, with no reality
       on the ground." Naipaul's Froudian thinking was sharply
       rebuked, along with "the ugly attitudes of the colonial cus-
       todians in the Caribbean," specifically the British and Ameri-
       cans. Searle argues that the revolution "brought a commit-
       ment to extend language resources, to find new ways of
       using words, to ensure full literacy in the standard language,
       to understand and use it as an international tool of communi-
       cation, to encourage reading and writing of literature and
       ideas from all over the world." Naipaul's work was more
       widely read after the revolution, ironically.

C206. Swinden, Patrick. The English Novel of History and Society,
       1940-1980, 210-252. London: Macmillan, 1984. Contents:
       Richard Hughes, Henry Green, Anthony Powell, Angus Wil-
       son, Kingsley Amis, V. S. Naipaul.
           Swinden argues that for over fifty years developments
       in the novel have not enjoyed such prominence. The book
       seeks to find out where these "fertile imaginations" came from,

and out of what kind of literary background. One of the developments the book probes is the spate of linguistic experiment. The section on Naipaul is extremely lucid, and gives a refreshing view of the plaudits and criticisms levelled at him in the past.

C207.   Thieme, John. "An Introduction to 'A House for Mr. Biswas.'" In A Sense of Place: Essays in Post-Colonial Literature, edited by Britta Olinder, 151-161. Gothenburg: Gothenburg University, 1984.

C208.   Jones, D. A. N. "The Enchantment of Vidia Naipaul." London Review of Books 6 (May 3-16, 1984): 15-16.
          Gives an overview of the essays. With reference to "Prologue to an Autobiography" cites A House for Mr. Biswas as a backdrop, noting that the introduction to its reissue "harmonises well with the mood" in Finding the Centre. In the second essay, "The Crocodiles of Yamoussoukro," Jones notes the delight with which Naipaul relates his adventures in the Ivory Coast "with more satisfaction than scepticism." One learns also of Naipaul's personal enchantment with the French language, which developed at school in Trinidad, and now prompts his visit to this African country. Suggests that the Ivory Coast President's style of leadership is perhaps due for further study.

C209.   Johnson, Patrice. "The Third World According to V. S. Naipaul." The Black Scholar 15 (May/June 1984): 12-14.

C210.   W. B. "A Note on Naipaul's Development; Naipaul will go on Ascending." Trinidad Guardian, August 22, 1984, p. 22.
          Suggests that in Naipaul's deeper fiction, In a Free State and Guerrillas, he views history as an impersonal process and human efforts as "futile, puny and ridiculous." Feels that the nihilistic outlook built into the form of the books, namely that "man as the plaything of history" constitutes the violence with which the novels are concerned. Notes that in A Bend in the River Naipaul provides the opportunity for individual action and regards the novel itself as a measure of success. Regards this a major improvement on the nihilism of his earlier work, and expects to see a more positive outlook emanating from his work in the future.

C211.   Hoagland, Edward. "Staking his life on One Grand Vision." The New York Times Book Review 89 (September 16, 1984): 1, 44-45.
          Notes Naipaul's abiding concern with poverty, and some moderation in his polemical stance against Third World countries he has visited. However, he raps Naipaul's contempt for Islam. Suggests that Finding the Centre does not openly connect his childhood wounds and petulant nature, though he

sees traces of upheaval in the book. Comments on the reasons which bring him to the Ivory Coast, upon which the second essay is based. Criticizes Naipaul for making disparaging remarks about Third World countries to appease segments of intellectual American opinion.

C212. Belcher, William F. "Jonathan Swift on Miguel Street." World Literature Written in English 24 (Autumn 1984): 347-349.
Regards "Man Man" as more closely matched to Jonathan Swift than "B. Wordsworth" is to the true poet. Also sees Man Man's experience on the cross as perhaps his most developed role, but considers his character to be more complex than first appears. Attributes this to the great influence Swift had on Naipaul. Notes one of the major differences between Swift and Man Man is that the former displays no political ambitions. Points out, however, the "telling resemblance" between Man Man's sermon before going on the cross, and the irony reflected in Swift's A Modest Proposal. Not the least important is Belcher's observation of the self-sufficiency which Swift advocates and Naipaul's allusion to Trinidadians' preferences for foreign products. Regards it as a more complex and "impressive achievement" than a casual reading of Miguel Street may suggest.

C213. Gottfried, Leon; Hughes, Shaun F. D., eds. "Special Issue: V. S. Naipaul." Modern Fiction Studies 30 (Autumn 1984): 439-596.
Contents: Leon Gottfried, "Preface: The face of V. S. Naipaul," pp. 439-443; Paul Theroux, "V. S. Naipaul," pp. 445-454; Bibhu Padhi, "Naipaul on Naipaul and the novel," pp. 455-465; Harveen Sachdeva Mann, "Variations on the Theme of Mimicry: Naipaul's 'The Mystic Masseur' and 'The Suffrage of Elvira,'" pp. 467-485; Keith Garebian, "The Grotesque Satire of 'A House for Mr. Biswas,'" pp. 487-496; John Thieme, "Naipaul's English Fable: 'Mr. Stone and the Knights Companion,'" pp. 497-503; John Thieme, "A Hindu Castaway: Ralph Singh's Journey in 'The Mimic Men,'" pp. 505-518; James R. Lindroth, "The Figure of Performance in Naipaul's 'The Mimic Men,'" pp. 519-529; Hana Wirth-Nesher, "The Curse of Marginality: Colonialism in Naipaul's 'Guerrillas,'" pp. 531-545; Lynda Prescott, "Past and Present Darkness: Sources for V. S. Naipaul's 'A Bend in the River,'" pp. 547-559; Amin Malak, "Among the Believers: Two Views V. S. Naipaul and the Believers," pp. 561-566; Leon Gottfried, "A Skeptical Pilgrimage," pp. 567-571; Shaun F. D. Hughes, "Two Books on V. S. Naipaul: An Essay Review," pp. 573-580; Harveen Sachdeva Mann, "Primary Works of and Critical Writings on V. S. Naipaul: A Selected Checklist," pp. 581-591.

Gottfried in his preface vividly restates some of the
established facts on Naipaul's early life and literary career.
Draws attention to the quality and structure of A House for
Mr. Biswas. Suggests that the first major charges of "arrogance and snobbery" against him by intellectuals occurred
after he wrote The Middle Passage. Expresses the highest
praise for Naipaul's journalism as exemplified in An Area of
Darkness. Notes that the essays in this issue trace the development of his literary career during the past twenty-five
years.

C214. Alwari, Karim. "Through Western Eyes: The Fiction of
V. S. Naipaul." Inquiry (November 1984): 72-73.
"Though acclaimed on the cover as a masterpiece, Guerrillas is a novel in which repetition passes for style and in
which the images are bland and imprecise. An example of
this is the way Roche is repeatedly described as a
"doer."

C215. Goodwin, Ken. "Political Power and Social Flexibility in
African and Australian Novels." World Literature Written in
English 23 (Winter 1984): 96-115.
This is a comparative study of the way conflict is treated
in the works of three African and three Australian novelists.
Conrad's Heart of Darkness features prominently in the dis-
cussions as it relates to interpretations of the book and his
English usage. Harris' view is that Conrad's biases stem
from "a frontier to a capacity which he never quite attained."
Harris also refutes Achebe's attack on "Conrad's addiction
to adjectives." Goodwin maintains that Conrad's narrative
voice is a communicative device he employs, and further establishes that the impact of social forces on the attitudes of
his characters are "embodied in the experience of the words."
Here Naipaul's own experience fits. He speaks of his difficulty understanding Conrad's words which he calls "impenetrable." According to Goodwin without Naipaul's consciousness "his response to Conrad's work is relevant to his
own work."

C216. Hamner, Robert. "Colony, Nationhood and Beyond: Third
World Writers and Critics Contend with Joseph Conrad."
World Literature Written in English 23 (Winter 1984): 113-
114.
Discussion centers on Wilson Harris' view on Conrad's
style and use of language. Hamner suggests that frequent
allusions by Conrad's critics to narrative and nuance of language are "inescapable filters through which his colonial
world reaches the reader." Touches also on Naipaul's ad-
mitted initial difficulty in understanding Conrad, and the
relevance of his own work to Conrad's.

C 217. Ramraj, Victor J. "V. S. Naipaul: The Irrelevance of Nationalism." World Literature Written in English 23 (Winter
1984): 187-196.
    Ramraj notes that Naipaul in discussing his reactions to
the first Association for Commonwealth Language and Literature Studies (ACLALS) Conference in 1964 states that he
finds too much national and political emphasis on the papers
presented, this he calls "irrelevant nationalism." Argues
that Naipaul in his own writing never indulges in issues of
nationalism. In the case of language Ramraj observes that
Naipaul develops a command of English and uses it to his
advantage. Focuses also on his appreciation of dialect "as
a literary tool, not a foundation for nationalism." Maintains
that while it is possible to delineate Trinidad and Tobago's
path from colony to independence through a chronological
reading of the novels, "there is no fusing of socialism and
nationalism."

C 218. Simpson, Louis. "Disorder and Escape in the Fiction of
V. S. Naipaul." Hudson Review 37 (Winter 1984/85): 571-
577.
    Gives a few biographical details about the author. Simp-
son believes too that Naipaul has come to the end of a phase
in his writing career, but that the new one has not yet be-
gun. Contends that the novels inform on the corruption and
violence in life, of the need to retreat, and to preserve one's
inner qualities.

C 219. Duyek, Rudy. "V. S. Naipaul and Joseph Conrad's Secret
Sharing." In Elizabethan and Modern Studies, edited by
J. P. Vander Motten, 119-130. Rijksuniversiteit, Ghent:
Ghent Seminarie voor English and American Literature, 1985.

C 220. Kimbahune, R. S. "V. S. Naipaul's Travelogues." In Indian Readings in Commonwealth Literature, edited by G. S.
Amur and others, 187-192. New Delhi: Sterling Publishers,
1985.

C 221. McWatt, Mark A., ed. West Indian Literature and Its Social
Context; Proceedings of the Fourth Annual Conference on
West Indian Literature edited by Mark McWatt, 33-140.
Barbados: Cave Hill, University of the West Indies, 1985.
    Contents: Mark McWatt, "The Two Faces of El Dorado:
Contrasting Attitudes Towards History and Identity in West
Indian Literature," pp. 33-47; Jeffrey Robinson, "V. S.
Naipaul and the Sexuality of Power," pp. 69-77; Elaine Fido,
"Psycho-Sexual Aspects of the Woman in V. S. Naipaul's
Fiction," pp. 78-94; Cheryl Griffith, "The Woman as Whore
in the Novels of V. S. Naipaul," pp. 95-106; John Small,
"Sexuality and Cultural Aesthetic in the Novels of V. S.
Naipaul," pp. 107-118; Gloria Lyn, "Naipaul's 'Guerrillas'
Fiction and its Social Context," pp. 130-140.

Since Naipaul's work is the subject of six of the fourteen studies published, these papers have been listed accordingly. McWatt deals with The Loss of El Dorado in an historical context, he also sees in it a search for identity, reads into it also a sense of loss and failure of Trinidad society. Explores this negative trend through to A House for Mr. Biswas, and suggests that in Guerrillas Naipaul's chilly depiction of West Indian society sinks quite low. Four papers address sexuality in Naipaul's work. Gloria Lyn's paper reflects on Naipaul's insights relating to behavior in contemporary society, while praising his skills as a novelist.

C222. Maja-Pearce, Adewalo. "The Naipauls on Africa: An African View." The Journal of Commonwealth Literature 20 (1985): 111-117.
    The late Shiva Naipaul's North of South: An African Journey, V. S. Naipaul's In a Free State and A Bend in the River are the books which are featured in this study. One of the criticisms of In a Free State is that Naipaul allows Africans only minor roles. Maja-Pearce disputes the views of academics that the slur about the boy's scent was not a personal disrespect. Cites passages in North of South to substantiate similar levels of thinking and intellectual behavior towards Tanzanians. Regards Shiva's language as subtle but offensive, and draws on the example of his summary on Nyerere. Dislikes the magisterial plaudit accorded A Bend in the River and the thought implicit in Salim's "feelings of unease at what might happen" after an African country achieves independence. Perhaps his principal objection is to the open-ended criticisms to which they subject Africans and their countries, the Amins and the Mobutus notwithstanding. That the Naipauls should acclaim the virtues of Western tradition and impose their values on Africa, India, and even on the West Indies from which they come, is unacceptable.

C223. Nathrekar, Alka S. "Naipaul's 'The Mimic Men' and Third World Politics." In Indian Readings in Commonwealth Literature, edited by G. S. Amur and others, 137-143. New Delhi: Sterling Publishers, 1985.

C224. Pyne-Timothy, Helen. "V. S. Naipaul and politics: his view of Third World societies in Africa and the Caribbean." College Language Association Journal 28 (March 1985): 247-262.
    Pyne-Timothy argues that Naipaul is in some ways "an "anachronism in Third World writing." Draws on four of his novels which deal with independent post-colonial societies in the Caribbean and in Africa, to examine his perceptions of Third World political philosophy, attitudes and movements; analyzes the factors which promote these attitudes and Naipaul's own contribution to a "larger understanding of the

Third World political person." Notes that the "assessment of Third World political action and interaction given in The Mimic Men is a devastating one"; those effects are further explored in Guerrillas. Naipaul's treatment of the natural environment in Africa, unstable governments, third-class facilities, the assessment of Third World societies by European standards, are all themes Naipaul deals with in In a Free State and further elaborates upon in A Bend in the River.

C225.   Tewarie, Bhoendradatt. "Sex and Politics in Naipaul's 'Guerrillas.'" Trinidad and Tobago Review (Literary Supplement Long Vacation) 8 (August 1985): 2, 3, 7.
         Contends that in Guerrillas vulgarity pervades "all interpersonal relationships." The article sets out to examine those relationships in terms of the purposes they serve, with particular reference to Naipaul's own principles regarding sex. Tewarie gives as one reason Naipaul's intention to introduce the element of shock, and sees the use of sex too as a medium to broaden the scope of his audience. Touches on one of Naipaul's main concerns that his work should not be viewed in a purely regional context, which probably explains some of the reasons for his extensive travels. Draws attention also to his experiment with metropolitan characters and "some interracial sex" and violence in Guerrillas, A Bend in the River, and, to a lesser extent, A Flag on the Island. Makes it clear that these methods are not intended to commercialize his work "at the expense of artistic integrity."

C226.   Healy, Jack J. "Fiction, Voice, and the Rough Ground of Feeling: V. S. Naipaul After Twenty-five Years." University of Toronto Quarterly 55 (Fall 1985): 45-63.

C227.   Pyne-Timothy, Helen. "Women and Sexuality in the Later Novels of V. S. Naipaul." World Literature Written in English 25 (Autumn 1985): 298-306.
         The discussion on women and sexuality in Naipaul's later novels seeks to establish the role they play in relation to the male as extremely vital. Suggests further that it is a "very disturbing key" to fully understanding his work. The three books addressed are In a Free State, Guerrillas and A Bend in the River. Notes that in spite of "the almost totally demeaning manner in which Naipaul presents his women, however, Linda and Jane, the Europeans are the most fully developed characters in these works." Zabeth, the African trader in A Bend in the River represents "the most intriguing and ambitious attempt at ethnographic personality." Pyne-Timothy draws attention to Naipaul's avoidance of the characterization of Black women in these novels. Concludes that in addition to the themes of displacement and isolation, he has provided an "extremely harsh, moralistic and judgemental" view of women.

C228.   Dasenbrock, Reed Way. "Creating a Past: Achebe, Naipaul, Soyinka, Farah." Salmagundi 68-69 (Fall-Winter 1985/86): 312-332.

C229.   Thorpe, Michael. "Echoes of Empire: Conrad and Caliban." Encounter 66 (March 1986): 43-51.

C230.   Suleri, S. "Amorphous India: Questions of Geography." Southwest Review 71 (Summer 1986): 389-400.

C231.   Bardolph, Jacqueline. "Son, Father, and Writing: A Commentary." In Commonwealth 9 (Autumn 1986): 82-90.
        This is an incisive comment on the novel which seems to focus principally on its structure. Bardolph talks of its tonal disparity, and varying types of irony, including "alternating moments of burlesque, satire, or passages of lyrical sadness." In summary, the book displays various styles and moods, it further demonstrates the father's role as guide and mentor, and illustrates the complicated switching of viewpoints which Naipaul adopts.

C232.   Diot, Rolande. "Fate and Futility: Derision and Black Humour." In Commonwealth 9 (Autumn 1986): 72-81.
        This is another in a series of recent in-depth analyses of A House for Mr. Biswas. Diot considers it an extremely derisive, controversial novel "because of its subject-matter and historical background." Suggests that Naipaul deliberately borrowed "derision and black or 'sick' humour which betray both a philosophical, ideological and aesthetic standpoint" as a narrative technique and mode of representation. Touching on Naipaul's techniques, Diot notes he has avoided any "characterization that might lead to a tragic catastrophe or a happy end."
        Focuses on his use of "the structural metaphor of the house" which he sees as a derisive symbol; further suggests the fluctuating rhythm of his sentences from negative to positive is "a conventional humourous technique" which he adopts to further his derisive and destructive ends.

C233.   Fabre, Michel. "By Words Possessed: The Education of Mr. Biswas as a Writer." In Commonwealth 9 (Autumn 1986): 59-71.
        A very analytical study of A House for Mr. Biswas which begins by recording the reactions of illiterates to the printed word. Its main focus relates to "the self-referential use of literacy and literature," and their role in creating a cultural model of accomplishment influenced by British cultural tradition. There are several allusions to "writing" and "the letter" which Fabre notes were used in Miguel Street as a theme of which Naipaul seems fond. Suggests that Naipaul wants the reader "to perceive Mr. Biswas as a creditable, even

adroit, user of the Queen's English." Here Fabre alludes to Selvon's Moses Ascending and the difference between Mr. Biswas and Moses Aloetta. Argues that "by transferring fictional situations and characters the reader becomes capable of mastering actual situations without the onus of real-life emotional involvement."

C234. Woodcock, Bruce. "Post-1975 Caribbean Fiction and the Challenge to English Literature." Critical Quarterly 28 (Winter 1986): 79-95.
Provides a cross-section of views on the direction and development of Caribbean fiction since 1975. It dismisses the prominence of Wordsworth's text on the English Literature syllabus at University of the West Indies, Mona as "utterly inappropriate." Woodcock questions the simplistic categorization of issues or anxieties of Caribbean writers and writing. Suggests that Naipaul's despair and nihilism should not obscure his contributions: a view Gordon Rohlehr previously enunciated.

C234A. Saakana, Amon Saba. "Education of a Colonial & The Lost Centre of V. S. Naipaul," in The Colonial Legacy in Caribbean Literature Vol. 1. Karnack Literary Criticism. London: Karnack House; Trenton, NJ: Africa World Press, 1987. Chapter 6, pp. 89-100.
Naipaul is the most famous Caribbean-born writer in the West, primarily because of his role in "satirising, ridiculing, and condemning both the Caribbean and Africa as 'barren societies.'" Saakana is concerned with understanding how Naipaul has evolved into what he is, a colonial in crisis of psychic trauma, viewing the world through the oppressor's lens, without any possibility "of a meaningful change."

INTERVIEWS

C235. Fraser, Fitzroy. "A Talk With Vidia Naipaul." Sunday Gleaner [Jamaica] (December 25, 1960): 14, 19.

C236. Bates, David. "Interview With V. S. Naipaul." Sunday Times Supplement (May 26, 1963): 12-13.

C237. Walcott, Derek. "Interview With V. S. Naipaul." Sunday Guardian [Trinidad] (March 7, 1965): 5, 7.

C238. Oberdeck, Stephen. "Angry Young Indian." Newsweek 65 (April 19, 1965): 103-104.
Based on Naipaul's year-long sojourn in India, this book is "a crushing compendium of compassionate rate," replete with hyperbole and metaphors. Discusses the social, human and symbolic aspects of the work. Favors Naipaul's novelistic

presentation because of "its brutal facts"; generally favorable.

C239. Wyndham, Francis. "Interview With V. S. Naipaul." Sunday
Times (September 10, 1968). See also item C46.

C240. Rouse, Ewart. "Naipaul. An Interview with Ewart Rouse."
Trinidad Guardian, November 28, 1968, pp. 9, 13.

C241. Lowell, Robert. "Et in America Ego." Robert Lowell talks
to the Novelist V. S. Naipaul. Listener 82 (September 4,
1969): 302-304.

C242. Rowe-Evans, Adrian. "The Writer as Colonial." Transition
40 (1971): 56-62.

C243. Hamilton, Ian. "Without a Place." Times Literary Supplement, no. 3622, July 30, 1971: 897-898. Rpt. in Savacou:
A Journal of the Caribbean Artists' Movement Nos. 9-10,
(1974): 120-126.
   Naipaul discusses his early life in England, his indiffer-
ence to events political which he calls a colonial attitude.
Draws a parallel between the security he enjoyed as a colonial,
and the colonialism he senses in the British because of the
security they feel being allied to America. Discusses also
the plight of West Indians in Britain, London as his literary
base and the problems of audience.

C244. Hamilton, Alex. "Living a Life on Approval." Trinidad
Guardian (October 4, 1971): 8.

C245. Shenker, Israel. "V. S. Naipaul, Man Without a Society."
New York Times Book Review (October 17, 1971): 4, 22-24.
Rpt. "V. S. Naipaul." In Words and Their Masters, Israel
Shenker, 64-70. New York: Doubleday, 1974. Rpt. in
Critical Perspectives on V. S. Naipaul, edited by Robert D.
Hamner, 48-53. Washington, DC: Three Continents Press,
1977.

C246. Henry, Jim Douglas. "Unfurnished Entrails--the Novelist
V. S. Naipaul in Conversation with Jim Douglas Henry."
The Listener 86 (November 25, 1971): 721.
   In the discussion, Naipaul again deals with the problems
of aspiring to be a writer. Regards luck, ideas, art of
shaping paragraphs, as essential ingredients in writing before one's work gains authority.

C247. Roach, Eric. "Fame a Short-Lived Cycle, Says Vidia."
Trinidad Guardian (January 1972): 1-2.

C248. Bingham, Nigel. "The Novelist V. S. Naipaul talks to Nigel

Bingham about his Childhood in Trinidad." The Listener
88 (September 7, 1972): 306-307.
The discussion centers on Naipaul's earliest recollections
of his childhood, and the strong relationship he had with his
father. This he links to his peculiar free-lance nature and
"sense of isolation." Suggests that his unsettled life could
be related to the movement of his parents from one house to
another during his formative years; he attributes those dis-
ruptions to his rather late school beginning.

C249.   Hamish, Keith.   "The Ridiculous Panic Behind Vidia Naipaul."
Trinidad Guardian (November 29, 1972): 9.

C250.   Bryden, Ronald.   "The Novelist V. S. Naipaul talks about
his work to Ronald Bryden." Listener 89 (March 22, 1973):
367-368, 370.
A wide-ranging interview which focuses on Rhys, Mailer
and Borges. Both The Overcrowded Barracoon and The Loss
of El Dorado feature in the discussion. Naipaul talks about
the stimuli which London offers him as a writer, some of his
ideals as a writer, the value of journalism to him, the need
to travel in order to expand, his impressions of the novel
form and the need for an alternative convention of "imaginative interpretation" to the novel.

C251.   Pantin, Raoul.   "Portrait of an Artist: What makes Naipaul
Run." Caribbean Contact, 1 (May 19, 1973): 15, 18-19.
A candid discussion which addresses several issues from
beggars to the urban sprawl. It confirms many of the enigmatic traits in his personality. Very useful for a close study
of Naipaul.

C252.   Grant, Lennox.   "Naipaul joins the Chorus."   An Interview
With Gordon Rohlehr. Tapia 5 (July 6, 1975): 6-7.

C253.   Grant, Lennox.   "For Naipaul there is a Challenge of Faith."
An Interview With Gordon Rohlehr. Tapia 5 (July 13, 1975):
6-7.

C254.   Mentus, Ulric.   "Is There Something Called Black Art?"
Caribbean Contact 3 (February 1976): 7, 17.

C255.   Gussow, Mel.   "Writer without Roots." New York Times
Magazine (December 26, 1976): 8-9, 18-19, 22. Rpt. "Who'll
nominate Naipaul for the Nobel Prize: He's a Writer Without
a Constituency." Trinidad Guardian (March 15, 1977): 4.
This profile on Naipaul highlights many of the controversial
statements attributed to him. He proposes a solution to solv-
ing Jamaican immigration to Britain, Trinidad he calls "that
crazy resort place," England he regards as "intellectually and
culturally bankrupt," India "unwashed." Comments favorably

on his sense of humor, discusses his condemnation of colonialism. Touches on both A House for Mr. Biswas and shares some insights with Gussow on the writing of Guerrillas. About his audience he says "I'm recording a disappointment, a very wounding one. I write out of a sense of duty to myself, to my talents."

C256.   Wheeler, Charles. "'It's Every Man for Himself'--V. S. Naipaul on India." The Listener 98 (October 27, 1977): 535, 537.

This is a very detailed and far-reaching interview which explores some of Naipaul's thoughts on India, based on his second book of that country. He defines his interpretation of a wounded civilization, expresses his dislike for magic. Regards analyses of Indian history based on European models of presentation as a weakness; this approach he feels, detracts from a comprehensive view of the subject. Sees a need for Indians to broaden their loyalties. Argues that the country's total independence struggle was directed at rekindling its past history, and this has resulted in many of the current problems. Talks of his identification with the Indian cause, subsequent abandonment of that effort, and his disillusionment due to the absence of a "sense of country" he found in India. He regards Narayan's work as a contradiction in terms; a writer who attaches no importance to man's condition, yet expresses views of the human condition through the novel "as though human life matters."

C257.   Pryce-Jones, David. "A Conversation with V. S. Naipaul." Radio Times (March 24-30, 1979): 7, 11.

Subjects discussed include Naipaul's early years in England, the houses in which he lived, his travels abroad, his life style. Naipaul explains that the darkness and despair associated with his work stem from the absence of anything funny about which to write anymore. Finds his birthplace destroyed by the government of the day, regards his freedom as a person and a writer a timely matter. Despairs as his travels reveal the violence and cravings that affect mankind.

C258.   Hyman, Ronald. "V. S. Naipaul in Interview." Books and Bookmen 24 (1979): 23-26.

C259.   Hardwick, Elizabeth. "Meeting V. S. Naipaul." New York Times Book Review 84 (May 13, 1979): 1, 36.

A very interesting discussion between Naipaul and Hardwick on various topics, including his impressions of the various countries to which he has travelled. His fastidiousness is very evident. Of Borges he says: "his real work is in the poems, not in the tales. The poems celebrate the glorious land." Commenting on the durability of an author's

work, he believes one has to possess "a certain clearsightedness" and a few prejudices. Naipaul also talks about
"a work of perfect clarity" fashioned on Gogol's fiction that
he would like to write. An important thematic interpretation
of his style.

C260. "Vidia Talks of His Early Years in London." Sunday Express
[Trinidad] (June 10, 1979): 24-25.

C261. Cudjoe, Selwyn. "Talking About Naipaul; Gordon Rohlehr
Interviewed by Selwyn Cudjoe." Carib 2 (May 6, 1981):
39-65.
An extremely long and perceptive interview. Subjects
discussed include the differences in style and philosophy of
Wilson Harris and V. S. Naipaul, the impact of Naipaul's
race and religion on his self-concept, his standards for
measuring success, the limits he sets for himself, experiments
in his writings, his concern with the ill-effects of colonialism, the influence of Conrad on his work, Naipaul's popularity.
Notes that there are striking differences and similarities between Conrad and Naipaul. Rohlehr believes Naipaul "is
fascinated by the notion of the grotesque." References are
made to Eric Williams, C. L. R. James and George Lamming.

C262. Medwick, Cathleen. "Life, Literature and Politics: An Interview with V. S. Naipaul: An Elusive Man of many Cultures
Talks About his--and our--World." Vogue 171 (August 1981):
129-130.
This is partly a narrative interview. It reflects on Naipaul, a citizen of the world, some of his peculiarities, finer
virtues, affectations, art of conversation. Recollects experiences of his visits to India and his disillusionment with
the place. Medwick suggests that air of pessimism may be a
weakness in his work. Naipaul disavows any dark vision in
his writing. Regards success not as something magical, but
as flowing from sheer effort and will.

C263. Mukherjee, Bharati; Boyers, Robert. "A Conversation with
V. S. Naipaul." Salmagundi 54 (Fall 1981): 4-22.
The conversation between Boyers, Mukherjee and Naipaul
deals essentially with writing, and Naipaul's reactions to his
own work.

C263A. Rambaran, Irma. "Pakistani with a Passion for Reggae Mu-
sic." Trinidad Guardian (October 25, 1981): 17.
Discusses with Mrs. Ranjibouy her plans for making a
documentary film on V. S. Naipaul. Alludes to the translation of his work, his style and the controversy which surrounds
him. Believes he has underscored the weaknesses of developing countries, but has "not reached far enough in identifying the causes of the weaknesses." Suggests that Europeans

derive support from his views of the Third World which are
parallel to their own.

C263B. Michener, Charles. "Dark Visions of V. S. Naipaul." Newsweek 98 (November 16, 1981): 104-105, 108-110, 112, 114-
115.
    Largely biographical. Interview accompanying review of
Among the Believers (D424). See entry C166 for fuller an-
notation.

C264. Cudjoe, Selwyn Reginald. "V. S. Naipaul and the West Indian Writer: Kenneth Ramchand speaks with Selwyn Cudjoe."
Antilia 1 (1983): 9-20.
    A far-ranging interview on Naipaul which touches on
many subjects: his limited vision, obsession with his own
view of the world, popularity in the United States, a general discussion on A House for Mr. Biswas, the Mudkar group,
the relationship of West Indian nationalism to literary development in the region, racism, the foreign critics who exceed
their limitations "and become placeless souls." Ramchand
concludes the interview by telling Cudjoe "it is the feeling
of humility which Naipaul elicits that I value most in his work
at this time."

C265. Levin, Bernard. "V. S. Naipaul: A Perpetual Voyager."
The Listener 109 (June 23, 1983): 16-17.
    Among other topics, Naipaul discusses his dislike of
Trinidad, including his family, his impatience with people
who lead instructive, placid lives, his father's influence on
his own life, his early literary inclinations, the chores in
becoming a writer. He makes some very positive observations about India. He comments on the delusion of a homo-
geneous world: "there is a good deal of misunderstanding
of one group by another because of this appearance that we
are talking about the same thing." About his future plans,
he says "I would like to do some comic novels before I fin-
ish."

C266. Gussow, Mel. "V. S. Naipaul: 'It is out of this Violence
I've Always Written.'" New York Times Book Review (September 16, 1984): 45-46.
    Reflects upon the impulses which prompted him to write
"Prologue to an Autobiography," the attendant problems in
his aspirations to be a writer, and gives some personal
views on the art of writing. Touches also on his belief in
justice, and expresses some disappointment with many London publishers and with his reading audience. He believes
he took writing too seriously, for which he has been punished.
He thinks his fortunes changed after 1962 when he became an
extraregional writer. Naipaul says he has neither views nor
attitudes towards Third World countries. Expresses his disdain

for sex literature, but admits that his "unnaturally violent" reactions enable him to function best as a writer.

C267. Von Barloewen, C. "Naipaul's World: Interview with C. Von Barloewen." World Press Review 32 (April 1985): 32-33.

C268. Atlas, James. "The Fierce and Enigmatic V. S. Naipaul Grants a Rare Interview in London. V. S. vs. The Rest." Vanity Fair (March 1987): 64-68.

THESES AND DISSERTATIONS

C269. Alisharan, Stephen Sheik. "V. S. Naipaul: A Study of Four Books." M.A. thesis, Mount Allison University, 1965.
    The thesis attempts to establish "some of the attitudes to large numbers of East Indians in Trinidad," in order to understand their situations in Naipaul's apprenticeship works. Alisharan uses as his criteria: structure, style, narrative technique and characterization to assess the books. It also examines Naipaul's role in the development of West Indian literature. There are eleven chapters.

C270. Boxhill, Herman Francis Anthony. "The Novel in English in the West Indies, 1900-1962." Ph.D. diss., University of New Brunswick, 1966.

C271. Broughton, G. "A Critical Study of the Development of V. S. Naipaul as a Novelist as Reflected in his Four West Indian Novels." M.Phil. thesis, University of London, 1967.

C272. Derrick, A. C. "The Uncommitted Artist: A Study of the Purpose and Methods of Satire in the Novels of V. S. Naipaul." M.Phil. thesis, University of Leeds, 1968.

C273. Ramraj, Victor Jammona. "A Study of the Novels of V. S. Naipaul." M.A. thesis, University of New Brunswick, 1968.

C274. Ramchand, Kenneth. "A Background to the Novel in the West Indies." Ph.D. diss., Edinburgh University, 1967. Revised and published under title: The West Indian Novel and Its Background. London: Faber and Faber, 1970.

C275. Hamner, Robert Daniel. "An Island Voice: The Novels of V. S. Naipaul." Ph.D. diss., University of Texas (Austin), 1971.
    An analysis of the structure and content of Naipaul's longer published fiction, which forms the basis of this study in six chapters. Chapter One introduces him, his critical reputation and the obstacles West Indian writers encounter;

Chapter Two examines the structural techniques adopted in each of his novels. Chapter Three touches on characterization, Chapter Four addresses the satirical content so prevalent in his earlier work, Chapter Five discusses the variety of his themes; Chapter Six, in summarizing, suggests "he transcends regional barriers and is a supranational author with concepts and principles which place him well within the main stream of contemporary Western thought and literary expression."

C276.   Erapu, L. O. "The Novels of V. S. Naipaul: A Symbolic Approach." M.Litt. thesis, Edinburgh University, 1972.

C277.   Sani, Ruta Mara. "A Bibliographical Survey of the West Indian Novel." M.L.S. thesis, Western Michigan University, 1972.
The thesis consists of four chapters and two appendices. The chapters are arranged chronologically in Part One; the appendices are arranged alphabetically by authors in Part Two. The survey lists two hundred and twenty novels by West Indian writers; eighty seven of those titles have been annotated.

C278.   Subramani. "Search for a Country: A Study of V. S. Naipaul's Fiction and Non-Fiction Writings." M.A. thesis, University of New Brunswick, 1972.

C279.   Zinkhan, Elaine Joan. "Vidia Naipaul: Artist of the Absurd." M.A. thesis, University of British Columbia, 1972.

C280.   Tiffin, Helen Margaret. "The Lost Ones: A Study of the Works of V. S. Naipaul and Alejo Carpentier." Ph.D. diss., Queens's University, 1973.

C281.   Ahmed, N. "The Quest for Identity in the West Indian Novel with Special Reference to John Hearne, V. S. Naipaul, George Lamming, Dennis Williams, Roger Mais." B.Litt. thesis, Oxford University, 1974.

C282.   Hanen, David J. Markham. "Naipaul's Unnecessary and Unaccommodated Man." M.A. thesis, University of Calgary, 1975.

C283.   St. Omer, Garth. "The Colonial Novel: Studies in the Novels of Albert Camus, V. S. Naipaul and Alejo Carpentier." Ph.D. diss., Princeton University, 1975.
St. Omer's thesis is that the "colonial writer," regardless of his ethnic background or stature, soon discovers that he cannot write in "a largely illiterate society." He cites Naipaul's realization of this; notes Camus' conviction "only after initial experience of trying to write for a readership in the

colony." Carpentier's ambivalence notwithstanding, the
colonial writer chooses to write for the more literate European
and North American societies, where, in addition, critical
evaluation is part of the tradition. He further notes that the
study examines the novels by Albert Camus, V. S. Naipaul
and Alejo Carpentier to demonstrate "the consequences in
the form and structure of their work, of writing out of one
semi-illiterate society for another society accepted as culturally, though not politically, superior."

C284.   Seukeran, Angela Ahylia. "The Development of V. S. Naipaul as a Writer." M.A. thesis, McMaster University, 1975.

C285.   Baksh, Mustakeen. "The Myth of El Dorado in Caribbean
Fiction." M.A. thesis, McGill University, 1976.

C286.   Cudjoe, Selwyn Reginald. "The Role of Resistance in the
Caribbean Novel." Ph.D. diss., Cornell University, 1976.
Revised and published under title : Resistance and Caribbean Literature. Athens, Ohio: Ohio University Press,
1980.
States "the purpose of the study is to present the literary development of the Caribbean novel that transcends linguistic barriers and bridge a gap created by a colonial condition."
It is essentially a political study divided into two parts. Part
I: Outlines briefly the history of Caribbean resistance.
Part II: Shows through dialect the link between resistance
and literature. Notes that the English-speaking aspect of the
work is limited to novelists regarded as "the authentic literary voices of the Caribbean." Three of V. S. Naipaul's
books receive attention: The Middle Passage, A House for
Mr. Biswas and Guerrillas particularly.

C287.   Thorpe, Marjorie Ruth. "Beyond the Sargasso: The Sig-
nificance of the Presentation of the Woman in the West Indian
Novel." Ph.D. diss., Queen's University, 1976. 191 pp.
Issued by University Microfilms under title: The Image of
the Woman in West Indian Fiction. Michigan: University Microfilms International, 1976.
States that "fiction is the most highly developed form of
West Indian literary expression" from which many aspects of
West Indian woman image can be studied. Cites Shama, Mrs.
Tulsi's daughter, as a focus. The work is divided into four
chapters. Chapter I: Deals with contemporary cultural
traditions in the society; Chapter II: Identifies and studies
novelists' perceptions of women as failures. The last two
chapters deal with "the imitative response" and "the cultural
response" as solutions to what Thorpe sees as "a West Indian cultural problem."

C288.   Nunez-Harrell, Elizabeth. "The 'Tempest' and the works of two Caribbean Novelists: Pitfalls in the way of seeing Caliban." Ph.D. diss., New York University, 1977.

"The first two chapters of the dissertation discuss reasons for West Indian interest in Shakespeare's Caliban and the difficulties involved in an interpretation of this character. The Third chapter formulates criteria for evaluating Third-World literature which are applied in the final two chapters to an analysis of the works of Lamming and Naipaul, emphasizing how the particular perspective of each of these artists distorts the real image of the West Indian."

C289.   Ayuen, Anthony Wing Chong. "V. S. Naipaul: A Study in Alienation." M.A. thesis, McGill University, 1978.

C290.   Carty, Deverita Elisabeth. "Selected West Indian novels: Thematic and Stylistic Trends from the Nineteen-Fifties to the Early Nineteen-Seventies." Ph.D. diss., University of Michigan, 1978.

An analysis of the concepts of "identity, madness and paradise" explored through the work of five West Indian novelists with varying degrees of thematic emphasis. The writers represented are St. Omer, Lamming, Mais, Barret and V. S. Naipaul. Carty notes that all the novels place emphasis on one central character. It is from Lamming's Natives of My Person that she records "a multiplicity of stylistic and linguistic forms," similarly treated in A Love Song for Mumu. Focuses also on the theme of "internal and psychological orientation" which runs through all five novelists' work. In Naipaul's A House for Mr. Biswas she suggests that Biswas's rejection of his ethnic grouping "is a departure from many West Indian novels which emphasize the search for racial identity."

C291.   Greenwald, Roger Gordon. "The Method of V. S. Naipaul's Fiction, 1955-1963." Ph.D. diss., University of Toronto, 1978.

This study analyzes Naipaul's first novels, out of which he sees a cycle in Naipaul's work. The study concentrates on the language and the overall narrative techniques used in the novels, in order to further an appreciation of each novel's recognition. The thesis in the introduction gives an overview of other critical approaches previously adopted towards Naipaul's work. Stresses that his focus, when discussing the books collectively, is to identify relations between the ways parts of one title relate to each other.

C292.   Rodriguez, Maria Christina. "The Role of Women in Caribbean Prose Fiction." Ph.D. diss., City University of New York, 1979.

Traces the social and political development of the Caribbean in the last twenty-five years, and the impact this development has had on women. The study cites the narrative work of Alejo Carpentier of Cuba, Rosario Ferre from Puerto Rico, and from the West Indies: Roger Mais, Jean Rhys and V. S. Naipaul, to underline the stereotype images into which these writers have placed female characters. Suggests that as Caribbean society progresses, literature will inevitably reflect female characters as humans.

C293. Aiyejina, Funso. "Africa in West Indian Literature: From Claude McKay to Edward Kamau Brathwaite." Ph.D. diss., University of the West Indies, St. Augustine, 1980.

C294. Deodat, R. "V. S. Naipaul's Fiction, 1954-71: Fragmentation and Ruthlessness." M.A. thesis, Simon Fraser University, 1980.

C295. Donawa, Margaret. "Childhood in the West Indian Novel." M.Phil. thesis, The University of the West Indies, Cave Hill: 1980.
The theme of childhood is the focus of this study. Donawa draws on some of the works of the following West Indian authors: Jean Rhys, George Lamming, Michael Anthony and V. S. Naipaul. Sees the children in Naipaul's novels represented as "victims of corrupt and atrophying traditions," those in Lamming's books hold "important and often dual symbolic functions," the children in Rhys' Wide Sargasso Sea like Naipaul's, share a certain degree of "isolation and alienation," whereas Anthony's exhibit the "capacity to give and receive affection" which reinforces them in a hostile world. Concludes that in many ways all are affected by the legacy of colonialism. Contains a list of juvenile books.

C296. Mason, Nondita. "The Fiction of V. S. Naipaul: A Study." Ph.D. diss., New York University, 1980. Calcutta: World Press, 1986. 131 pp.
Several of Naipaul's books are used in each of six chapters into which the thesis is divided. It emphasizes a particular aspect of his growth and maturity as a writer. Pays attention to "structure, themes, motifs and imagery in his works." Concluding chapter discusses Naipaul as "a life-affirmer" in spite of his pessimism. Notes Naipaul's characters "continue to live, accepting the imperfections and divisions in life."

C297. Rambachan, Niala. "Through Commonwealth Eyes: Naipaul's Narayan in Perspective." M.A. thesis, The University of the West Indies, St. Augustine, 1980.
The thesis is organized in three sections. Section one examines the basis for Naipaul's early affinity with Narayan; Section two looks at the divergence of attitude between both Naipaul and Narayan: Section three analyzes Naipaul's views on Narayan to determine their validity, in order to better

understand the value of his work and what he has accomplished.

C298. Roderique, Vernette. "The Image of the Colonial in the Works of V. S. Naipaul." M.A. thesis, The University of the West Indies, St. Augustine, 1980.
Focuses on Naipaul's vision of the colonial. Uses In a Free State to underline the universal human condition of the dispossessed and the displaced. A Bend in the River is used to focus on Africa and its colonial relation with North America. Argues that Naipaul's geographical shift underlines his need "to examine man's position, to understand exactly where he belongs in the universe."

C299. Campbell, Elaine. "West Indian Fiction: A Literature in Exile." Ph.D. diss., Brandeis University, 1981.
Outlines the historical relationship which evolved between Great Britain and the Empire; also discusses the dual loyalties and the methods some writers have adopted to rationalize that relationship. Discusses English as the medium of communication in relation to the "burgeoning literature" from the area. Deals with four novelists: George Lamming, Jean Rhys, Wilson Harris, and V. S. Naipaul "to demonstrate that the overseas/local motherland duality has provided the tension generating a metaphor of exile utilized by West Indian novelists" who use England as their base to write and publish their work.

C300. Fitch, Nancy Elizabeth. "History in a Nightmare: A Study of the Exilic in the Life and Work of James Joyce, V. S. Naipaul and Edna O'Brien." Ph.D. diss., University of Michigan, 1981.
"It is a topical investigation of how the common experience and background of colonialism, especially British colonialism, affected these three particular authors--all writing in the English language but whose tradition was other than English." Focuses specifically on alienation, deracination, mimicry, dislocation and inequality in Ireland, India and Trinidad which the study argues were the root causes of their exile.

C301. Nasta, S. M. "Basement, Attic of Suburban Hotel? London and the Question of Appropriate Form in Samuel Selvon's 'The Lonely Londoners' and in V. S. Naipaul's 'The Mimic Men.'" M.A. thesis, University of Kent at Canterbury, 1981.

C302. Charles, Henry James. "A Theological-Ethical Apprisal of the Disclosure of Possibility for the Post-Colonial Caribbean Via an Analysis of Selected Literary Texts." Ph.D. diss., Yale University, 1982.

The thesis discusses and analyzes in a theological and eth-
ical context the future potential for post-colonial Caribbean
states, through selected literary works. The authors represented are H. Orlando Patterson, Roger Mais, Wilson Harris
and V. S. Naipaul. Charles assesses some of Naipaul's writing "through an explication of the way of negation in the
apophatic tradition and through Aquinas' moral reflection on
'acedia.'"

C303.   Gonzalez, Anson John. "Race and Colour in the Pre-
Independence Trinidad and Tobago Novel." M.Phil., University of the West Indies, St. Augustine, 1982.

C304.   Williams, Ronald Alexander. "Third World Voices: An
Analysis of the Works of Chinua Achebe, George Lamming,
and V. S. Naipaul." Ph.D. diss., Lehigh University, 1982.
The study compares the works of Achebe, Lamming and
V. S. Naipaul. The key focus of the study is "the literary
reaction" of each writer to his colonial experience discussed
under four critical headings: confrontation and change, the
uses of the past, the function of the mother country, the
failed rebellion--and attempts to use these to investigate
post-colonial societies. Regards the work of Achebe and
Lamming as totally anticolonial; suggests that Naipaul's reactions are entirely different: "he records only the squalor
of the colonized people's past, and his characters tend towards absurdity." Regards their work as "a significant comment on the psychology of people in colonial societies."

C305.   Boyle, JoAnne Woodyard. "The International Novel: Aspects
of its Development in the Twentieth Century with Emphasis
on the Work of Nadine Gordimer and V. S. Naipaul." Ph.D.
diss., University of Pittsburgh, 1983.
Traces the development of the international novel in the
twentieth century from Henry James's The American to V. S.
Naipaul's Guerrillas and A Bend in the River. Suggests that
in this "sub-genre" the theme of revolution is usually found,
that their characters are marginal figures, caught up in
ideology and cultural conflicts. Notes that "the sympathy of
the landscape reinterprets the causes and outcomes of the
revolutions and reveals the unstable conditions of the marginal men and women who participate in them."

C306.   Husten, Larry Alan. "From Autobiography to Politics: The
Development of V. S. Naipaul's Fiction." Ph.D. diss., State
University of New York at Buffalo, 1983.
A chronological discussion of Naipaul's fiction, starting
with his exploration of the Third World and theme of alienation from an autobiographical viewpoint. Suggests that these
apprenticeship novels record life in Trinidad and his own "extremely complex attitude" to that world. Notes his writing

undergoes a series of changes after A House for Mr. Biswas, when he focuses on Third World social and political questions. An analysis is continued of the various context in which the autobiographical theme is presented in Naipaul's fiction.

C307.   Tewarie, Bhoendradatt. "A Comparative Study of Ethnicity in the Novels of Saul Bellow and V. S. Naipaul." Ph.D. diss., Pennsylvania State University, 1983.
Tewarie's study, based on the work of Saul Bellow and V. S. Naipaul, examines the "ethnic dilemma of protagonists" in their novels. Firstly they are considered as novelists whose consciousness evolved from their own experience and the "historical experience of their ethnic groups in the New World." Secondly they are treated as writers "marginal to the dominant culture flow in their societies." The study regards marginality as a "crucial ingredient" impacting upon "their artistic vision and social consciousness" in their work.

C308.   Lim, Ling-Mei. "V. S. Naipaul's Later Fiction: The Creative Constraints of Exile." Ph.D. diss., Indiana University, 1984.
The study focuses on the emergence of his later fiction "from his acceptance of permanent exile towards a socio-historical analysis as a means of confronting the problems of the larger post-colonial Third World." Chapter One reviews "the overall pattern in the development of Naipaul's writing." Chapters Two to Four analyze his later novels from The Mimic Men to A Bend in the River. Concludes that in the absence of a literary tradition Naipaul fashions his writing "in response to the constraints upon his relation to the world and to the problems of both personal and literary response to the Third World."

C309.   Morgan, Paula Eleanor. "The Love Relationship: A Study of Male/Female Interaction in Selected West Indian Authors." M.Phil. thesis, University of the West Indies, St. Augustine, 1984.
The thesis examines the works of Jean Rhys, John Hearne, George Lamming and V. S. Naipaul in the context of their ethnic and cultural affiliations. Uses their "patterns of interaction" as microcosms of relations in the broader society. The study also looks at the changing patterns of family relations in "the normless, multicultural society."

C310.   Wilson-Tagoe, Veronica Nana. "The Historical Sense in Selected West Indian Writers." Ph.D. diss., University of the West Indies, St. Augustine, 1984.
Tl ⌐ study discusses aspects on the theme of history as they relate to selected works of Edward Brathwaite, Derek Walcott and V. S. Naipaul. There are five chapters as follows: "The Historical Novel in the West Indies," "Displacement

and Possibility in <u>A House for Mr. Biswas</u>," "Determinism as Vision and Form in V. S. Naipaul's later works," "Walcott's Progress Towards a Concept of History," "Edward Brathwaite's Vision of History in the Caribbean."

C311. Dhahir, Sanna. "Women in V. S. Naipaul's Fiction: Their Roles and Relationships." Ph.D. diss., University of New Brunswick, 1986.

Suggests that "Naipaul's fictional women reflect and propagate his significant themes and viewpoints through their different roles and relationships." Sees his preoccupation with displacement and alienation having great influence on "his presentation of women's relationships with men." On the other hand, argues that "Naipaul's male characters are often portrayed as ineffectual, even petty, creatures."

C312. Hassan, Dolly Zulakha. "West Indian Response to V. S. Naipaul's West Indian Works." Ph.D. diss., George Washington University, 1986.

Hassan's dissertation gives "detailed treatment of this wide range of materials" on Naipaul, which has appeared as journal articles, lectures by West Indians overseas, "and criticisms in West Indian journals, periodicals and newspapers." Chapter one gives an overview of the East Indian social, political and cultural life in the Caribbean. The second chapter addresses "the constraints placed on Naipaul" as a Caribbean writer living in self-imposed exile. Chapter five covers "all of Naipaul's West Indian journalistic non-fiction." Concludes that "the current dominant preception among critics is that his books are anti-West Indian, his standards Eurocentered, and his sensibility Brahmin."

C313. Mustafa, Fawzia. "Africa Unbound: Works of V. S. Naipaul and Athol Fugard." Ph.D. diss., Indiana University, 1986.

C314. Firth, Kathleen. "Aspects of V. S. Naipaul's Caribbean Fiction." Ph.D. diss., University of Barcelona, 1987.

This study, the first Ph.D. dissertation on V. S. Naipaul to be presented in Spain, comprises an analysis of the purely Trinidad fiction, that is to say, the works up to and including <u>A House for Mr. Biswas</u>. Dedicating a chapter to Seepersad Naipaul's short stories, it is part of this study's intention to convey the importance of his father, not only to Vidia Naipaul's early career, but also to his finally having come to an acknowledgement of the past he believed he had eschewed when he left Trinidad to become a writer in the metropolis.

* * *

The dissertation titles and (portions of) abstracts contained here are published with permission of University Microfilms International, publishers of <u>Dissertation Abstracts International</u> (copyright © 1965 through 1987, by University Microfilms International), and may not be reproduced without their prior permission. Full text copies are available from University Microfilms International, 300 North Zeeb Rd., Ann Arbor, MI 48106.

D. SELECTED BOOK REVIEWS

THE MYSTIC MASSEUR (1957 MM)

D1. Quinton, Anthony. "New Novels." New Statesman 53 (May
     18, 1957): 648-649.

D2. Bayley, John. "New Novels." Spectator 198 (May 24, 1957):
     687-688.

D3. "Out of Joint." Times Literary Supplement 2833 (May 31,
     1957): 333.
        Traces the vicissitudes in Ganesh's life, including his
     stint as a mystic, "which leads him finally to Lake Success."
     Comments favorably on Naipaul's sense of humor, "and con-
     siderable feeling for, as well as insights into characters."
     Suggests that the end of the book shows signs of being
     rather hastily concluded.

D4. "Ganesh in the Years of Guilt." Sunday Guardian [Trinidad]
     (June 16, 1957): 23, 27.
        Suggests that Ganesh's character and circumstances are
     reminiscent of those of several Trinidadian politicians. Draws
     attention to Naipaul's keen sense of observation, gift of hu-
     mor, and mastery of satire. Sees the book as "a mature
     first novel." Further describes it as "woven into Oriental
     Trinidad tapestry which displays fresh brilliant insights into
     Hindu politics."

D5. Ross, Angus. "A Shaggy Mystic." Public Opinion (August
     24, 1957): 7.

D6. Amis, Kingsley. "Fresh Winds from the West." Spectator
     200 (May 2, 1958): 565-566.
        Comments favorably on Naipaul's originality and effective
     use of humor with "stylistic quietude" throughout the book.
     Touches also on the bewilderment and inefficiency which as-
     sails the characters, thus negating their shrewdness and pro-
     moting their noisy reactions.

D7.   Collymore, Frank A. "Mystic Masseur." <u>Bim</u> 7 (January/
       June, 1958): 119-120.
           Naipaul's satirical novel uses as its background the poorer
       East Indian community reflecting the characteristics of the
       poorer classes "of almost any West Indian island." Empha-
       sizes Naipaul's understanding and sympathy for their predica-
       ment.

D8.   Seymour, Arthur J. "Mystic Masseur." <u>Kyk-Over-Al</u>, 8,
       no. 24 (December 1958): 84-85.
           A very light-hearted book in which "the spirit of poking
       fun at hero and reader alike" predominates. Regards this
       as a relief from "the diet of sex offered by the majority of
       West Indian writers." Focuses on the sympathy Naipaul at-
       taches to his hero, Ganesh. Comments favorably on the
       dialogue and the control Naipaul exercises over his charac-
       ters.

D9.   "Huckster Hindu." <u>Time</u> 73 (April 6, 1959): 89.
           Ganesh's portrayal receives high praise. He is the embodi-
       ment of "that growing family of ex-colonial heroes who have
       their feet firmly planted in the muck of local tradition, and
       their heads lifted to the sweet smell of Western excess."
       His careers range from author to U.N. representative for
       his country. Describes the book as "often too clotted with
       local colour."

D10.   Levin, Martin. "How the Ball Bounces Down Trinidad Way."
       <u>New York Times Book Review</u> (April 12, 1959): 5.

D11.   Nyren, Karl. "Mystic Masseur." <u>Library Journal</u> 84 (May
       1, 1959): 1533.
           It is essentially a plot summary. Much of the book con-
       sists of Caribbean dialect. Seen as a pleasant off-beat at-
       tempt "which tells a humorous, low-pressure story of human
       folly." Detects a weakness towards the end of the novel.
       Criticizes Naipaul's "attitude towards his central character
       whom he satirises most of the time."

D12.   Balliett, Whitney. "Mystic Masseur." <u>New Yorker</u> 35 (May
       30, 1959): 103-104.
           Discusses jointly Naipaul's novel, The Mystic Masseur and
       Selvon's <u>Turn Again Tiger</u>, both of which deal with "the
       rise of a poor Trinidadian." Ganesh emerges as the hero in
       the former title. Focuses on Naipaul's technique of handling
       his characters. Regards Selvon's vivaciousness in his novels
       towards his fellow-citizens as "a rare and attractive quality."

D13.   Baro, Gene. "Ganesh's Beguiling Exploits." <u>New York
       Herald Tribune Book Review</u> 35 (June 7, 1959): 6.
           Touches on the vividness and wit of Naipaul's characters.

Apart from the entertainment value of this book, he notes that Naipaul establishes his talent in excellent fashion.

D14.   Wood, Percy. "Mystic Masseur." Chicago Sunday Tribune Magazine of Books (July 12, 1959): 5.
Expresses satisfaction with the standard Naipaul establishes in his first book, its comical nature notwithstanding. Describes it as an appreciative and tender story of Hindus in Trinidad, made more effective by his vivid mind, academic background and race.

D15.   "Briefing." Observer (October 18, 1964): 22.

THE SUFFRAGE OF ELVIRA (1958 SE)

D16.   Richardson, Maurice. "New Novels." New Statesman 55 (April 19, 1958): 510-511.

D17.   "New Fiction." The Times (April 24, 1958): 13.

D18.   Powell, Anthony. "Electoral Roll." Punch 234 (April 30, 1958): 587-588.

D19.   "Tropical Heat." Times Literary Supplement No. 2931 (May 2, 1958): 237.
The story is centered on Naparoni, a small neglected county in Trinidad. Comments favorably on the comic traits in Naipaul's writing, while observing that "the dialogue of his racy yet earnest compaigners is an almost aural delight."

D20.   Panton, George. "Satire on Trinidad." Sunday Gleaner [Jamaica], June 22, 1958, p. 11.

D21.   Newby, P. H. "The Suffrage of Elvira." London Magazine 5 (November 1958): 82-84.
A mixed, ironical review on elections in a Trinidad community, in which Newby notes that Naipaul "has not yet acquired Narayan's ability to subordinate detail to a memorable whole." Believes the author's cynical attitude towards the election detracted from the quality of the book. However, his compassion for his characters is immense.

MIGUEL STREET (1959 MS)

D22.   Shrapnel, Norman. "This Mr. Cambridge Go Bawl." Manchester Guardian April 4, 1959, p. 4.

D23.   "Street Scene." Times Literary Supplement, no. 2982 (April 24, 1959): 237.

A collection of seventeen short sketches centered on a series of highly comical characters, many of whom form "a continuous thread of communal or street life running through the book." Naipaul captures the dialogue and use of the language with remarkable vividness.

D24. Richardson, Maurice. "New Novels." New Statesman 57 (May 2, 1959): 618.
  Richardson describes Miguel Street as "a string of delightfully drawn character sketches of Trinidadian back street eccentrics." Generally favorable review which anticipates more substantial writing from Naipaul. Praises his style, humor and "pleasing philosophical detachment."

D25. "Naipaul Does it Again." Sunday Guardian [Trinidad], May 17, 1959, p. 22.

D26. Collymore, Frank A. "Miguel Street." Bim 8 (July/December 1959): 67.
  Apart from the book's originality and lucid style, Collymore observes some of Dickens' "rich prodigality of characterization." Further detects "a certain Rabelaisian humour" which is absent in Dickens' novels.

D27. Wyndham, Francis. "Miguel Street." London Magazine (September 6, 1959): 80-81.

D28. Poore, Charles. "Books of the Times." New York Times (May 5, 1960): 33.
  Presents a vivid version of the book. Poore alludes to a comparison with "Porgy and Bess." The scene is set in a slum section of Port of Spain during the Second World War. Concedes the book "presents a world of its own excellently."

D29. Malone, Robert M. Library Journal 85 (May 15, 1960): 1938.
  Displays a brilliant satirical insight into the lives of the characters living on Miguel Street. Sees them as a "vivid and enchanting picture of an unfamiliar background."

D30. Rodman, Selden. "Catfish Row, Trinidad." New York Times Book Review (May 15, 1960): 43.

D31. Wood, Percy. Chicago Sunday Tribune Magazine of Books (May 15, 1960): 6.

D32. Wickenden, Dan. "Stories Told Under the Sun of Trinidad." New York Herald Book Review 36 (May 22, 1960): 10.

D33. "Mixed Fiction." Time 75 (May 30, 1960): 77.
  This comprises a string of sketches peopled by very ludicrous characters. Naipaul "understands well that his comical

characters do not live comic lives and his best sketches are
shaded with compassion."

D34.   Payne, Robert. "Caribbean Carnival." Saturday Review 43
        (July 2, 1960): 18.
        Provides a summary of the book and draws attention to
        several of the characters. "They have a flair for conversa-
        tion, and sometimes even the dullest of them will arrive at
        the edge of a revelation." Naipaul's vividness of mind re-
        ceives high praise, prompting Payne to suggest "the mantle
        of Chekhov has fallen on Naipaul's shoulder."

D35.   Balliett, Whitney. "Soft Coal, Hard Coal." New Yorker
        36 (August 27, 1960): 98, 100.
        The book "consists of a series of funny, unpretentious,
        parabolical sketches about the inhabitants" in a section of
        Port of Spain. The characters are for the most part misfits.
        Describes Naipaul's humor as suspended from "his dialogue"
        and "a strong, effortless sense of irony." Concludes that
        "Miguel Street dances like a diamond its whole length."

D36.   W. B. "The Descent and Ascent of Naipaul; Vidia Naipaul's
        'Miguel Street.'" Trinidad Guardian (July 18, 1984): 22.
        Offers fresh insights for a reading of this novel. Sees
        Naipaul as a disciple of James Joyce uncomfortably aware,
        like Joyce, "of the susceptibility of his small archaic com-
        munity to exotic fictional treatment." Touches on the "author-
        ial distance" he adopts before his treatment of a character
        or situation.

D37.   Moore, Gerald. "Miguel Street." Black Orpheus 9 (June
        1961): 66-67.

                    A HOUSE FOR MR. BISWAS (1961 HB)

D38.   Gilbert, Morris. "Hapless Defiance." New York Times Book
        Review (June 24, 1961): 30.

D39.   "High jinks in Trinidad." Times Literary Supplement, no.
        3109 (September 29, 1961): 641.
        The book is an exhaustive account of the Trinidad East
        Indian community. Its vividness, technical details and satir-
        ical style make it a first-rate social commentary. Thinks
        Biswas is a "rather stupid little man" upon whom Naipaul
        lavished too many details, bordering on inconsistencies. Com-
        ments favorably on his superb handling of power conflicts
        between the sexes; credits the universality of the book's
        theme.

D40.   Jacobson, Dan. "Self Help in Hot Places." New Statesman
        62 (September 29, 1961): 440-441.

D 41. Wyndham, Francis. "A House for Mr. Biswas." The Listener
1 (October 1961): 90-93.
Regards Biswas as an original character "whose extreme
individuality illuminates" mankind's general experience.
Likens the embodiment of his experiences to those of Trinidad's Hindu society. Champions Naipaul's skill in producing
this novel, "one of the clearest and subtlest illustrations ever
shown of the effects of colonialism." Comments on the flow
of his writing, while praising his avoidance of "the sex-cam
sensationalism." Cautions on too much criticism of the novel's
"exotic background." His characters receive much praise.

D 42. Lamming, George. "A House for Mr. Biswas." Time and
Tide (October 5, 1961): 1657.

D 43. "New Fiction." The Times (October 5, 1961): 16.

D 44. Mitchell, Julian. "Everyman's Island." Spectator 207 (October 6, 1961): 472.

D 45. Keown, Eric. "New Fiction." Punch 241 (October 25, 1961):
624.

D 46. Walcott, Derek. "A Great New Novel of the West Indies."
Sunday Guardian [Trinidad] (November 5, 1961): 17.
A biographical sketch touching on Naipaul's relationship
with the Caribbean; it also dwells on the make-up of his
major characters, with brief comments on his previous works.
A sympathetic assessment.

D 47. Walcott, Derek. "The Man Who Was Born Unlucky." Sunday
Guardian [Trinidad] (November 5, 1961): 17.
Walcott regards this the first major novel produced by an
indigenous writer. It deals essentially with the Indian ele-
ment in Trinidad society, "and dramatises the complexity in
its half-comic hero," Biswas. The pathos in this tragic
farce Naipaul skillfully immerses amidst the book's humor.
Both his judgement of human nature and his creativity receive praise.

D 48. Panton, George. "West Indian Writing Comes of Age."
Sunday Gleaner [Jamaica] (December 3, 1961): 14.

D 49. Dobbs, Kildare. "West Indian Exiles." Saturday Night 77
(February 3, 1962): 31-32.
Naipaul's natural wit, fluency of style and objectivity re-
ceive much praise. His handling of the main character, Mr.
Biswas, is excellent. Dobbs regards Biswas as "one of those
fictional people who make themselves part of our own experi-
ence." Detects some biographical similarities reminiscent of
Naipaul's father. An extremely favorable review.

D50.   "A House for Mr. Biswas." Kirkus 30 (March 1, 1962): 249.

D51.   Owens, J. R. "A House for Mr. Biswas." Caribbean Quarter-
        ly 7 (April 1962): 217-219.
            Provides a summary of the plot, and praises the book as
        "far and away his best." Comments on the subtleness and
        effectiveness with which he uses irony. Concludes that "the
        merit of this sad, sympathetic and intelligent book is that we
        are impelled to make comparisons with our own situation."

D52.   Mann, Charles. "A House for Mr. Biswas." Library Journal
        87 (May 15, 1962): 1917.

D53.   Rogers, W. G. "Be it Ever so Humble." Saturday Review
        45 (June 9, 1962): 37.
            Much of the review is devoted to Mr. Biswas's life strug-
        gle and his determination to acquire his own house. Sees
        "Mr. Biswas's failings in Trinidad as his successes." Views
        as a fine smooth flowing story, peopled by characters remi-
        niscent of P. H. Newby's books on Egypt.

D54.   "Also Current." Time 79 (June 22, 1962): 74.

D55.   Archer, Rosanne K. "A House for Mr. Biswas." New York
        Herald Tribune 38 (June 24, 1962): 6-7.

D56.   Chapin, Louis. "Fiction of South India and the West Indies:
        'A House for Mr. Biswas.'" Christian Science Monitor 54
        (July 19, 1962): 11.

D57.   Eimerl, Sarel. "A Trinidadian Dickens." The Reporter 27
        (July 19, 1962): 56-57.
            Regards the novel as a strong social commentary on East
        Indian life in Trinidad. Biswas's idiosyncracies apart, Nai-
        paul presents in Biswas a remarkable character and example
        of determination. Believes it is to Naipaul's credit that he
        has assimilated "the comedy and the horror, the fun and the
        misery into a coherent whole." The novel's major flaw is
        its length and repetition, clearly one of Dickens' traits.

D58.   MacInnes, Colin. "House for Mr. Biswas." Bim 8 (July/
        December 1962): 221-223.
            Praises Biswas's fortitude to reject a social structure ex-
        panding in wealth, complicated by colonial restrictions. Re-
        gards the book as the "unforced pace of a master at work."
        Rpt. in London Sunday Observer (October 1, 1961): 31; Rpt.
        in Public Opinion (October 7, 1961): 3.

D59.   Balliett, Whitney. "Books: Wrong Pulpit." New Yorker
        38 (August 4, 1962): 70-71.
            Balliett describes it as an "exceptional ironic work." He

gives an objective assessment of Naipaul's style. The major
character, Mr. Biswas, represents a "steady succession of
gentle failures." Regards Naipaul's portrayal of the East
Indian community in Trinidad as a kind of "microscopic pano-
rama" reminiscent of Victorian novelists. Admires his skill
in maintaining a balanced flow throughout; perhaps the major
accomplishment in this novel is the link between Biswas's
inner thoughts and his major goal in life.

D60. Bagai, Leona Bell. "A House for Mr. Biswas." Books Abroad
  36 (Autumn 1962): 453.

D61. Krikler, Bernard. "V. S. Naipaul's 'A House for Mr. Biswas.'" The Listener 71 (February 13, 1964): 270-271.
   An extremely detailed and forceful assessment of the story.
  Projects the significance of the book far beyond Biswas's
  life, and regards it as "one of the few major English novels
  to have appeared since the war." Apart from its immaculate
  satirical style and depth, Krikler senses in Naipaul a profound
  compassion. Detects in the book elements of Dickens and
  E. M. Forster's influence on Naipaul. It is his effective use
  of the novel as a vehicle of communication which touches
  Krikler most. Concludes that "the delicacy and honesty"
  with which he has made the complexities of his novel felt,
  would make A House for Mr. Biswas endure.

D62. Carr, Bill. "A House for Mr. Naipaul." Public Opinion
  (March 20, 1964): 8-10.

D63. Harris, Wilson. "Comedy of Pathos." In Tradition and the
  West Indian Novel, 13. London: West Indian Students'
  Union, 1965.
   Harris was addressing an audience at the West Indian Students' Union where he gave a stirring analysis of Lamming's
  Of Age and Innocence. He compares Shephard, its main
  character with Mr. Biswas in Naipaul's book. Shephard is
  "stark and tragic" where Biswas is "a mixture of comedy
  and pathos." He suggests that Naipaul's world is free of
  any exceptional and "corrosive sensibility"; it centers essentially on a Trinidad Hindu lifestyle in its historical context.
  Sees his characters as made to measure, never erupting "into revolutionary or alien question of spirit."

D64. Enright, D. J. "No Matter the Place or Time, To Write is
  To Learn." The Listener 111 (May 3, 1984): 22-23.
   Discusses Naipaul's early years at the B.B.C. and his
  father's influence on his career. Questions the self-pity which
  pervades Naipaul's mind. Sees the foreword to A House for
  Mr. Biswas as a clearer micro-version of "Prologue to an
  Autobiography." In "The Crocodiles of Yamoussoukro" "no
  one is quite certain about the significance" of the practice in

the Ivory Coast of feeding live chickens to the reptiles as a ritual, writes Enright, who offers some explanations of his own. See also item D 446.

D 65.   Stevenson, Anne. "Heart of Darkness." Times Educational Supplement (June 1, 1984): 22.
        In the foreword to this edition of A House for Mr. Biswas, Naipaul writes it is the most personal of all his books; "created out of what I felt as a child." Stevenson observes that out of it he was able to create situations and characters and also another way "of looking and feeling himself into alien societies." Appreciates his patience, instinct, feeling. Likens his writing skills to those of a painter. Comments on his technique of developing characters.

THE MIDDLE PASSAGE (1962 MP)

D 66.   Allen, Walter. "Fear of Trinidad." New Statesman 64 (August 3, 1962): 149-150.
        Naipaul's penchant for details predominates. Much of the review is devoted to social and racial attitudes in the Caribbean. On British Guiana Naipaul excels. Allen finds in Jamaica that Negro racism appears in the most extreme form of all the territories. Regards his account about Trinidad as the least pleasing section of the book.

D 67.   Bryden, Ronald. "New Map of Hell: 'The Middle Passage.'" Spectator 209 (August 3, 1962): 161.

D 68.   "Credit Balance." Punch 243 (August 8, 1962): 213.

D 69.   "The Re-Enactment of Mr. Naipaul." Times Literary Supplement, no. 3154 (August 10, 1962): 578.
        Regards as "the most challenging book that has been written about the West Indies." It is sentimental, gloomy and objective. Praises the novelist's characterization, sincerity and vivid mind qualities reminiscent of Graham Greene's Journey without Maps.

D 70.   Lucie-Smith, Edward. "The Middle Passage." The Listener 68 (August 16, 1962): 254-255.
        Refers to the work as a clever sociological observation. Touches on Naipaul's accent, rhythm and vocabulary. Praises his handling from within, the problem which most writers of West Indian travel books have been glad to ignore: race, class and colonialism. Commends the book for its refreshing and lively approach.

D 71.   "The Middle Passage." Encounter 19 (September 1962): 84.

D72.   Knight, Norman. "The Middle Passage." Chronicle of the
        West India Committee 77 (October 1962): 523.

D73.   Hearne, John. "The Middle Passage." Caribbean Quarterly
        8 (December 1962): 65-66.
            Hearne unleashes a vigorous attack on both Naipaul and
        his book, calling him "the most rigid and severe of moralists--
        the aesthetic Puritan." Questions Naipaul's infallibility and
        many of his assumptions, particularly as they relate to the
        Negro. It is a thorough analysis of a book which Hearne
        regards as lagging far behind A House for Mr. Biswas in
        quality.

D74.   Marshall, Harold. "Middle Passage." Bim 9 (January/June
        1963): 290-292.
            Not a particularly favorable review which partly high-
        lights Naipaul's unfamiliarity with some places discussed in
        the later section of the book. Still regarded as a potentially
        able writer.

D75.   "Middle Passage." The Bajan (June 1963): 24-28.

D76.   Harrison, John. "From the West Indies." Bim 10 (July/
        December 1963): 60-63.
            Focuses on the learning experience Naipaul gains on his
        return visit to the West Indies. Discusses the observations
        he makes about Trinidad: "always there is the constant
        reality that his country remains a materialistic, immigrant
        society"; touches also on the country's transition. Notes
        that after he leaves Trinidad his vision becomes blurred in
        the places he visits. Regards his style as immaculate "when
        he stays within the orbit of his particular field." Radio
        talk originally given in Suva, Fiji.

D77.   Dolbier, Maurice. "The Middle Passage." New York Herald
        Tribune (September 3, 1963): 19.

D78.   Poore, Charles. "A Native's Return to the Caribbean World."
        New York Times (September 7, 1963): 17.
            Suggests Naipaul's training as a novelist clouded his ob-
        jectivity. Provides a brief summary of the book and notes
        that he was restless everywhere he went. A major criticism
        of the book "was that in his determined effort to see the
        dark side of everything Mr. Naipaul sometimes seems" to over-
        emphasize the situation.

D79.   Jabavu, Noni. "Return of an Insider." New York Times
        Book Review (September 22, 1963): 14.

D80.   "The Middle Passage." Booklist 60 (October 1963): 134.

D81.   N.J. "The Middle Passage." Mexican Life (October 1963):
        36-37.
        Substantially agrees with Naipaul's book in relation to the
        reviewer's own experiences in the Caribbean. Concedes the
        political and social freedoms West Indians enjoy. Suggests
        his "tribal loyalties" and language afford the African "a
        fortunate sense of continuity." An exploration into the
        Caribbean consciousness.

D82.   "Briefly Noted Fiction." New Yorker 39 (October 12, 1963):
        312-314.

D83.   Malan, Harrison B. "The Middle Passage." Library Journal
        88 (October 15, 1963): 3842-3843.

D84.   Di Giovanni, Norman Thomas. "Return of a West Indian."
        Nation 197 (October 26, 1963): 262-263.

D85.   Johansson, Bertram B. "Caribbean Counterpoint." Christian
        Science Monitor 55 (October 30, 1963): 9.

D86.   Bedford, Sybille. "Stoic Traveller." New York Review of
        Books 1 (November 14, 1963): 4-5.

D87.   Carr, Bill. "The Annoying Ironist." Public Opinion (March
        26, 1964): 8-9.
        Regards this book a major contribution to understanding
        Commonwealth Caribbean society. Questions Naipaul's tone
        and some of his assumptions about this region which according
        to Carr was "consistently exploited, and never given confi-
        dence in itself"; Carr also suggests Naipaul's main theme on
        the region's preference "to enslave itself with ruthlessness
        and inertia" is refutable. However, this succinct and ana-
        lytical review creates a more rational understanding of The
        Middle Passage.

D88.   Archibald, Charles. "Eye of a beholder." Trinidad Guardian,
        July 24, 1973, p. 10.
        Essentially a review of Shiva Naipaul's book, North of
        South: An African Journey; in it Mr. Archibald reflects
        on the high standard of prose and style of V. S. Naipaul's
        The Middle Passage. Attributes both their fierceness in tone
        of writing to their being victims of an illusory world.

MR. STONE AND THE KNIGHTS COMPANION (1963 MSK)

D89.   "Mr. Stone and the Knights Companion." Essays and Re-
        views from Times Literary Supplement 2 (1963): 76-78.

D90.   Brooke, Jocelyn. "Two Comedies." The Listener 69 (May 30,
        1963): 934.

Naipaul's book is a "comedy of contemporary suburban life which seems curiously uncontemporary." Sees Mr. Stone as a "dull and conventional man" at odds with his station in life. Brooks questions the aura which Naipaul creates: "recitations after dinner and comic songs from the men." Impressed by the quality and lucid style of Naipaul's writing.

D91. "New Fiction." The Times (May 30, 1963): 16.
Discusses Naipaul's concern with the common man. It is a tragi-comedy of the protagonist, Mr. Stone, who "lives an impeccably, respectable and uneventful life." Credits the force of Naipaul's pen and the tact with which he handles his somewhat unpleasant material.

D92. "Sunk in Suburbia." Times Literary Supplement 3196 (May 31, 1963): 385.
The scene is set in England. The novel discusses Mr. Stone and his retirement scheme which Excal, his employer, finally approves. It also describes Mr. Whymper's appointment to help implement the scheme which "in the process is subtly but irretrievably damaged," and ironically of Whymper's confidence in Mr. Stone. Reflects on Naipaul's tenderness in handling his characters even when they are funny. His economy of "word and phrase," his gift of humor receive high praise.

D93. Raphael, Frederick. "The Later Spring of Mr. Stone." Sunday Guardian [Trinidad] (June 9, 1963): 15.
"Mr. Naipaul writes with a controlled wit which extracts the modest maximum from the autumnal spring of Mr. Stone and from the romance which forms a domestic counterpoint to his business success." At sixty-two he marries rather unceremoniously. Here one sees a parallel between Mr. Biswas and Mr. Stone. He is clearly a man of fantasies however, he sells a brilliant idea to his employers which Whymper later develops.

D94. Mitchell, Adrian. "Styles and Dreams." Spectator 210 (June 21, 1963): 815.

D95. Walcott, Derek. "Naipaul's New Book." Sunday Guardian [Trinidad] (July 7, 1963): 15.
Discusses Naipaul's reticence in writing a book about England or the English and the likely responses to it. Mr. Stone, an aging man, occupies center stage. His life's achievement Walcott calls "the creation of a chivalric order for decaying pensioners." Sees the wider vision of the novel as being a disregard for the individual.

D96. Ross, Alan. "Mr. Stone and the Knights Companion." London Magazine 3 (August 1963): 87-88.

D 97. "Mr. Stone and the Knights Companion." The Bajan (September 1963): 26.

D 98. Wood, Percy. "A Gem in an English Setting." Chicago Sunday Tribune Magazine (February 9, 1964): 4.

D 99. "A Short, Painful Life." Time (February 28, 1964): 75-76.
The novel's hero is Mr. Stone, a middle-age librarian obsessed with the prospect of old age and his wish to make a worthwhile contribution in life before his retirement; so he marries rather impulsively. Later he proposes to his employer a retirement scheme as a protection for the later years of life. The review stresses the universality of the novel.

D 100. Pryce-Jones, Alan. "Mr. Stone and the Knights Companion." New York Herald Tribune (March 7, 1964): 13.

D 101. Gleason, J. "Mr. Stone and the Knights Companion." San Francisco Chronicle (March 15, 1964): 41.

D 102. Allen, Walter. "London Again." New York Review of Books 2 (March 19, 1964): 21.

D 103. Frakes, James. "10K Golden Years." Book Week (March 22, 1964): 16.

D 104. Walcott, Derek. "The Achievement of V. S. Naipaul." Sunday Guardian [Trinidad] (April 12, 1964): 15.
Naipaul's style receives very favorable comment. Describes the book as "a murmur galvanised occasionally by spasms of terror." In spite of the novel's depressing mood, Walcott regards it as technically successful. Suggests the book is important from Naipaul's view as an alien and an artist.

D 105. Crutwell, Patrick. "Reviews." Hudson Review 17 (Summer 1964): 303, 311.
Analyzes some causes of Naipaul's measured acceptance among West Indians. Considers the book a transition in his attempt to shed his characterization as a regional writer.

D 106. Willis, Davis. "A Compassionate Spectator." Sunday Guardian [Trinidad] (January 10, 1971): 9.
Praises Naipaul's flair for sketching scenes and characters. Discovers also a pause in his quest for identity, a theme which characterizes much of his earlier work. Instead the book is centered on the aging Mr. Stone, a restless and sometimes eccentric person. Suggests Naipaul's calm and sobriety "give him room to produce a narrative of deep compassion."

AN AREA OF DARKNESS (1964 AD)

D107.   Walsh, William.   "Meeting Extremes."   Journal of Commonwealth Literature (1964): 170-172.

D108.   Pritchett, V. S.   "Back to India."   New Statesman 68 (September 11, 1964): 361-362.
A highly complimentary review of a book Pritchett calls
"the most compelling" on India in a long time.   Naipaul's
virtues as a novelist and his journalistic instincts combine
to produce a fusion of the two genres.   He is seen as "one
of those disturbed egotistical travellers" in quest of the
"reality that lay behind the dying hearsay of his family."
As elsewhere Naipaul returns to such themes as negation and
mimicry.   The strength of this book owes much to "his interpretation of the present dazed state of the lives and minds
of the Indians he met."

D109.   Wain, John.   "Mother India."   Observer (September 13, 1964):
24.

D110.   "West Indian Writer visits Home of his Ancestors."   The Times
(September 17, 1964): 17.
The reviewer praises the quality of the book and feels
few could have surpassed Naipaul's standard.   Notes his objectivity "not sparing of the world of illusions in which he
finds most of India."   Focuses also on many other positive
attributes of the book: the simplicity and dignity and sweet-
ness of people everywhere in stark contrast to "the artificial
assertiveness of the modern Indian as a direct and unhappy
effect of the later years of British rule."   Naipaul has brilliantly portrayed his stay in Kashmir and introduced a different mood, concluding with a visit to his grandfather's
home town.   Believes Naipaul has "a better sense of place
than anybody."

D111.   Walcott, Derek.   "Mr. Naipaul's Passage to India."   Sunday
Guardian [Trinidad] (September 20, 1964): 4, 5.
Rates the work as a significant analysis of the "dispossessed colonial."   It echoes very graphically the pain Naipaul
endured during a year's residence in India.   Naipaul admits
he should never have undertaken the journey, which broke
his life in two.   Walcott calls this "his hysterical exaspira-
tion at India's mixture of bureaucracy and caste."   Comments
favorably on the book's construction, precision and regards
its style as "so finely tuned that it has bordered on prim-
ness."

D112.   "Mr. Naipaul's Passage to India."   Times Literary Supplement, no. 3265 (September 24, 1964): 881.

D113. Reed, Henry. "Passage to India." Spectator 213 (October
       2, 1964): 452-453.
       Impressed with the beauty of the book's middle section,
       particularly its similarity of "comic vividness" and strength
       of characterization depicted in The Mystic Masseur. Contends
       that in spite of being a truly comic artist Naipaul could not
       but produce the type of account he has. Regards him "too
       honest a man and too good an artist to try to manipulate
       what he hated." Notes that a constant concern for Naipaul
       is "the bland Indian habit of public defecation." Completely
       vindicates Naipaul and regards him "a notable artist making
       that harrowing choice between the sorry things that can just
       be laughed at and those that can only be wept at."

D114. Williams, Eric. "Bookshelf." Nation 7 (November 13, 1964):
       11.
       Criticizes the extent to which the book dwells on defeca-
       tion in India. However, regards Naipaul's statements in it on
       English Literature as valuable. Sees the juxtaposition of In-
       dia and Trinidad as rude and devoid of sympathy.

D115. Enright, D. J. "Who is India?" Encounter 23 (December
       1964): 59-62, 64.
       In spite of its controversial nature, this review accords
       the book high critical acclaim, calling it "a rarity in its genre."
       The brilliance of Naipaul's recollections are never in doubt.
       He displays a tendency to generalize, shades of which ap-
       peared in The Middle Passage. The review meticulously
       analyzes his conclusions and defends Naipaul's predicament
       by saying "he who wrote comfortably of India would not be
       writing about India." His recorded accounts in Kashmir are
       very palatable. Regards Naipaul's more sobering views
       towards the end of the book as "an honourable attempt to
       expiate sins of omission." His pessimism, even his rage, are
       never far removed.

D116. "Too Great a Burden." Economist 213 (December 12, 1964):
       1257.
       A mixed review which tends to rationalize Naipaul's re-
       pugnance to social conditions in India. Speculates that dis-
       illusionment with his own common culture, coupled with the
       adverse heat were overriding factors. Visits to Kashmir
       reflected a more moderate tone. However, the reviewer ac-
       cuses Naipaul of lacking also in a historical perspective.

D117. Biswas, Robin. "Exhaustion and Persistence." Tamarac Re-
       view 35 (Spring 1965): 75-80.
       A detailed review which focuses on Naipaul's harsh and
       blunt perceptions of India. Notes his ironic gifts, status as
       a novelist, intelligence and "sensitive honesty" are the spe-
       cial qualities in the book. But suggests that Naipaul achieved

"a genuinely inward understanding only twice in the book"
which ends "in rejection and failure." A balance assessment.

D118. Bram, Joseph. Library Journal 90 (April 15, 1965): 1904.

D119. Prescott, Orville. "The Land of his Ancestors." New York
Times 114 (April 16, 1965): 27.

D120. Pryce-Jones, Alan. "An Area of Darkness." New York
Herald Tribune 125 (April 20, 1965): 25.

D121. "Current and Various." Time 85 (April 23, 1965): 95-96.

D122. Hitrec, Joseph. "A Disenchanted Journey." Saturday Review
48 (May 1, 1965): 42.
The triumph of the book is in observing Naipaul's perceptions fully at work. He contends that "India deals in
symbols." Gandhi was one of them, "reverenced for what he
was, his message was irrelevant." Describes the book as a
"blistering document." Hitrec sympathizes with Naipaul's
dilemma. With the exception of the books on India by E. M.
Foster and Aldous Huxley, regards Naipaul's account as devoid of "intellectual arrogance."

D123. "An Area of Darkness." Booklist 61 (May 15, 1965): 897-898.
Naipaul launches a scintillating attack on the social and
political conditions existing in India. Briefly mentions his
"empathy and affection" for the people.

D124. Gupta, K. "An Area of Darkness: an experience of India."
Canadian Forum 45 (June 1965): 70.
By his own admission Naipaul's first visit to India "had
broken his life in two." A reluctant acceptance of Naipaul's
sordid account about India, so magnified by the brilliance of
his writing. Attributes his views to preconceived notions.
Accuses him of perverting the truth and not recognizing the
new direction Gupta believes India is following. Sees one of
Naipaul's faults as his concern with palpable matters.

D125. Mander, John. "The Anglo-Indian Theme." Commentary
39 (June 1965): 94-97.

D126. Natwar-Singh, K. "Unhappy Pilgrim." New York Times
Book Review (July 11, 1965): 35.
An unfavorable review assailing Naipaul's negative picture
of Indian life, and for implying he did not meet "a single
worthwhile human being." Calls the book "fine prose and
rough nonsense." Detects a strong Western bias, believing
that if the Taj Mahal were transported "slab by slab to the
United States and re-erected it might be wholly admirable."
The review ends positively, noting Naipaul as saying he
would like to try living in India for a while.

D127. Rao, Raja. "Out of step with Shiva." Book Week 2 (August 29, 1965): 4, 14.

D128. Rau, Santha Rama. "Two Descriptions of the Elephant." The Reporter 33 (September 9, 1965): 40-43.
This review provides a good comparison of two books on India: Ronald Segal's The Anguish of India and V. S. Naipaul's An Area of Darkness. It is Rau's view that both authors' facts were misconceived. Of Segal's he seemed more suspicious since he was born white in South Africa. To characterize India as "a political arrangement of widely divergent states and people loosely bound," was a conclusion they both reached, much to Rau's chagrin.

D129. Benda, Harry J. "India and Indonesia." Yale Review 55 (October 1965): 121-123.

D130. Dathorne, O. R. "An Area of Darkness." Black Orpheus 18 (October 1965): 60-61.

D131. Muggeridge, Malcolm. "Books." Esquire 64 (October 1965): 28.

D132. Delaney, Austin. "Mother India as Bitch." Transition 5 (1966): 50-51.

D133. Sheehan, Edward R. F. "Cities of the Dreadful Night." Nation 202 (March 14, 1966): 300-302.
Reviewed along with Ronald Segal's Anguish of India. Praises the book's literary quality and questions many of its conclusions. Sheehan advances some powerful moral and political arguments to counter Naipaul's account on the country's "defecating multitudes." Shows extreme sympathy for India's predicament. A balanced assessment.

A FLAG ON THE ISLAND (1967 FI)

D134. Miller, Karl. "Naipaul's Emergent Country." The Listener 28 (September 1967): 402-403.
Miller combines a detailed analysis of the title story with the recurrent themes of Naipaul's work focused primarily on despair, and the "strains of pessimism" found in both The Middle Passage and A House for Mr. Biswas. He regards the latter book as an anti-colonial statement. The Mimic Men expresses doubt "about independence and about Caribbean nationalism." He describes A Flag on the Island as "a story written in a rather jagged hallucinatory style." Notes that each title represents a literary experiment; the novella form is successfully demonstrated in A Flag on the Island.

D135. "Movietone." Times Literary Supplement 3420 (September 14, 1967): 813.

Commissioned by a film company, the little story appears the most beautifully written in the collection. Its composition includes a leading American character, subsidiary characters, explicitness, much dialogue and sex--the latter a new departure for Naipaul. Notes the sadness in most of the other stories, despite their humorous vein. Regards "The Nightwatchman's Occurrence Book" the funniest.

D136. MacNamara, Desmond. "Flayed Skin." New Statesman 74 (September 15, 1967): 325.

D137. Buchan, William. "Out of School." Spectator 219 (September 22, 1967): 328-329.

D138. Price, R. G. G. "New Novels." Punch 253 (September 27, 1967): 484.

The patronizing attitude towards its characters detracts slightly from an otherwise highly complimentary review. He singles out the references made to "the limitations of West Indians and the British working class." The book conveys "many historical and sociological points." Admires Naipaul's professionalism. Dismisses his "stream of fantastic events technique" used in the title story as old fashioned.

D139. Panton, George. "West Indian Satirist." Sunday Gleaner [Jamaica] (December 3, 1967): 4.

Provides a summary of the stories, the majority of which are set in Trinidad. Commends the author's "quiet satirical humour." Thinks the title story disappointing.

D140. "A Flag on the Island." Kirkus 36 (January 1, 1968): 25.

D141. "A Flag on the Island." Publishers' Weekly 193 (January 15, 1968): 83.

D142. Knight, G. Norman. "A Flag on the Island." West Indies Chronicle 83 (February 1968): 78-79.

D143. McInnis, Raymond. "Fiction." Library Journal 93 (March 1, 1968): 1021.

Comments on Naipaul's "acute perception" of the unfortunate characters in both Trinidad and London where the stories were set. They depicted vivid and forceful scenes of "human weaknesses and conceits." The title story was intended for a film. The humorous "Nightwatchman's Occurrence Book," and "Greenie and Yellow" appealed most to the reviewer.

D144. Marsh, Pamela. "Fiction Concentrate." Christian Science Monitor 60 (March 29, 1968): 13.

D 145. Wain, John. "Characters in the Sun." New York Times Book
Review (April 7, 1968): 4.

D 146. Hartman, John. "Flag on the Island." Best Sellers 28
(April 15, 1968): 29.

D 147. Plant, Richard. "Potpourri of the Antilles." Saturday Review 51 (June 8, 1968): 52.
Briefly outlines the plot of the title story originally commissioned for a film. Naipaul's incessant use of self-pity in
The Mimic Men is a flaw he repeats here. The other stories
receive high praise. "Greenie and Yellow" and "The Heart"
represent a delicate blend of language and style reminiscent
of Guy de Maupassant and Gogol. Such is Naipaul at his
best.

THE MIMIC MEN (1967 MIM)

D 148. "The Mimic Men." Essays and Reviews from Times Literary
Supplement 6 (1967): 106-109.

D 149. Boston, Richard. "Caribbean and Aegean." The Times
(April 27, 1967): 16.

D 150. "Suburbia in the Sun." Times Literary Supplement 3400
(April 27, 1967): 347.
Summarizes the novel and suggests it "may be praised
with due diffidence as 'Commonwealth literature.'" Book
based on the memoirs of Ralph Singh who is "Naipaul's low-
spirited narrator." Believes the "childhood section will be
generally found the most impressive." Comments on the international application of the book's theme.

D 151. Wilson, Angus. "Between two Islands." Observer (April
30, 1967): 27.

D 152. Gray, Simon. "A Man of Style." New Statesman (May 5,
1967): 622.
Charts vividly the course of events in Singh's life. It
is an autobiographical account in which "there is no climax of
self-revelation." Regards the novel as "a complex and mas-
terful achievement of style."

D 153. Seymour-Smith, Martin. "Exile's Story." Spectator 218
(May 5, 1967): 528-529.

D 154. Price, R. G. G. "New Novels." Punch 252 (May 10, 1967):
696.

D 155. Roach, Eric. "As Naipaul Sees Us." Trinidad Guardian
(May 15, 1967): 7.

Regards the work as a socio-political novel reflecting a dense, complex view of life on a Caribbean island named Isabella. Focuses on Naipaul's technique of allowing "a defeated and exiled playboy politician from his own ethnic group" to write his life story. Notes the development of Naipaul's style of writing.

D156.   Corke, Hilary. "The Mimic Men." The Listener (July 1967): 693.

D157.   "The Mimic Men." Kirkus 35 (July 15, 1967): 831.

D158.   "The Mimic Men." The Bajan 168 (August 1967): 26.
The theme of insecurity figures prominently in the review. It also states that the book is not about a society which mimics "precisely because its initiation depended on the destruction of a system which was the scapegoat of the past." Stresses Naipaul's skill in depicting how well the status quo prevailed over its adversaries.

D159.   Nancoo, Joseph. "Magnificent 'Mimic.'" Trinidad Guardian (August 25, 1967): 14.
Considers The Mimic Men an excellent book about the imaginary island of Isabella in the West Indies. Comments favorably on its symbolism and on the intelligence of the characters, as well as the quality of the book as a statement of placelessness and its implications beyond the West Indies.

D160.   Curley, Arthur. "The Mimic Men." Library Journal 92 (September 15, 1967): 3057.

D161.   Beloff, Max. "Verandahs of Impotence." Encounter 29 (October 1967): 87.
A perceptive and detailed review which advances several thematic interpretations in the novel. Beloff also speculates on the autobiographical significance of the book. Sees the novel as concerned with "the inevitable figure of the age of imperial retreat."

D162.   Blackburn, Sara. "Bookmarks." Nation 205 (October 1967): 247-348.
Describes the book as "serious, urbane and beautifully written." Despite its concern for contemporary society, Blackburn regards it as too academic and devoid of any perceptible reality. Sees Ralph Singh as an extension of V. S. Naipaul's cultural background.

D163.   Rickards, Colin. "On a Novel Departure." Books and Bookmen 13 (October 1967): 47.

D164.   Maloff, Saul. "Yesterday in Isabella." New York Times Book Review (October 15, 1967): 55.

D 165. Wain, John. "Trouble in the Family." New York Review of Books 9 (October 26, 1967): 33-35.
Briefly describes the plot and charts the fortunes of the book's egotistical hero-politician. Naipaul's departure from the canons of novel writing "for long stretches" results in a "mixture of essay and plot-summary," leading to monologue. Emphasizes that the book contains "patches of pure novelistic virtuosity," in spite of the narrator's negative impact on the other characters.

D 166. Lask, Thomas. "Shadow and Substance." New York Times (December 16, 1967): 39.

D 167. Plant, Richard. "Caribbean Seesaw." Saturday Review 50 (December 23, 1967): 32-33.
Believes Naipaul's attempt "to coerce a number of related themes" in Marcel Proust's style "has denaturalized his fertile Caribbean material through excessive introspection and definition." Speculates on his motive for keeping "his fragmented narrative in disorder." Projects a philosophical overview of Ralph Singh's life. Plant also comments on Naipaul's use of satire and the venom he showers "on all races and ideologies."

D 168. Moore, Gerald. "Book Reviews." Bim 12 (January/June 1968): 134-136.
Mr. Moore draws a parallel between Naipaul's book and Orlando Patterson's An Absence of Ruins. Suggests Singh's notoriety and failure in domestic and political life were symbolic of colonial societies.

D 169. Pritchett, V. S. "Crack-Up." New York Review of Books 10 (April 11, 1968): 10, 12-14.
Regards The Mimic Men as "a resourceful, compassionate, intensely critical and imaginative statement of a colonial crackup." In comparing Naipaul's success with that of other Commonwealth writers, suggests "his advantage is that he shares with many English novelists natural and serious feelings for the fantasy life of his characters." Notes that the book also has a strong autobiographical note.

THE LOSS OF EL DORADO (1969 LE)

D 170. "Vision and Reality." Essays and Reviews from Times Literary Supplement 8 (1969): 35-40.

D 171. Greene, Graham. "Terror in Trinidad." Observer (October 26, 1969): 34.

D 172. May, Derwent. "A Black Tale." The Times (November 1, 1969): 5.

D173. Bryden, Ronald. "Between the Epics." New Statesman 78 (November 7, 1969): 661-662.

D174. Innes, Hammond. "For God and Profit." Spectator 223 (November 8, 1969): 647-648.

D175. Miller, Karl. "Power, Glory and Imposture." Listener 82 (November 13, 1969): 673-674.

D176. Patterson, James H. "Hot Little Offshore Island." Sunday Guardian [Trinidad] (November 16, 1969): 5.

D177. Hosein, C. "Naipaul's Latest Called a Novel about History." Sunday Guardian [Trinidad] (December 14, 1969): 20.

D178. Clasp, Bertram. "Another view of the Loss of El Dorado." Sunday Guardian [Trinidad] (December 21, 1969): 8-9.
    Naipaul places in historical perspective the roles played by Antonio de Berrio, Miranda, Fullarton, Raleigh and Picton, including Luisa Calderon's torture. Trinidad became the staging post for those adventurers in search of that elusive City of El Dorado. Clasp believes that the depth of Naipaul's research "inhibited his imagination and constricted his style."

D179. "The Failings of an Empire." Times Literary Supplement 2539 (December 25, 1969): 1471.
    Regards the book as a pioneering effort "to weave together in so subtle a manner the threads of the most complex and turbulent period of Caribbean history"; also credits it with reviving an interest in the area. The book's theme centers on the origin of modern Trinidad viewed in terms of the El Dorado myth.

D180. "The Loss of El Dorado." Publishers' Weekly 197 (February 2, 1970): 86.

D181. "The Loss of El Dorado." Kirkus 38 (February 15, 1970): 224.
    Traces Naipaul's use of two incidents, three centuries apart, "to relate to the futility of the colonial experience." Focuses on Luisa Calderon's brutal treatment and its consequences for Chacon and Fullarton. Considers the study more important for an English audience.

D182. Boromé, Joseph A. "The Loss of El Dorado." Library Journal 95 (April 1, 1970): 1367.

D183. Plumb, J. H. "A Nightmare World of Fantasy and Murder." Book World 4 (April 19, 1970): 1, 3.

D184. Elliott, J. H. "Triste Trinidad." New York Review of Books 14 (May 21, 1970): 25-27.

A rather lengthy and mixed review which characterizes the book as "simultaneously indescribable, idiosyncratic and unique." Naipaul's venture into "a kind of historical re-creation" depicts not only Berrio's and Raleigh's quest for El Dorado, but presents a thoroughly researched account of Picton's fierce administration and subsequent trial in London. Praises Naipaul's handling of his "themes and motifs." His sense of humor, compassion and sensitivity have combined to produce a brilliant account of a past era in Trinidad's history. For Mr. Elliott's part, however, some reservations remain about the canons of historical writing Naipaul employs.

D185.   Rabassa, Gregory. "The Dark, Obverse Side of the Shining Myth." New York Times Book Review (May 24, 1970): 7, 22.

D186.   "To Dream no More." Time 95 (May 25, 1970): 0-3.
This vivid review sketches Trinidad's history from the Spanish occupation to the first few years after the British rule. It is a tale of colonialism, exploitation, corruption and abuse of power, particularly by Thomas Picton. Notes that Naipaul's purpose was to portray "a sense of the ambiguity" which existed. Praises his effectiveness in "describing the fantasy life that resulted from the island's plantation culture."

D187.   Millar, Neil. "Slavery's High Cost." Christian Science Monitor (May 28, 1970): 11.

D188.   Lask, Thomas. "Brave New World." New York Times (June 20, 1970): 27.

D189.   "The Loss of El Dorado." The Bajan 203 (July 1970): 22.
The review calls it "a tale of non-society, an image of what could never be," since it existed only in the imagination. Both Picton and Fullarton figure prominently in the book. Draws a parallel to all the territories which Columbus discovered, as none of them achieved the status of real societies.

D190.   Updike, John. "Fool's Gold." New Yorker 46 (August 8, 1970): 72-76. Rpt. in Critical Perspectives on V. S. Naipaul, edited by Robert D. Hamner, 153-158. Washington, DC: Three Continents Press, 1977.
Naipaul was originally requested to write a historical handbook on the City of Port of Spain. Updike writes that Naipaul's masterly anomaly, though brilliantly researched and well presented, "resembles less a work of history than a piece of poetry." It reveals much about Trinidad society under Antonio de Berrio and later Thomas Picton as it does biographically about those men. Updike challenges many of Naipaul's assumptions.

D191. "The Loss of El Dorado." Booklist 67 (September 1, 1970): 34.

D192. Cheuse, Alan. "The Realms of Gold." Nation 211 (October 5, 1970): 311-312.
Provides a summary of the book and praises its author's painstaking research, sincerity, detail and creative imagination. "Naipaul portrays the action of Caribbean conquest as a movement from medieval adventure to bourgeois trading and shopkeeping." It makes a striking contrast between the Spanish, French and British occupation of the island. Regards the book as a significant historical account of the territory.

D193. Rodman, Selden. "Three on Latin America." National Review 22 (October 6, 1970): 1064-1065.

D194. Kappan, Edward W. "Colonial Victims." Progressive 35 (April 1971): 49-51.

D195. Carnegie, J. A. "Rediscovery from Outside." Savacou 1 (June 1971): 125-128.
A forceful review which criticizes several aspects of the book. Suggests Picton's career in Trinidad, published as a memoir, would have earned that section "deserved standing as a biographical classic." Naipaul's historical understanding comes into question in relation to his A House for Mr. Biswas. His scholarly, novelistic, witty and biographical skills receive high praise. Carnegie feels Naipaul's most glaring weakness as a writer has been his tendency to sacrifice "analytical thought to the masterly turned phrase."

D196. Marshall, Peter. "The Loss of El Dorado." American Historical Review 76 (June 1971): 848.

D197. Jebb, Julien. "Prophet in Another Country." Books and Bookmen 19 (December 1973): 57.

IN A FREE STATE (1971 FS)

D198. "Fiction of 1971." Essays and Reviews from Times Literary Supplement 10 (1971): 41-44.
The scenes set in Africa, England and America are peopled by transients, exiles and tourists, all of whom pine for home. The review states some of the possible reasons for Naipaul's lack of popularity in the United States. Notes that in the entire book, "irony and pathos are assimilated to a version of placelessness." Regards the most striking feature of the book as Naipaul's inclination to become "more wide-rangingly itinerant." Praises his ability to incorporate into the narrative some of the intricacies of colonialism.

D199. "In a Free State." Publishers' Weekly 200 (July 12, 1971):
65.

D200. "In a Free State." Kirkus 39 (July 15, 1971): 768.

D201. Mann, Charles W. "In a Free State." Library Journal 96
(September 1, 1971): 2671-2672.

D202. Wyndham, Francis. "V. S. Naipaul." Listener 86 (October
7, 1971): 461-462.

D203. Calder, Angus. "Darkest Naipaulia." New Statesman 82
(October 8, 1971): 482-483.

D204. "Nowhere to Go." Times Literary Supplement, No. 3632
(October 8, 1971): 1198.
Suggests not only has Naipaul's treatment of the race
question been marginal, but that his attempt to expand his
theme prior to writing In a Free State was not without its
limitations. Uses the unpopularity of his work in America
at that point in time to support such a claim. Touches on
the universality of Naipaul's "placelessness" theme. Notes
he "has managed to become more wide-rangingly itinerant,"
devoid of the "strain of fabrication." Admires not only the
structure of the "novel," but the treatment of his subject
as it relates to Africa, Britain and the United States. A
forceful and searching yet favorable review.

D205. Waugh, Auberon. "Auberon Waugh on V. S. Naipaul."
Spectator 227 (October 9, 1971): 511.

D206. Whitley, John. "Naipaul's New Book." Sunday Guardian
[Trinidad] (October 10, 1971): 10.
The scene set in Central Africa centers on the decline of
empire and its attendant humiliations. Bobby, one of the
main characters, embodies many of those humiliations. Naipaul's brilliant descriptions of Equatorial Africa, Whitley regards as the best he had ever read. The other two pieces
extend the colonial theme, and receive equally good comments.

D207. Webb, W. L. "Exiles." Guardian 105 (October 16, 1971):
23.

D208. Gordimer, Nadine. "White Expatriates and Black Mimics: 'In
a Free State.'" New York Times Book Review (October 17,
1971): 5, 20.

D209. Larson, Charles R. "In a Free State." Saturday Review
54 (October 23, 1971): 91-92.
The five pieces are loosely linked by themes of exile,
freedom and prejudice. Regards Naipaul's attempt to blend

fiction and fact into one volume as a disappointment. Both the story "One out of Many" and its "first person point of view" receive much praise, the others less so. Assails the title story, suggesting its racial overtones not be seen through the characters, but through Naipaul's comments.

D210. McGuinness, Frank. "A Rough Game." London Magazine 11 (October/November 1971): 156-158.
Notes the sad comic plight of a stranger in a country that is different, if not hostile to him. This is a common theme which predominates among these stories. Comments highly on the construction of Naipaul's dialogue and delineation of character.

D211. "Unstable Sequence." Economist 241 (November 6, 1971): iii-iv.
The book contains two of Naipaul's travel journals, two short stories and a novella. Collectively it is not a novel. Credits the variations of the author's theme approach to his intelligence and shrewdness which he utilizes so effectively. Regards the Washington narrative, written in the first person "a literary performance" told with "delicacy and light-handed humour." A perceptive review.

D212. Parker, Dorothy. "All very far from Home." Christian Science Monitor 63 (November 26, 1971): B4.

D213. Adams, Phoebe. "In a Free State." Atlantic Monthly 228 (December 1971): 135.

D214. Maloff, Saul. "Critics' Choices for Christmas." Commonwealth 95 (December 3, 1971): 232.

D215. Theroux, Paul. "To Be Without Roots." Book World (December 5, 1971): 22.

D216. Dopson, Andrew. "I'll stop writing for less...." Sunday Guardian [Trinidad] (December 12, 1971): 18-19.
The book is essentially one on homelessness and exile. Dobson describes it as "a prize-winning exploration into the psychology of alienation." The review embodies the thoughts of many Naipaul observers. His skills receive high praise. Each story is a model in itself.

D217. Lask, Thomas. "Where is the Enemy?" New York Times 121 (December 25, 1971): 15.

D218. Kazin, Alfred. "Displaced Person." New York Review of Books 17 (December 30, 1971): 3-4.

D219. Gonzalez, Anson. "Another Step to Silence." The Mausican 4th issue (1972): 14-17.

The book consists of a Prologue, an Epilogue and three other pieces, the longest of which takes its name from the title story, "In a Free State." Gonzalez calls the organization of this book a creative departure from Naipaul's other books. Life's journey and its futility is a symbolic theme throughout the work, unlike Conrad's Heart of Darkness and Harris's The Palace of the Peacock, where in both instances there is a sense of achievement. Naipaul's detachment from the "narrator" in the "Piraeus" piece receives favorable comment. The use of the first-person narrative in "One out of Many" and "Tell Me Who to Kill" is quite telling. Both these stories demonstrate a new dimension in Naipaul's work, the use of sex. Gonzalez concludes by asking, "who is to argue if one can create art out of his futility?"

D220. Thorpe, Michael. "Current Literature 1970-71." In English Studies 53 (1972): 282.
Describes the novella as "a tense narrative of an ill-assorted European couple." The other two stories set in Washington, DC, and London dwell on the theme of alienation. Praises Naipaul's characterization, which he calls uncommon "in fictional indictments of social and political injustice."

D221. Cheuse, Alan. "This Was the Famous View." The Nation 214 (January 17, 1972): 87-88.
It explores Naipaul's broadened themes of exile and freedom, away from the "muted comedies of islanders and expatriates." Commends the descriptions of people and places, notes his ability to convert the natural landscape into "symbolic turf." Advances several thematic interpretations of the stories. Touches on the limited attention his writing has attracted in the United States. His successful experimentation with the novella in the title story does not go unnoticed.

D222. May, Derwent. "Amis, McCarthy, Naipaul." Encounter 38 (January 1972): 74-78.

D223. McDowell, Frederick. "In a Free State." Contemporary Literature 13 (Summer 1972): 379-380.

THE OVERCROWDED BARRACOON (1972 OB)

D224. Bryden, Ronald. "The Hurricane." Listener, 88 (November 9, 1972): 641.

D225. MacInnes, Colin. "Not Just for Today but long Tomorrows." Sunday Guardian [Trinidad] (November 12, 1972): 6.
Discusses the skills necessary to write essays effectively, such as Naipaul possesses, and of the essay's "vanishing form

in England." Focuses on his opposing views to Kipling who
champions the British Empire, while Naipaul "describes the
social and human wreckage" which follows its demise. Attributes Naipaul's writing success to his experience, analytical intelligence and a keen ear "for subtleties and absurdities
of all the varieties of ex-colonial."

D226.   Hearne, John. "In Search of Another Country." Times Literary Supplement no. 3689 (November 17, 1972): 1391.
        Paul Theroux's V. S. Naipaul is reviewed along with The
Overcrowded Barracoon. The former is one of interpretation, highlighting many of Naipaul's themes: creation, travel,
fantasy. "Cannery Row" is one of the twenty-one articles
contained in the book. Explores the symbolism which struck
Naipaul when he visited the place. "Here indeed are fantasy,
mimicry, an illusion of history," states the review.

D227.   Potter, Dennis. "The Writer and his Myth." The Times
(December 4, 1972): 6.

D228.   Glover, Elaine. "Recent Fiction." Strand 14: 2 (1972/73):
39.
        One of Naipaul's major concerns in the essays, Glover notes,
is the inability of Third World countries "to make realistic
assessments." Naipaul singles out Indians who he feels "de-
lude themselves by blind adherence to stultified tradition."
He despises acceptance of Gandhi's faith in progress through
individual self-sacrifice, and Indians who have progressed by
equal acceptance of Western habits.

D229.   Harrison, Tony. "Fantasia-Asia." London Magazine 12 (De-
cember/72-January/73): 135-40.
        The essays are essentially based on "self-contempt" and
the "identity crisis" which confront West Indians and people
from India even after independence. The review demon-
strates the "myth-faculty" as identified in the essay on
"power."

D230.   Pantin, Raoul. "The Ultimate Transient." Caribbean Contact 2 (January 1973): 4, 23.
        Regards the book as "the finest literary work produced
in recent times." The first article on London draws attention to Naipaul's abhorrence with the place, yet regards it
as "the best place to write." This sets the tone for the
book: Naipaul's views on India, Black Power in Trinidad,
Mauritius. Naipaul receives a sympathetic ear.

D231.   "The Overcrowded Barracoon." Publishers' Weekly 203 (January 22, 1973): 62.

D232.   "The Overcrowded Barracoon." Kirkus 41 (February 1, 1973):
171.

D233. "The Overcrowded Barracoon and other Articles." British Book News (March 1973): 212.

D234. Parker, Dorothy L. "To Be a Member of a Minority Always seemed to Be Attractive." Christian Science Monitor 65 (March 14, 1973): 13.

D235. Mukherjee, Bharati. "Colonies: Caste Adrift." Book World 7 (March 18, 1973): 4, 8.

D236. "Overcrowded Barracoon." Choice 10 (June 1973): 610.
Praises the quality of the Steinbeck and Mailer pieces, observing that the essay form of writing articles has "almost disappeared from magazines and newspapers in this country." Regards the "Columbus and Castro" section on the West Indies as significant to Americans in terms of information. In spite of the contemporary nature of the essays, Mukherjee suggests that the reader is likely to feel a remoteness of the type one experiences when rereading Addison and Steele.

D237. McSweeney, Kerry. "The Editors Column." Queen's Quarterly 80 (Autumn 1973): 494-97.
Offers a literary biographical capsule of both Greene and Naipaul. Criticizes the quality and unevenness of the articles many of which should have been excluded. Describes "A Second Visit" and the final section of the collection as the best.

D238. "The Overcrowded Barracoon." New York Times Book Review (September 16, 1973): 18.

D239. Thorpe, Michael. "Current Literature 1973." English Studies 55 (1974): 554-555.
Suggests the book fills a gap in Naipaul's publications and gives "a fair cross-section of the themes and interests of a most industrious author-journalist." Focuses on some of Naipaul's continuous concerns which are reflected on in "The Regional Barrier."

D240. Figueroa, John. "The Overcrowded Barracoon." Caribbean Studies 13 (January 1974): 135-140.
The book comprises of a range of journalistic articles written on a variety of subjects. "The Election at Ajmer" and "Jasmine" touch Figueroa's fancy; the former on politics in India, the latter on language and literature. Expresses reservations about Naipaul's "excellent sharp probe" as the most suitable method of correcting the problems in the countries he examines in the work. Sympathizes with many of Naipaul's views, but emphatically rejects the notion that "there is simply nothing but fantasy and consumerism in the Caribbean," the very area out of which Naipaul has emerged.

Recommends a thorough reading of the book which is forceful, subtle and sometimes funny.

GUERRILLAS (1975 GU)

D241. Lopez de Villegas, Consuelo. "Guerrillas." Revista/Review Interamericana 5 (Fall 1975): 500-502.
Describes setting for the novel as a small derelict Caribbean island which the reviewer suggests is Trinidad. The plot is itself based on a "racially inspired killing in Trinidad." Regards this novel as a "story of failure" except for Meredith, whom Lopez de Villegas regards as the most successful character in the book. Views Naipaul's lack of compassion in the novel as a disturbing feature. Praises Naipaul's prose, but chides him for indulging in "an overriding obsession with depravity" in the book. Concludes that Guerrillas is devoid of "certain realistic details." Among those she cites are Jane's devotion to Ahmed in spite of the abuse she suffers at his hands and Meredith's unknown fate, an omission which she regards as significant to the plot.

D242. "Guerrillas." Kirkus 43 (September 1, 1975): 1016.

D243. Jones, D. A. N. "Little Warriors in search of a War." Times Literary Supplement 3835 (September 12, 1975): 1013.
Fully supports Naipaul's treatment of his subject--the exploration of "people's feelings about race, sex and power." Jones explores rather fully the genesis of this novel stemming from the exploits of Michael de Freitas, and maintains a rather objective viewpoint of the book. Naipaul's characters receive high praise, as does his prose. Shades of Graham Greene's work appear. Very favorable.

D244. Ackroyd, Peter. "On Heat." Spectator 235 (September 13, 1975): 350.

D245. Thwaite, Anthony. "The Heart of Darkness." Observer (September 14, 1975): 25.

D246. Wyndham, Francis. "Services Rendered." New Statesman 90 (September 19, 1975): 339-340. Rpt. in Critical Perspectives on V. S. Naipaul, edited by Robert D. Hamner, 255-259.
Considers Naipaul's attitude towards Jimmy sympathetic, but he believes Naipaul is far less charitable towards Jane. Sees shame as the recurring motif in an otherwise gloomy book.

D247. Bannon, Barbara. "P. W. Forecasts." Publishers' Weekly 208 (September 22, 1975): 130.

D248.   Vaizey, John. "Good Works." The Listener 94 (September
        25, 1975): 410.
            The reviewer, by admission, disfavors this book. Finds
        the introductory chapters dull, the main characters Jane,
        Roche and Jimmy uninspiring, and charges that its treatment
        of sexual politics: "succeeds in being vulgar without being
        forthright." Suggests that the theme of "moral awareness of
        world's plight" somewhat betrayed. For sheer beauty of lan-
        guage, it is Vaizey's view that chapters nine and ten over-
        shadow the entire book.

D249.   Walsh, William. "Unhealing Powers." New Review 2 (Octo-
        ber 1975): 64-65.

D250.   Hamner, Robert D. "Guerrillas." Library Journal 100 (Octo-
        ber 1, 1975): 1846.

D251.   Pantin, Raoul. "The Waste Land of Naipaul." Caribbean Con-
        tact 3 (November 1975): 3, 8.
            Deals at length with the plot. Three of the main charac-
        ters, Roche, Jane and Ahmed, receive full attention. Com-
        ments on Naipaul's habitual criticism of the Caribbean, and
        appears to sympathize with "the physical and moral deteriora-
        tion of the society" which seems to pain him. Concludes it
        is a novel of despair, one into which too much has been
        crowded.

D252.   DeMott, Benjamin. "Lost Words, Lost Heroes." Saturday
        Review 3 (November 15, 1975): 23-24.
            Sees the author and Jimmy, a major character, as both
        well suited to their respective roles. The book conjures up
        "many reminders of golden pages in his earlier novels."
        Credits Naipaul's views on the psychology of race tension
        to "a penetrating mind" and graceful style. DeMott, however,
        does not consider Guerrillas "a successful novel," principally
        because of "the relative emptiness" of Roche's characteriza-
        tion. In spite of its imperfections, as a political statement,
        its implications are profound.

D253.   Epstein, Joseph. "Nowhere Men." Book World (November
        16, 1975): E11-E12.

D254.   Theroux, Paul. "An Intelligence from the Third World."
        New York Times Book Review (November 16, 1975): 1-2.
            Mr. Theroux presents a brief, vivid overview of Naipaul's
        work. Guerrillas he describes, however, as "a violent book
        in which little violence is explicit," regarding it also as per-
        haps one of his most complex. The parallel Theroux draws
        between Jane and Patty Hearst accentuates the depth of
        Naipaul's creativity and imagination. The review expresses
        a certain warmth, "deep sympathy and keen understanding"

for the characters. Concludes by calling it a brilliant novel "shimmering with artistic certainty."

D255. Broyard, Anatole. "The Authors vs. His Characters." New York Times (November 20, 1975): 39.
The reviewer clearly is not enthused with the tone of this book. He also sees Naipaul as a victim of "overgeneralization," and regards his characters' motives as "obscure or non-existent." Naipaul appears to have been withholding from them the roles for which they were created. In spite of its shortcomings, Broyard admits that the book contains "inspired details and passages that only a good novelist could have written." Otherwise favorable.

D256. "Guerrillas." British Book News (December 1975): 926.

D257. Spurling, John. "Novelist as Dictator." Encounter 45 (December 1975): 73-79.

D258. Gray, Paul. "Burnt-Out Cases." Time 106 (December 1, 1975): R8.

D259. Jefferson, Margo. "Misfits." Newsweek 86 (December 1, 1975): 102, 104.

D260. Miller, Karl. "In Scorn and Pity." New York Review of Books 22 (December 11, 1975): 3-4.

D261. Larson, Charles R. "Watching the Revolution go by." The Nation 221 (December 13, 1975): 627-628.
This very favorable review sketches the range and consistency of Naipaul's themes. Guerrillas essentially addresses two familiar subjects: restlessness and political strife. Larson credits Naipaul's astute observations for a "significant treatment" of Black Power, despite its triteness. The reviewer is convinced that in the final analysis it is the economic factors that will prevail in the Caribbean region, not Black Power movements.

D262. "Briefly Noted Fiction." New Yorker 51 (December 22, 1975): 95.

D263. Bell, Pearl K. "Guerrillas." New Leader 58 (December 22, 1975): 10-11.

D264. Knickerbocker, Brad. "Guerrillas." Christian Science Monitor 68 (December 24, 1975): 23.

D265. Broyard, Anatole. "Everybody is not a Guerrilla." Sunday Gleaner [Jamaica] (December 28, 1975): 3.

D266. "Guerrillas." New York Times Book Review (December 28, 1975): 1-2.

D267. Brockway, James. "The End of the Day." Books and Bookmen 21 (January 1976): 55.

Brockway regards Guerrillas as a very sensitive, profound and passionate book, and provides some very interesting insights into Naipaul's treatment of his subject. The characterization receives high praise. The review draws a sharp distinction between the scope of Naipaul's characters and those of Graham Greene. In Naipaul's work "the real world is the plot." Guerrillas represents a radical shift in Naipaul's mood, away from his earlier satirical style. Generally favorable review.

D268. Coombs, Orde. "Madness Among the Made-Up People." National Observer 15 (January 31, 1976): 21.

A stimulating review which focuses on the texture of West Indian identity. Naipaul should have elevated the tone of Caribbean perceptions rather than negate them by using such a plot. Coombs assails him and argues that "people who have been forced to make up themselves as they go along need to receive more than derision." For Coombs a less rigid stance would have been more palatable.

D269. LaSalle, Peter. "How Far the Poet's Writ Runs." The Nation 222 (February 28, 1976): 248-249.

It was only a matter of time before the Black Power movement would infiltrate the Caribbean, as it did in 1970. Naipaul's Guerrillas therefore may not have been that prophetic after all. It showed again the accuracy of Naipaul's timing, and ability to utilize so effectively the material culled from a real situation masterminded by Abdul Malik earlier on in Trinidad. LaSalle observes though that Naipaul "offers no solutions but he wisely probes where the uneasiness lies." The book, however, has implications far beyond the Caribbean. Graham Greene's The Quiet American, like Guerrillas, also accurately reflected the times. A searching review.

D270. "Guerrillas." Virginia Quarterly Review 52 (Spring 1976): 56.

D271. Pritchard, William H. "Novel Auguries." Hudson Review 29 (Spring 1976): 148.

Draws some comparisons between Guerrillas and Under Western Eyes, suggesting "it is possible to read Guerrillas without much sympathetic suffering." Focuses closely on Naipaul's treatment of his characters and observes "if anything he is all too ruthlessly clear-eyed about their limitations." Pritchard is disappointed that Naipaul's job "of evaluating and devaluating" is absent.

D272. Jones, D. A. N. "Reader's Guide." Yale Review 70 (March 1976): xiv-xv.

D273. Kramer, Hilton. "Naipaul's 'Guerrillas' and Kramer's Assassins." Commentary 61 (March 1976): 54-57.
Extolls Naipaul's virtue as "a novelist who creates a world, who conjures up compelling characters and commands our assent in their complex fate." He further reminds the reader that "Naipaul's fiction has the centrifugal power of carrying us beyond the boundaries of its vividly rendered microscopic events." Guerrillas is just such a book. The review has also given much attention to his use of "the sexual-political equation." Concludes that "Guerrillas stands in the great tradition of novels that anatomise the effect of ideology on the lines of those it has thoroughly 'possessed' and destroyed."

D274. Reedy, Gerard C. "The Best Springtime Reading: 'Guerrillas.'" America 134 (May 1, 1976): 385.

D275. "Short Notices." Queen's Quarterly 83 (Winter 1976): 701.
Detects a gloomy influence creeping into Naipaul's work. Sees the dominant theme as "the willed exterioration of the picture of the country," assumed to be Trinidad. Contains biographical elements of Michael de Freitas, one of the principal characters of the original story.

D276. Warner-Lewis, Maureen. "Guerrillas." Caribbean Quarterly 23 (June-September 1977): 103-105.
Gives an overview of the novel and its main characters, with some inferences to A House for Mr. Biswas. Praises "the accuracy and sureness of detail" in his technique, but concedes that it is not as forceful as in Biswas. Dislikes Naipaul's incessant, repulsive descriptions of Blacks, regarding this as one among many other issues. Suggests Naipaul's resemblance to "these perversely arrogant characters he creates so well."

INDIA: A WOUNDED CIVILIZATION (1977 IN)

D277. Gowda, H. H. Anniah. "India: A Wounded Civilization." Ariel 10 (January 1977): 98-101.
An insider's view describing the book as a type of "novel-biography." Accuses Naipaul of distorting Karma's doctrine in a novelistic fashion to defend his concept of Indian tradition. Sees a link between Naipaul's bias and his displacement. Gowda suggests that the basic misconception arises from his "inability to understand Indians in terms of the deepest cultural values." A passionate response.

D278. Garebian, Keith. "Passages to India." Montreal Star (March 12, 1977): D1, D4.

For Garebian "Naipaul's book remains one of the leading documents about Indian failure." The review presents a study in contrasts between Bharati and Clark Blaise's Days and Nights in Calcutta, and V. S. Naipaul's India. These comparisons are essentially one of style, interpretation; he notes "Mr. Blaise doesn't miss the things Naipaul sees, but he colours his vision differently." A stirring comparison which he concludes is a necessary balance to Naipaul's perceptive but disproportionate documentary."

D279.   Bannon, Barbara. "P. W. Forecasts." Publishers' Weekly 211 (March 28, 1977): 70.

D280.   "India: A Wounded Civilization." Kirkus Review 45 (April 1, 1977): 399.

D281.   "Briefly Noted." New Yorker 53 (June 6, 1977): 136.
It is safe to suggest that Naipaul's background plays no positive role in this latest account of India. His gloomy insights are unmistakable. Believes "India's ills" are more far-reaching than its political structure, that its intellectual dissipation is the result of foreign conquests. Concludes that the differences of opinion expressed in the book do not detract from its strength.

D282.   Jefferson, Margo. "India's Tragic Flaws." Newsweek 89 (June 6, 1977): 84, 86.
"The book combines reporting, analysis, literary criticism and theory to contrast the elaborate mythologies of India's past with the intractable realities of its present." The rage and force demonstrated in the book Jefferson attributes to Naipaul's own "sense of alienation." Its rigidity and anguish are offset by the elegance, precision and his facility for observation.

D283.   Lelyveld, Joseph. "For Naipaul a Difficult Country." New York Times Book Review (June 12, 1977): 10, 44.
Sees the book as both an extension and expansion of An Area of Darkness. However, infers that Naipaul leaves the reader to believe that the country is "less unsettling and unnerving than it was on first encounter." Credits his ability to analyze the Indian patterns of thought and resulting complacency. Questions his judgements of Gandhi's contribution to the Hindu society, believes Mrs. Gandhi's social reforms were equally "as borrowed and bankrupt" as that of the pro-Gandhian forces. In spite of its gloom, offers a reader "the most notable commitment of critical excellence" and scrutiny the country has experienced since independence.

D284.   Scott, Paul. "India's Collective Amnesia." Washington Post Book World (June 19, 1977): K1, K2.

D285.   Hayward, H. S.   "India."   Christian Science Monitor (June
        20, 1977): 23.

D286.   Smith, William E.   "Lest the Past Kill."   Time 109 (June
        20, 1977): 71-72.

D287.   Fuller, Edward.   "Compelling Studies of Troubled India."
        Wall Street Journal 189 (June 23, 1977): 20-22.

D288.   Novak, Jeremiah.   "India: a Wounded Civilization."   America
        136 (June 25, 1977): 570-571.
        Ved Mehta's Mahatma Gandhi and His Apostles reviewed
        with Naipaul's India.   While Mehta discredits Gandhian in-
        fluence as a spent force in the country, Naipaul focuses on
        his work and its contributions to the Emergency.   The
        March 1977 elections helped to exonerate Gandhi and weakened
        many of their arguments.   Assails Mehta and Naipaul for de-
        liberately omitting material damaging to Mrs. Gandhi.   Con-
        cludes that these books "come across as apostles for [Indira
        Gandhi's] regime."   An evenhanded view.

D289.   Adams, P. L.   "India: A Wounded Civilization."   Atlantic
        240 (July 1977): 87.

D290.   Mollinger, Shernaz.   Library Journal 102 (July 1977): 1478.
        Extremely favorably reviewed.   Praises its perceptive,
        humane and moral values.   "It is a rigorous dissection of the
        assumptions and attitudes that have prevented India from
        ever fully making it into the 20th century."

D291.   Gordon, Leonard A.   "The Marginal View."   The Nation 225
        (July 2, 1977): 26-28.
        Reviews India with Ved Mehta's Mahatma Gandhi and His
        Apostles.   Emphasizes Naipaul's concern with Gandhi's brand
        of ideology, "a world without creative intellect and change."
        Sees contradictions and unfair generalizations in his argu-
        ments.   Agrees the Emergency raised "some fundamental
        questions" for India.   Not enough credit given to its tech-
        nological progress.   A poignant review.

D292.   Berger, Peter L.   "India: a Wounded Civilization."   New
        Republic 177 (July 9, 1977): 30-32.
        Regards Naipaul's forceful command of English and his
        strength of depicting characters as just a few of the quali-
        ties which make his writing so successful.   Considers India
        to be as fascinating as it is disturbing and a work that
        "raises questions that go beyond the validity of its particular
        interpretation."   Thinks Naipaul sees India, a world in equi-
        librium, too overwhelmed by Hinduism.   The reviewer re-
        iterates a previously held view that the Indian world repre-
        sents "the most complete antithesis to modern ideals of liberty

and freedom." But suggests Naipaul's own "defect of vision" obscures "a critical view of modern reality." Balanced and interesting observations.

D293. Towers, Robert. "India's Long Night." New York Review of Books 24 (July 14, 1977): 6, 8, 10.

D294. Ayre, John. "India; A Wounded Civilization." Globe and Mail (July 16, 1977): 33.
Draws parallel with Richler as satirist in his early novels, and later as crusader of moral and social issues. Expresses disappointment on Naipaul's book, however, which reflected more "about ideas than people." Regards it as a rehash of a previous work, An Area of Darkness, tightened into a "grand despairing condemnation of his Hindu ancestry." Thinks the limit of his popularity in North America to be directly related to this "infallible aversion to Third World images," rather than to his writing abilities.

D295. Woodcock, George. "India Through a Glass Darkly." The New Leader (July 18, 1977): 17-18.

D296. Adachi, Ken. "India's Mortal Wound is Fascinating, Painful." Toronto Star (July 23, 1977): H7.
Expresses some reservation about Naipaul's conclusions. Chides his preoccupation with the "Indian predicament." Hinduism, cultural and regional differences, Gandhian philosophy, a thousand years of "invasion and defeat" are factors Naipaul has attributed to the country's present political and social direction. Still regards Naipaul "one of the most significant and original fiction writers." Attributes the book's "brilliant insights" to the author's strength of characterization and aptitude for detail.

D297. Taylor, Jeremy. "'India: A Wounded Civilization.' Another Superb Novel by Naipaul On India." Express [Trinidad] (August 13, 1977): 9.

D298. Borders, William. "Books of The Times." New York Times 126 (August 17, 1977): C19.
This is a valuable addition to previous accounts on India. For all its intensity and pain, Borders suggests it is a less gloomy picture than the one painted in An Area of Darkness. Naipaul senses a ray of optimism. Though he has not provided any solutions to the questions he raises, he "ponders them with startling clarity," and journalistic perceptions.

D299. "Books Briefly." Progressive 41 (September 1977): 44.
Sees Naipaul as "a bitter and devastating critic of India, his ancestral country." The review also recognizes the brilliance and vividness of his writing, but suggests the thesis

of his book to be confused on the premise that "India has
always been wounded, invaded over the centuries, and has
never been the golden civilization whose resurrection many
Indians foolishly long for." Naipaul strikes hard at those in
India whose misuse spirituality as an excuse for mindlessness
and misinterpret Gandhi's philosophy.

D300.   Amis, Martin. "In a State of Emergency." New Statesman
94 (October 21, 1977): 543-544.
        Provides a summary of the book and praises its compelling
and elegant style. Deplores its depressing theme as "the
complete and graphic failure of Mahatma," reflected in the
development of contemporary India.

D301.   Stokes, Eric. "The High-Caste Defector." Times Literary
Supplement 3943 (October 21, 1977): 1229.
        Traces the development of Naipaul's style after A House
for Mr. Biswas, notes he "consciously looked for a fresh
copy and a less constricting mode of expression." Questions
his special freedom as conducive to objective judgements as
well as his interpretation of Hinduism, but credits his treatment of those areas with which he is fully versed. Feels his
present book restates many of the arguments found in An
Area of Darkness, but believes the incidents and dialogue
fall short of its "freshness and vivacity." Detects a super-
ficial view of the book "other than the occasional visit to a
village." Suggests Naipaul to be a victim of his own charge
that Indians "had abandoned intellect, observation and reason."
Ends on a philosophical view of Naipaul, the man.

D302.   Grigg, John. "Expatriate." Spectator 239 (October 22,
1977): 23.
        Suggests that Naipaul's obsession with India has resulted
in an excellent, "but emotionally charged polemic." Naipaul
singles out Hinduism as the major barrier to the country's
advancenent and Gandhi as the instrument of that creed.
Grigg makes a stirring defense of Gandhi's political beliefs;
regards some of Naipaul's analysis as oversimplified and mis-
calculated. A refreshing view.

D303.   Locke, Richard. "The Democratic Imagination." New York
Times Book Review (October 23, 1977): 3, 42-43.
        Naipaul "writes with ease and eloquence in the first per-
son." Sees the major themes as India's need to recognize
her inadequacies and her limited intellectual capacity to ad-
vance. Emphasizes the importance of the book's critical intelligence in "awakening American readers to contemporary
reality." Equates the work of Naipaul and Bellow in terms of
their "distinctly literary methods."

D304.   Oates, Quentin. "Critics Corner." Bookseller 3749 (October
29, 1977): 2654-57.

D305. McTair, Roger. "India: A Wounded Civilization." Caribbean
Contact 5 (November 1977): 3.
An objective interpretation of the essay which focuses on
Naipaul's perception of India; admitting that his view of the
country is a dual one. Suggests that Naipaul "reduces the
traditional Hindu response of Karma to intellectual depletion
and absurdity throughout the book." Naipaul's pessimism is
clear. He offers little hope for solution of the country's
problems since "all solutions have to come up against the
fact of the pervasive influence of old India."

D306. Mellors, John. "Indian Emergencies." London Magazine 17
(November 1977): 79-84.
Naipaul visited India during the Emergency of Mrs.
Gandhi's administration. After that visit he wrote India:
A Wounded Civilization which describes his disenchantment
with the place and the inability to handle the problems. Naipaul attributes Hinduism as totally responsible for these
problems, and recommends radical changes in attitude to life
there. Mellors suggests that against this background Naipaul attempts to be objective, but is hampered by "the de-
terminist view of history," and the influence of his previous
gloomy book, Guerrillas.

D307. Mosley, Nicholas. "In Place of Taboos." Listener 98 (November 3, 1977): 591-92.
Regards this book as tough, sharp-witted and brilliantly
illuminating. "Main thesis is that the political and economic
ills of Indians will not be remedied unless some change of
mind takes place." Deplores Naipaul's attitude towards them
and their implicit belief in Hinduism. Considers Naipaul a
"highly skilful writer."

D308. "Defect of Vision." Economist 265 (November 5, 1977): 132.
Amidst the power and depth to Naipaul's writing, albeit
controversial, there is a sense of "love and understanding."
A major thrust of his argument centers on India's seeming
inability to cope with contemporary problems, due mainly to
its "hermetic philosophical system." The state of emergency
he saw as rallying point against the perceived fatalism of the
Indian nation. While admitting there is much substance in
Naipaul's account on which to ponder, the review concludes
that some of his vision appears blurred. An honest assessment.

D309. Heren, Louis. "The Blight of the Caste." The Times (November 17, 1977): 12.

D310. Paton, David. "Suffering Subcontinent." The Times Educational Supplement (December 2, 1977): 24.

D311. "India: A Wounded Civilization." Queen's Quarterly 84 (Winter 1977): 705-706.
Clark Blaise's Days and Nights in Calcutta and India are reviewed jointly. The latter reflects much of the pessimism recorded in An Area of Darkness. Naipaul's sensibility and masterly use of language stand in sharp contrast to the rigid analysis of the country he has offered. Blaise is reported to have said that "the nature of India is such that it can shrivel the compassion even of a Naipaul."

D312. Sastry, Srinivasa K. "Naipaul on India." Crosscurrents 27 (Winter 1977/78): 477-80.

D313. Kiernan, Victor G. "Passage from India." Journal of Contemporary Asia 8 (1978): 374-380.

D314. McTair, Roger. "Vulnerability, Defeat, Withdrawal." Last Post 6 (January 1978): 50.

D315. Yapp, M. E. "India: A Wounded Civilization." British Book News (January 1978): 77.

D316. Massey, Thomas. "China and India and Me." Washington Monthly 10 (March 1978): 44-47.

D317. Agarwal, R. "V. S. Naipaul's India." World Literature Today 52 (Spring 1978): 343.

D318. Bridges, Linda. "Books in Brief." National Review 30 (May 26, 1978): 667.
A straightforward review which focuses primarily on Moslem conquests over time, the devout acceptance of Hinduism and the impact these factors have had on the country's ability to accept change. Believes the book achieved at least one objective, "to give the Western reader a compassionate sense of what is going on there."

D319. Hodson, H. V. "A Nation Trapped by History." Round Table 270 (April 1978): 192.

D320. Haynes, Edward S. "India: A Wounded Civilization." American Historical Review 83 (October 1978): 1079-1080.

D321. Thorpe, Michael. "Current Literature 1977." English Studies 60 (1979): 64-65.

D322. Van Praagh, David. "New India?" Pacific Affairs 52 (Summer 1979): 315-318.

D323. Wise, Donald. "New Sickles and Old Cows." Far Eastern Economic Review (August 31, 1979): 73.

D324.   Paulin, Tom. "The Fire Monster: Recent Fiction." En-
        counter 54 (January 1980): 62-64.

        A BEND IN THE RIVER (1979 BR)

D325.   Bannon, Barbara. "P. W. Forecasts." Publishers' Weekly
        215 (March 26, 1979): 68.

D326.   "A Bend in the River." Kirkus Review 47 (April 1, 1979):
        407-408.
             Provides a brief but gloomy summary of the novel. Be-
        lieves the genre is too listless as a framework for ideas.
        However, records high praise for the author's prose. Touches
        on Naipaul's vivid characterization of Salim "who remains an
        uninvolving personality throughout."

D327.   Howe, Irving. "A Dark Vision." New York Times Book
        Review 84 (May 13, 1979): 1, 37.
             "For sheer abundance of talent there can hardly be a
        writer alive who surpasses V. S. Naipaul." Concedes though
        that his knowledge of India is limited, but sees him divorced
        from "the moral charms of primitives" or colonial nostalgia.
        Naipaul masterfully describes the "rhetoric, guile, sorcery and
        a strong helping of terror" by which the Big Man, as Presi-
        dent, rules for life. According to the review, meditation and
        narrative form a shadowy parallel. Considers this novel com-
        paratively "much better and deeper" than Guerrillas. A very
        penetrating account.

D328.   Clemons, Walter. "Black Africa's Outcasts." Newsweek
        (May 21, 1979): 90.
             Describes it as a "political novel of a subtle and unusual
        kind," a chilling description of life in an unnamed African
        country. In spite of its imperfections, this "enormously
        disturbing book confirms Naipaul's position as one of the best
        writers now at work."

D329.   Sheppard, R. Z. "Notes from the Fourth World." Time
        113 (May 21, 1979): 52, 54, R4.
             A favorable assessment stressing the novel's dominant
        theme of homelessness. Contains some biographical information
        on the author while commending the clarity of his work.
        Characterizes Naipaul's nonfiction works as the "Baedekers
        of forgotten history and cultural schizophrenia."

D330.   Updike, John. "Books." New Yorker 45 (May 21, 1979):
        141-144.

D331.   Hoagland, Edward. "Displaced Persons." New York 12
        (May 28, 1979): 82.

Sees the conclusions as consistent and well founded, their presentation subtle. Does not regard Salim a particularly interesting character; however, he fits his role very well. Commends the vividness of Naipaul's style and grasp of human nature.

D332. Larson, Charles R. "A Novel of Hope and Fear in the Third World." Chronicle of Higher Education 18 (May 29, 1979): R11.

Suggests the themes of "displacement, abandonment and denial of hope" found increasingly in Naipaul's works may stem from his grandfather's status in Trinidad as an indentured laborer from India a century ago. Provides a good summary of the novel and admires "the ease with which Naipaul handles the language, the deceptive simplicity of his narrative skill."

D333. Thompson, John. "Bankruptcy and Revolt." New York Review of Books 26 (May 31, 1979): 6, 8.

D334. Adams, P. L. "A Bend in the River." The Atlantic Monthly 243 (June 1979): 98.

The narrator of this novel is the son of an Indian merchant who has prospered for generations on the East coast of Africa. Correctly foreseeing disaster there, the young man sets up business in a newly independent state in the interior of the continent, where he and his Afro-Indian assistant run into all those problems of developing Africa which have become familiar in the news, plus a few that still lurk in the bush. Mr. Naipaul's hero is a stoic, but as he describes a world where everything is in a state of uncertainty, where no one feels safe at home and where progress, retrogression, or disintegration are all equally possible, his tale becomes both absorbing and convincing.

D335. "A Bend in the River." Booklist 75 (June 1, 1979): 1479.

D336. Beatty, Jack. "A Bend in the River." New Republic 180 (June 9, 1979): 38-39.

Provides a summary of the novel's major themes and events, its political uneasiness, reminiscences of Conrad's Africa, Salim's memoirs and the negative elements of European control. Suggests the novel enacts Naipaul's own vision of the world. His literary prowess also receives high praise.

D337. Cheuse, Alan. "A Bend in the River." Saturday Review 6 (June 9, 1979): 63.

D338. Domowitz, Janet. "Bushwhacked." Christian Science Monitor 71 (June 11, 1979): B7.

Provides a summary of a book that surpasses African

politics. Praises the universality of the theme: "insecurity and freedom of choice." Commends Naipaul's prose style and his presentation of Salim. A positive evaluation.

D339. Adachi, Ken. "Naipaul Is One of the World's Very Best." Toronto Star (June 16, 1979): B7.

The novel "vividly serves up the absurdities and tragedies that undermine those so-called Third World countries." Core of the review centers on Salim's quest for a new life as a businessman in an unknown African state. He cultivates a wide circle of friends, "but as an outsider he remains detached." Adachi provides a short biographical insight of Naipaul, who offers "not even a glimpse of hope in his vision of the new Africa." Praises Naipaul's skill. Views the book favorably.

D340. Snider, Norman. "A Bend in the River." Globe and Mail (June 23, 1979): 26.

Salim embodies the Indian of East African descent trading and determined to succeed in spite of adverse circumstances. Stresses the forcefulness and originality of the novel, and Naipaul's unique gift of being able "to burrow inside the conscience of the ordinary man." A thoroughly forthright and concise review of a depressing book, tempered by Naipaul's facility for observation and style.

D341. Green, Benny. "News from Nowhere." The Nation 228 (June 30, 1979): 791-793.

Perceives Naipaul's characters as prototypes whose interrelationships are vague. Salim is perhaps the most ambivalent. Homelessness is a central theme in this book. Examines the after-effects of "the colossal experiment of the British Empire." Touches on Naipaul's great gift of expressing "complex ideas in clean, simple language." Generally favorable.

D342. Rand, Peter. "The Brothers Naipaul look into Africa." Washington Post (Book World) (July 1, 1979): F1, F3.

Feels this book "might have provided us with a new vision of Africa" if Naipaul had inquired deeper into the history of the coastal Asians and Arabs in East Africa. This insider's view of the novel praises the reporting but questions the currency of his news. While Salim's voice is one of many colonial refugees which attracts "Naipaul's sympathy, [it] seems not to have the author's vital attention."

D343. Taylor, Jeremy. "Brilliant, Superbly Written, Structured." Sunday Express [Trinidad] (July 15, 1979): 16.

D344. De Santana, Hubert. "Tool Cool a Heart for the Heart of Darkness." MacLean's 92 (July 16, 1979): 51.

D345.   Raymond, Judy. " 'A Bend in the River': Once More Nai-
         paul Sees Life Through the Eyes of an Exile." People 5
         (August 1979): 55.

D346.   Wickham, John. " 'A Bend in the River' by V. S. Naipaul:
         A Superb Artist at Work." Sunday Sun (August 5, 1979):
         24.

D347.   Marshall, Douglas. "In Brief." Books in Canada 8 (August/
         September 1979): 17, 20.

D348.   Enright, D. J. "Naipaul's Grief." The Listener 20 (Sep-
         tember 1979): 382.
             A perceptive and philosophical evaluation which touches
         on many of the novel's themes and the elements of its style.
         Discusses the false use of mottoes, the sense of belonging,
         recollections of Conrad's Africa, political intrigue. A com-
         parison with In a Free State suggests that "Naipaul is not
         being merely satirical." This is an austere novel which re-
         flects some of his inner depth and courage.

D349.   La Salle, Peter. "A Bend in the River." America 141 (Sep-
         tember 22, 1979): 139.
             This is an "interesting, running commentary" narrated
         by Salim, the East Indian businessman. It bears Naipaul's
         stamp of "precise detail and probing intelligence." La Salle
         accepts many of Naipaul's harsh conclusions, having seen some
         of Africa at first hand, but believes there are hopeful signs
         too. Praises the value of the novel, particularly Naipaul's
         non-indulgence in the fantasy John Updike employed in The
         Coup.

D350.   Caute, David. "Late into the World." New Statesman 98
         (September 28, 1979): 464.
             Naipaul is "one of the finest and most consistently re-
         warding talents in the modern novel." Viewed through Salim's
         experiences, this novel represents another of Naipaul's tragic
         creations. Notes that "nothing in Naipaul's Africa is false,
         nothing distorted or evaded." However, the book lacks the
         exquisite form of In a Free State. Believes Naipaul gave
         "less than a total commitment." Otherwise favorable.

D351.   Evanier, David. "Heart of Darkness." National Review 31
         (September 28, 1979): 1241-42.
             A sincere review which focuses on "the Asian outsider in
         Third World countries exemplified by Salim, the narrator."
         Described as "a conduit for Naipaul's vision," Salim is seen
         as a dull, vague character. The dominant theme centers on
         "the human condition just underneath the cloak of leftist or
         national rhetoric." Admires "his particular knowledge, com-
         passion, and psychological insights into the region."

D352. Cooke, John. "Trinidad." World Literature Today 53 (Autumn 1979): 736-737.
The narrative vividly summarizes Salim's plight and his failure to find a sense of place in Africa. Naipaul "offers an even bleaker picture of post-colonial societies." Notes that the leader, Big Man, creates a "highly regimented and unstable" state. This novel, unlike Naipaul's previous works, foreshadows that deterioration spreading to Metropolitan London which was once a safe place to retreat to. A perceptive review.

D353. Milton, Edith. "Looking Backwards: Six Novels." Yale Review 69 (Autumn 1979): 100-103.
The theme of exile dominates this novel. In it, described as circular in movement and musical in arrangement, Naipaul implies that there is "a conflict between change and stasis which is always in equilibrium, so that nothing can progress and nothing can stay still." Suggests the nomadic tendencies of its characters to be a facet of the longer journey through life and history. Praises Naipaul's "force and integrity." It is a novel as without hope as it is flawless.

D354. "Bend in the River." Choice 16 (October 1979): 1023.
Naipaul has provided perhaps "the most accurate available single account of what life feels like in parts of Central Africa." Commends the objectivity, "narrative excitement" of his style and story-telling ability. Advances several opinions concerning his sentience about "both non-communist worlds." Favorable.

D355. Tomalin, Charles. "Out of Africa." Punch 277 (October 10, 1979): 638.

D356. Garebian, Keith. "Exchanged Deceptions." CACLALS Newsletter 11 (November 1979): 6-13.
Offers an existential reading of the novel. Commends Naipaul's skill in fusing contemplation with fiction before the reader realizes its "peculiar didactic force." Regards the civilization theme a new direction for Naipaul, away from his preoccupation with colonialism. The book centers around a small African town. Expresses doubt about the author's development of his female characters. Salim, the protagonist is not without his limitations either. A lengthy, favorable and erudite review, stressing the universality of the work.

D357. Murphy, Rae. "The Message is the Problem." Last Post 7 (November 1979): 45-46.

D358. Schieder, Rupert. "Scrupulous Fidelity." Canadian Forum 59 (November 1979): 26-27.
Traces the development of Naipaul's style from his "social

comedies" through to In a Free State, which Naipaul inaccurately described as a final statement of earlier topics. Notes the "broadening of his interest" and modification of his tone during the decade after Biswas. Regards Naipaul's experiment In a Free State as the most subtle and challenging of his presentations. A Bend in the River reaffirms both Naipaul's themes and attitudes. Schieder regards Salim, the narrator as the "most fully developed and psychologically complex character." A very forceful review.

D359. Thieme, John. "A Bend in the River." Caribbean Contact 7 (November 1979): 3.
        Provides a brief summary of the book, and attempts to place it in its geographical setting. Notes Conrad's continuous influence on Naipaul's writing since The Mimic Men. Sees Conrad's Africa as "a metaphor for man's symbolic journey into the innermost depths of self," and Naipaul's concern with "the vivid evocation of an actual terrain." Focuses on thematic significance of African life.

D360. Ryle, John. "Going with the Current." Times Literary Supplement 4002 (November 30, 1979): 77.
        The plots in both Updike's The Coup and Naipaul's A Bend in the River bear some resemblance. The novels are set near an African town on an imaginary river far into the interior and governed by a dictator. The water hyacinth analogy adds some vividness to the accounts. Commends Naipaul's style and his characterization of Salim, the narrator. Ryle believes Updike set out to make "a sympathetic and credible narrator" out of Colonel Ellellou. The themes of power and sovereignty predominate in both works, which were written from differing viewpoints. Credits Naipaul in treating his subject with "sombre passion" and "a tone of even-handed disenchantment." Ryle regards the two books as "among the best things their authors have done." A positive review.

D361. Scott-Kilvert, Ian. "A Bend in the River." British Book News (December 1979): 1032.
        A short, favorable review. Praises Naipaul's objectivity and insights of the native African predicament.

D362. Stewart, Ian. "Recent Fiction." Illustrated London News 267 (December 1979): 139.
        A look at post-colonial Africa from another leading novelist, V. S. Naipaul. By contrast with Updike's satirical novel, The Coup, Naipaul's is a rather gloomy episode seen through the eyes of the Asian trader, Salim, the major character. Praising the author for his brilliance and skill, the review concludes that "from it emerges a disturbing picture universal in its significance."

D363. West, Richard. "One of the Dark Places." Spectator 243
(December 1, 1979): 20.
Gives a clear overview of the novel and the vicissitudes
of Salim's fortune in Africa. Sees a distinct parallel with
Conrad's Heart of Darkness; both have portions set in London and Kurtz, like Raymond, is a central character with a
missionary calling in the Congo. Both Conrad and Naipaul
have chosen the Congo as a base to express "the human condition." Commends Naipaul's depth and his ability to make
one "question many assumptions about the world today."

D364. Park, Clara C. "Fiction Chronicle." In: Hudson Review
32 (Winter 1979/80): 580-581.
A perceptive view of a penetrating novel from Naipaul on
life in post-colonial Africa. Salim represents a remarkable
portrait of characterization, someone in which the reader becomes quite submerged. It seems to question the degree of
Naipaul's account.

D365. "Notes on Current Books." Virginia Quarterly Review 56
(Winter 1980): 14.
Naipaul's attention has shifted to European colonialism and
its effects on the ex-Belgian Congo. The reviewer commends
his political vision and his feeling for ordinary people caught
in extraordinary situations which "make him one of the most
important novelists writing English today."

D366. Williams, Wyck. "Rootless in Africa." Trinidad and Tobago
Review 4 (1980): 23.

D367. McWatt, Mark, comp. "The West Indies." Journal of Commonwealth Literature 15 (December 1980): 145.
Praises Naipaul's consistency of style and high standard
of writing. Comments on his "personal theme of placelessness and insecurity, slavery and freedom." Regrets his
singular voice among Caribbean writers raising "persistently
eloquent questions." Expresses some reservations about the
influence of Naipaul's "journalistic obsessions" on his fiction.

D368. Hope, Christopher. "After Conrad." London Magazine 19
(December/January 1979-80): 124-128.
Establishes a link with Conrad's Heart of Darkness. In
Naipaul's Africa nothing is pre-ordained. Three elements
come under scrutiny: Salim's insecurity about his "African"
identity, his "ironic understanding of the vanity of foreign
settlements" and "the predicament of Africans under their
dictator." Praises Naipaul's skill in weaving such an intri-
cate pattern from such a complex society, very favorable.

D369. Paulin, Tom. "The Fire Monster." Encounter 54 (January
1980): 62-64.

D370. Zweig, Paul. "Naipaul's Losers." <u>Harpers</u> 260 (January 1980): 69-72.

D371. Weathers, Winston. "Another Tide of World History." <u>Commonwealth</u> 107 (May 23, 1980): 317-318.

D372. King, Bruce. "A Vision of Dispossession." <u>Sewanee Review</u> 88 (Winter 1980): vi-vii.

D373. Tam, Ann-Louise. "Naipaul's Self-Portrait." <u>National Target</u> (January 7, 1981): 18.

RETURN OF EVA PERON:
WITH THE KILLINGS IN TRINIDAD (1980 RP)

D374. Leonard, John. "The Return of Eva Peron." <u>Books of the Times</u> 3 (1980): 199-200.
"Half-made societies" is a dominant theme in the review. "According to Mr. Naipaul there is no history in a half-made society, nor archives: there are only graffiti and polemics and school lessons." Addresses issues in colonial history and other Third World phenomena with objectivity and contempt. A favorable assessment.

D375. "The Return of Eva Peron: with the Killings in Trinidad." <u>Kirkus Review</u> (February 1, 1980): 196.
Naipaul seeks to describe the "unreal world of imitation" in Argentina, the Congo, and Trinidad and Tobago. The first of these essays epitomizes racial politics and their negative qualities. To the unsuspecting, one gets the impression that this brand of politics is condoned "especially in Black-majority Trinidad." A different type of treatment is reserved for Argentina and the Congo. The former is represented as a sterile society, "where torture is rigorously defended both officially and unofficially." Mobutu's Congo, a country trapped between its recent past and a precarious future, has its present existence supported by a "sham Africanism." Semblances of Conrad's writing are discernible in this last essay. A forceful collection, "one may also discover in Naipaul himself less bitterness than appeared on first, early 1970's reading, and more torment." These essays first appeared as a series of articles in both <u>The London Times</u> and <u>The New York Review of Books</u> between 1972 and 1975.

D376. "The Return of Eva Peron: with the Killings in Trinidad." <u>Publisher's Weekly</u> 217 (February 1, 1980): 98.
Traces Conrad's influence on Naipaul's own development. These essays also reflect the author's investigative ability. Seems to suggest that in each of the three countries discussed, "myth and madness often pass for history and civilization."

D377. Windrich, Elaine. The Return of Eva Peron: with the Killings in Trinidad." Library Journal 105 (March 1, 1980): 615.

There is some correlation between the four essays in this collection. Naipaul states that: "the themes repeat, whether in Argentina, the Congo or Trinidad and Tobago." Although praising Naipaul's elegant style in writing about these countries, Windrich sees his approach to them as "somewhat idiosyncratic," but rates him "indisputably one of the greatest practitioners of English today."

D378. Hunter, Frederic. "V. S. Naipaul Wanders the Post-Colonial World." Christian Science Monitor (March 10, 1980): B2.

This collection of essays upholds Naipaul's skill and perception as a writer. However, Hunter observes that "the factual lapses here are unsettling," this is in reference particularly to the piece on Mobutu's Congo; certain reservations, therefore, overshadow the depth of their analysis. The comparative perceptions of both Conrad and Naipaul on the Congo, Hunter describes as "a neat literary reversal, beautifully set forth." He believes Naipaul made a genuine effort "to understand Argentina," and sees Eva Peron as the catalyst which triggered the rupture of an already fragile relationship between its major factions. Offers a crisp biographical account of Michael de Freitas, the chief character in the Trinidad essay.

D379. Clemons, Walter. "Half-Made Societies." Newsweek 95 (March 31, 1980): 73, 77.

Naipaul's rather humble remark that the essays "bridged a creative gap from 1970 to the end of 1973" is not shared by Clemons who sees them "by no means casual make-work, and brought together they become something more than a collection of journalism." Suggests this book be the starting point for newcomers to Naipaul's work.

D380. Gornick, Vivian. "Terror and Rhetoric in Hot Places." Esquire 93 (April 1980): 22.

Focuses on Naipaul's early satirical style and the marked transition reflected in his later work, much of this attributed to his travels. Gornick notes that gradually the "tone of his voice changed; he was no longer amused." Based on a series of journalistic articles, this book receives much credit for "the transforming difference between the descriptive journalism and the creative fiction." Naipaul underscores the decline of imperialism and its impact on the political figures who have emerged from its demise, but regards their behavior in part as a reflection of those Third World societies. What follows is both painful and gloomy reading. A forceful review. Nowhere is Conrad's influence on Naipaul as much in evidence as towards the end; a true study in similarities.

D 381. Sheppard, R. Z. "Half-World." Time (April 7, 1980): R2-
R 4.
Underlines familiar but parallel themes such as "social
upheaval, solitude, madness and evil in the work of Conrad
and Naipaul, who unlike Conrad, relates them "to the
colonised, not the colonisers." One sees Mobutu as "the
remote leader," a futurist and ancestor worshipper, De Freitas
as the demagogue. Both these men were more fully described
in A Bend in the River, 1979 and Guerrillas, 1975. In his
description of Argentina Naipaul is depicted as walking "on
a decaying planet where a succession of carnivores feed on
a gullible mass." To Naipaul, degeneration and illusion are
everywhere. Even Jorge Luis Borges is rapped for appearing to cling "to a bogus past of noble battles fought for the
establishment of the fatherland."

D 382. Beatty, Jack. "The Return of Eva Peron." New Republic
(April 12, 1980): 36-39.
Attacks Western standards in judging alien cultures, and
regards Naipaul, therefore, as "an indispensable writer"
who takes "a less parochial perspective." The review offers
an existentialist view of the novel. Although the essays pre-
date the book, this affects neither its quality nor its permanence. It deals with themes such as: national character,
societies, and "the imperialism of Western moral styles."
Commends Naipaul's skill and lucidity in constructing this
novel from the essays. Sees the essay on Trinidad as the
most powerful in the collection "for its masterfully sustained
irony as well as for its final chord of pathos." Naipaul
though is not without his hang-ups.

D 383. Kramer, Jane. "From the Third World." New York Times
Book Review 85 (April 13, 1980): 1, 30-32.
Combines a caustic attack on Naipaul's style with an
equally sarcastic view of the book. His last three books are
not unscathed. The review does not discuss form or technique. Regards him as "our scourge for truth, a Solzhenitsyn
of the Third World." Seems to suggest that blanket approval
of his work reinforces his vengeance. Chides Naipaul's re-
cycling of his journalism into books: "a cartoon for the fin-
ished canvas of his work."

D 384. Said, Edward W. "Bitter Dispatches from the Third World."
Nation (May 3, 1980): 522-525.
Sets the tone of this review by dwelling on one of Naipaul's favorite themes, colonialism. Traces the gradual transition in his early novels. Naipaul never really lost the inward
antagonism which was "derived as much from his compromised
colonial situation" as from his subject matter. Examines this
colonial theme in Guerrillas, India, In a Free State, A Bend
in the River and Return of Eva Peron. Attacks Naipaul's

blatant insensibility to the Third World, his seeing its people only in negative terms. Chides Irving Howe who regards Naipaul "as an exemplary figure from the Third World." A highly critical, but perceptive view of Naipaul which Said expresses "with pain and admiration."

D385. "General." New Yorker 56 (May 19, 1980): 158-159.
Naipaul's literary prowess as an interpreter in English again draws praise. His scenarios are based on a series of journalistic essays he wrote in the early 1970's after visits to Trinidad, Zaire and Argentina. Trinidad's "counterfeit revolutionary," Michael X, Naipaul uses as an analogy to delineate a way of life there; his reviewer describes it as "a painfully telling contemporary parable," Argentina Naipaul presents as "an illusion of being European," and Zaire as vandalized by "Europhobia" under Mobutu's spell. Attributes their replica society to past colonial history, structures built on words and predominated by "the politics of plunder" and imitation. But above all, Naipaul sees implications for other countries as well.

D386. Jones, Frank. "Naipaul's Pursuit of Rogues." Toronto Star (June 7, 1980).
Highlights the disillusionment Naipaul discovered on his visits to Argentina, Zaire and Trinidad. Jones commends Naipaul's sustained attack on those in privileged positions who foist illusions on their followers. His portraits of Peron, Mobutu and "Malik" underline his mastery of characterization. His vantage position and sensitivity to the problems of the Third World strengthens this novel. The review suggests that the Western world also could learn from these unenviable situations.

D387. Didion, Joan. "Without Regret or Hope." New York Review of Books (June 12, 1980): 20-21.
Not very often does one agree with Naipaul, let alone defend some of his views. This review does precisely this. Observes "he lets no one off." Also sees Gale Benson's secure middle-class as the villains who helped to fashion the "Maliks," "continue to simplify the world and reduce other men." A philosophical reaction to the book.

D388. Conrad, Peter. "The Exhumation of a Secret Life of Dream and Desires." Listener 103 (June 26, 1980): 835-836.

D389. Schieder, Rupert. "The Return of Eva Peron." Globe and Mail (June 28, 1980): 13.
Schieder says of Naipaul: "although one of the most cosmopolitan writers, [he] is singularly equipped to be the most sensitive and percipient observer of the Third World." Believes it is his alien position that has influenced the

ruthlessness in his writing. The study centers on the structural and thematic significance of his essays. Their beauty
also is such that their "intensity and obsessional nature have
a strong direct impact on the reader." De Freitas, who was
hanged for murder in Trinidad, Naipaul describes as "the
creature of words," and the killings as "a literary murder, if
there ever was one."

D390.   Amiel, Barbara. "The Return of Eva Peron: with the Killings
in Trinidad." Maclean's 93 (June 30, 1980): 48.
        An excellent discussion on the conflict which confronts
Naipaul in writing about the bitter realities of the Third
World. Touches upon the incisiveness and ruthlessness with
which he handles the problem, a credential he holds almost
exclusively. Symbolism he employs as the central theme
exemplified by "the pimping-con world of Michael X, a Trinidadian hanged for murder in May 1975; a desolate Argentina
centered on the paraffin-injected corpse of Eva Peron; and
the Zaire of the dinner-jacketed, crypto-cannibal chieftain-
president Mobutu." Naipaul manages to display an unusual
measure of charity towards both De Freitas and Mobutu in
his biographical sketches of them, but not at the expense of
his objectivity.

D391.   Amis, Martin. "More Bones." New Statesman 100 (July 4,
1980): 19-20.
        Amis predicts that, despite the present work's high jour-
nalistic quality, Naipaul's An Area of Darkness "is likely to
remain his best book on the Third World." Observes that
Naipaul's human quality has gradually given way to a more
rigid style. Notes his youthful political unease has developed
into a "rhetorical attitude."

D392.   Marnham, Patrick. "Half Made." Spectator 245 (July 5,
1980): 18-20.

D393.   Stuewe, Paul. "Foreign Affairs." Quill & Quire 46 (August
1980): 35.
        A favorable assessment of the author's journalistic articles
condensed "in a most coherent and informative way." Naipaul brings to his subject "the agonised intelligence of a
knowledgeable but often horrified observer who is not afraid
to contradict the conventional wisdom of Western liberalism."

D394.   Wachtel, Eleanor. "Third World: Myths as History." Vancouver Sun (August 8, 1980): 36L.

D395.   Herstein, Harvey. "Half-Made Societies Ape Western Nations."
Winnipeg Free Press (August 23, 1980): 4L.

D396.   "Return of Eva Peron: with the Killings in Trinidad." Choice
18 (September 1980): 92.

Comments on the topical nature of Naipaul's work and its freedom from sectional interests. Regards the essay on Conrad as an original assessment worthy of note. A positive review.

D397.   Barratt, Harold.   "The Return of Eva Peron: with the Killings in Trinidad." Dalhousie Review 60 (Autumn 1980): 549-551.
A penetrating interpretation of the essays which underline Naipaul's obsession with the human condition. Regards his brilliant analysis of Michael X's macabre life as the best essay in the collection. Praises his "ability to recognize and crystallize for the reader the bizarre ironic contrasts in areas of human darkness." Sees the piece on Conrad very instructive, shedding "rewarding light on the fascinating craft of novel writing."

D398.   Rose, Phyllis.   "Of Moral Bonds and Men." Yale Review 70 (Autumn 1980): 149-156.
Vividly illustrates the moral strata which underlines Naipaul's work. His tendency has been to apply this philosophy to audiences least concerned about its relevance. Believes this absolute moral stance to be as much in the Matthew Arnold tradition as Conrad's. Warns it would be a mistake to read the indictments in these essays "as directed at the Third World alone." Malik's fourteen-year sojourn in England is a case in point. Also apportions some responsibility to the "First World" for having interfered in Third World history "so wantonly." Very perceptive review which discusses many of the book's themes.

D399.   McTair, Roger.   "Critical Response to Naipaul." Caribbean Contact (October 1980): 3, 18.
Severely critical of Naipaul's Third World bias against developing countries. Notes his constituency is largely in the metropolitan countries, where his journalism and fiction are well received. Concludes that his assumptions are to be questioned, but not his professionalism.

D400.   Scott-Kilvert, Ian.   "The Return of Eva Peron: with the Killings in Trinidad." British Book News (October 1980): 597.

D401.   Garebian, Keith.   "False Redeemers." Canadian Forum 60 (November 1980): 33.
The book explores Naipaul's "concern with metaphysical problems of history." These essays according to Garebian are "fascinating in themselves and magnify their intrinsic worth by offering us insights into the non-fictive sources for Guerrillas and A Bend in the River.

D402.   Rodman, Selden.   "The Bush Moves Closer." National Review 32 (November 14, 1980): 1406.

Believes that Naipaul has allowed his Third World detachment to blemish some of the more positive elements of these societies. Challenges that his attack on Borges, and on slavish tendencies in Africa and Caribbean countries have gotten out of hand. Deplores Naipaul's metaphysical stance. An objective review.

D403. Guinness, Gerald. "The Black Power Killings in Trinidad; Naipaul's New Book of Essays." Caribbean Review 10, No. 2 (April 1981): 36-37, 52.

Presents a lucid interpretation of the Black Power essay, and praises its literary quality and content. Guinness notes the interesting phenomenon that "Naipaul's fame has grown as his novels get worse." Respects his journalistic abilities, but not his talents as a novelist. Guinness fiercely refutes claims by others who compare Conrad to Naipaul; prefers instead to speak of "the affinity between the two men."

AMONG THE BELIEVERS (1981 AB)

D404. "Among the Believers: An Islamic Journey." Booklist 77 (July 15-August 1981): 1419-1420.

Examines the extent of influence Islam commands in Iran, Malaysia, Pakistan and Indonesia. The book assesses the current political and commercial situation in relation to the renaissance of Islamic dogma.

D405. "Among the Believers: An Islamic Journey." Publishers Weekly 220 (September 4, 1981): 51.

D406. Harris, Robert R. "Western Scorn at Islamic Rage." Saturday Review 8 (October 1981): 70, 73.

Cites A Bend in the River and The Return of Eva Peron as brilliant examples of "the chaos that reigns throughout the contemporary Third World." With respect to the present work, Harris launches a vigorous rebuttal of some of Naipaul's Third World views on Islam as seen through his established Western values. Regards the book as boring, lacking in "grand summation" characteristic of his earlier writings. Suggests that Naipaul's bitterness and impatience, including his antagonism towards Muslims, occur "when his sense of humor wanes." Questions Naipaul's frequent use of anecdotes in the book as "substitutes for careful historical and political analysis."

D407. Enright, D. J. "Islam is a Complete Way of Life: It Comprehends Everything." The Listener 106 (October 1, 1981): 375-376.

States that Naipaul's main concern was to determine the way in which Islam works. Enright notes that in those states

Naipaul visited, two ideologies are at work: Marxism and
Islam. The former predominates in practical ways, while the
power of Islam is unsurpassed in any secular system. Touches
on Naipaul's sensitivity to the "feeling of completeness, which
the Islamic resurgence has brought into people's lives." Regards his style as elegant, lucid and easy.

D408. Hayford, Elizabeth R. "The Contemporary Scene." Library
Journal 106 (October 1, 1981): 1911-1912.
       A brief favorable review which stresses Naipaul's insights
and sensitivity. Also notes the brilliance of his writing set
in sharp contrast to the mood in the Islamic world he depicted as "enraged, ignorant and parasitic."

D409. Cameron, James. "Trans-Arabia." Spectator 247 (October
3, 1981): 21-22.

D410. Nordell, Roderick. "Vivid. Opinionated Journey Through
the World of Islam." Christian Science Monitor 73 (October
13, 1981): B3.

D411. Carey, John. "Naipaul Among the Moslem Zealots." Trinidad
Guardian (October 14, 1981): 26.
       Describes the book as an attempt to investigate the bar-
barism of the Islamic revolution, and to explore the zeal of
young Moslem fundamentalists, particularly in Iran. Reflects
on Naipaul's low-keyed approach in gathering his information,
and the effective use of his critical eye as he moves through
Iran, Pakistan, Malaysia and Indonesia. Naipaul notes that
technology is seen through the eyes of the Islamic purist as
"a Western corruption." He finds mullahs and ayatollahs in
their life of prayer six centuries behind Europe. Carey observes that Naipaul never lacks sympathy in spite of his often
hostile conclusions.

D412. MacLeod, Sheila. "Islam Laid Bare." Times Educational
Supplement (October 16, 1981): 28.

D413. Said, Edward. "Expectations of Inferiority." New Statesman 102 (October 16, 1981): 21-22.

D414. De Santana, Hubert. "Dark Chorus in Greek Tragedy."
Maclean's 94 (October 19, 1981): 72, 75.
       Naipaul's journalism comes in for high praise in this book,
which De Santana regards as "a firsthand account of the religious, social, and political forces that have shaped the contemporary history of the Third World." He sees the book as
Naipaul's best nonfiction writing since An Area of Darkness.
In spite of Naipaul's brilliant diagnosis of social problems,
De Santana regrets that he "offers disappointingly few cures
beyond vague generalities." Otherwise favorable.

D415. Lehmann-Haupt, Christopher. "Books of the Times." New York Times (October 19, 1981): C21.

D416. James, C. L. R. "Ignoring History." New Society 58 (October 22, 1981): 162-163. Rpt. in Vanguard (March 5, 1982): 11.
Explains how Naipaul decided to write the book. James sees no confusion in it; he says "history is simply ignored." Regards "the most indicative piece of writing in the book," to be Naipaul's account of an Indian novel. Does not seem favorably impressed with Among the Believers.

D417. Halliday, Fred. "Misanthrope." Nation 233 (October 24, 1981): 415-416.
Sees the Iranian account as the least thorough of the four countries discussed. Argues that the Arab world "remains the core of Islam," yet the book excluded Arab countries. Attacks Naipaul's "same tangential method of inquiry." Underlines several other points of difference with his conclusions, stating "what disappears from Naipaul's world is purpositive action." An incisive review.

D418. Ajami, Fouad. "Among the Believers." New York Times Book Review 86 (October 25, 1981): 7, 30, 32.
"Displays all of Naipaul's major themes, his great talent as a writer and his increasing limitation of vision." Believes Naipaul's predictability to be damaging to his reputation. Challenges many of his assumptions including his misconstruing the Moslem mind. Ajami prefers to see their behavioral patterns as "part of the painful process of history that people are always made by the world they reject." Attributes Naipaul's success partly to his accurate timing and ability to convey a credible story.

D419. Gray, Paul. "Partisan Report." Time 118 (October 26, 1981): 106, 108, 110.
Seems to imply that Naipaul's trained mind and pro-Western background conflicts with his book, which otherwise is "filled with fascinating details." Questions Naipaul's value judgements about the Koran alone, as a satisfactory "blueprint for a functioning state." Accords the book a sympathetic ear, but does not think it will find many converts among the believers.

D420. Pipes, Daniel. "The Islamic Disturbance and the Dying West." Wall Street Journal (October 28, 1981): 28.

D421. Kedourie, Elie. "Faith and Fanaticism." New Republic 185 (November 4, 1981): 31-33.
Expresses high praise for the book, calling it "the most notable work on contemporary Islam to have appeared in a very

long time." Regards it as a "faithful report" whose application to those societies differ only by degree. Naipaul's vivid presentation congeals a web of complex and conflicting experiences.

D422.   Trevor-Roper, H. R. "Born Again." New York Review of Books 28 (November 5, 1981): 8, 10-11.

D423.   Kashmeri, Zuhair. "Among the Believers." Globe and Mail (November 14, 1981): 17.
Focuses on Naipaul's presentation of Islam not with little concern about "some rather incomplete, contentious and repulsive portions of Islamic history" included in the book. Much of the review is devoted to Naipaul's ideal Islamic followers, "characters who are confused, angry, bitter." Regards some of his judgements as hasty. A mixed review praising the mastery of his journalistic style.

D424.   Michener, Charles. "A Journey Through Lands of Rage." Newsweek 98 (November 16, 1981): 105. (Published together with C166.)

D425.   Manor, F. S. "Islamic Rage Sweeping Through Asia." Winnipeg Free Press (November 28, 1981): 4L.

D426.   Rousseau, Richard W. "Civilization." Best Sellers 41 (December 1981): 346.

D427.   Moore, Arthur J. "A Journey to Islam Marred by Western Bias." Business Week 2714 (November 16, 1981): 21, 24, 28.
Contains many "fascinating characters and passages of brilliant writing," Behzad, a student guide in Iran, is one such character. Naipaul's tendency to defend Western values here detracts somewhat from the objectivity of his writing. The exclusion of Arab nations also biases the book, thus reducing its value as a source for a profound understanding of modern Islam."

D428.   Yapp, M. E. "With the Revivalists." Times Literary Supplement 4106 (December 11, 1981): 1433.
Describes the book as "a quite remarkable perceptive account of certain features of modern Islam," although it lacks the humor of An Area of Darkness or the clarity of India. Highlights the initial disadvantages Naipaul encountered on the Islamic journey. The book portrays strong elements of discredit for the revolution.

D429.   Tehranian, Majid. "Among the Believers: An Islamic Journey." Journal of International Affairs 35 (Fall/Winter 1981-82): 261-263.

D430. Kelly, J. B. "Born-Again Muslims." Commentary 73 (January 1982): 76, 78.
       Draws attention to the "equally pervasive though slightly different brand of illogicality" and rage Naipaul discovers in each of the Islamic countries visited. Suggests that Islam acts as "a vehicle for protest," a type of defense mechanism against the problems of the modern world and particularly "the corrupting influence of the West." Naipaul's presentation, sincerity, humanity and understanding of the numerous complexities of Islamic receive high praise. Contains a pro-Western slant.

D431. Stuewe, Paul. "Among the Believers." Quill & Quire 48 (January 1982): 39.
       Expresses timeliness of the book and praises the power of Naipaul's perceptions. Observes a shift from his "intellectual impatience" to a less critical attitude towards Third World countries than previously held. Very complimentary.

D432. Pritchett, V. S. "Books." New Yorker 57 (January 4, 1982): 86-88.

D433. "Unbeliever." Economist 282 (February 6-12, 1982): 92-93.

D434. Hopwood, Derek. "Geography and History." British Book News (March 1982): 189.

D435. Brookhiser, Richard. "A Cynic Abroad." National Review (March 19, 1982): 302-303.
       A rather cautious review which focused mainly on the "need-hate relationship" adopted by the Islamic fundamentalists towards the West. Naipaul also draws attention to their lack of knowledge about their own history.

D436. Gerson, Frederick. "In search of Marginal Peoples." Canadian Forum 62 (May 1982): 33.
       Contends that the rebirth of Islam was influenced by the rejection of Western values. Expresses Naipaul's view that Islam is "heading towards retrograde fundamentalism." Praises the strength of his "marginal characters." Voices some misgivings about the book's enhancement in the form presented.

D437. Mohan, Dinesh. "Naipaul--the Flawed Mirror." Trinidad Guardian (July 8, 1982): 12-13.
       Focuses on the more positive aspects of the book while he explores the virtues of Islam to Muslim states. Dislikes Naipaul's generalizations, misunderstanding about Islam, his "superficial and Eurocentric view of Eastern civilizations." Sees in the work an implicit questioning of the tradition of Islam, a religion Mohan regards as the weapon of a pastoral people with limited skills and money. Suggests that Naipaul

simply converted his "homelessness and anguish" artistically
and is wealthier for it. Dismisses his demand for institutions
and less dependence on faith as being devoid of any solutions. Concludes that his insights are forceful but some of
his judgements are questionable.

D438.   John, George R. "In Defence of Naipaul. His Critics Should
Concentrate Their Ire on Our Corrupt Professional Flag-
Wavers." Trinidad Guardian (August 22, 1982): 8.

D439.   Pantin, Manuel. "Naipaul and the Blind Poet of Argentina."
Trinidad Guardian (September 19, 1982): 4.

D440.   Nazareth, Peter. "Among the Believers: An Islamic Journey."
World Literature Today 56 (Autumn 1982): 742-743.

D441.   Callam, Daniel. "Among the Believers." The Canadian Catholic Review 1 (January 1983): 27-28.
Naipaul's journalism, lucid style and "eye for significant
detail" receive high praise. His concern with the paradox
of Moslem belief in the "existence of paradise" and professed
"living by the Koran alone" while indulging in secular Western
practices is profound. Mr. Callam questions some of Naipaul's
humanism represented by Western values and questions the
explosiveness of its "spiritual poverty."

THREE NOVELS (1982 TN, Omnibus Edition)

D442.   "Three Novels." Publishers Weekly 222 (October 8, 1982):
54.

D443.   Schaire, J. "Brief Reviews." Harper 265 (December 1982):
71-72.

D444.   "Three Novels." Fiction Catalogue (1983 Supplement): 59.

FINDING THE CENTRE (1984 FC)

D445.   Boyd, William. "World of the Night." London Magazine
(April/May 1984): 128-130.
A very incisive analysis of the book. In "Prologue to an
Autobiography," the first of the two narratives, Naipaul discusses how the stories in Miguel Street came to be written,
the insights into his late father's life, the impact this had on
his own career. Boyd observes that V. S. Naipaul's account
has been particularly potent because of his terse style, its
scrupulous reserve and refusal to display any emotion. The
Ivory Coast piece, the second narrative is "an attempt to understand the nature of this fetish, a crocodile pond and the

abiding presence and influence of magic in the lives of
Africans."

D446. Enright, D. J. "No matter the Place or Time, to Write is to
Learn." The Listener 111 (May 3, 1984): 22-23.
Touches on Naipaul's regret that as a colonial subject he
was deprived of knowledge and had to co-exist "in an intellectually restricted world," unlike his European counterparts.
Chides Naipaul's self-pity when set against his success and
his recognition. Discusses Seepersad Naipaul's contribution
to his son as exemplified by V. S. Naipaul's famous book:
A House for Mr. Biswas. The second narrative, "The Crocodiles of Yamoussoukro" receives high praise for its style. In
it Naipaul explains what the value of travel means to him.
Regards the Ivory Coast as a successful African experiment.
His satiric traits are noticeably absent. Portrays tremendous
sympathy and appreciation for the life-style he finds there.
(See also item D64.)

D447. Oakes, Philip. "Into the Interior." New Society 68 (May 3,
1984): 188.
Regards as a "remarkable piece of self-scrutiny which not
only explains a complicated process, but also justifies it calm-
ly and comprehensively." The first of two narratives is called
"Prologue to an Autobiography" in which Naipaul talks about
his early life in Trinidad, and his ambition to become a writer.
Oakes notes that Naipaul's father willed him "a sense of voca-
tion, a refusal not to be extinguished." The second piece,
"Crocodiles of Yamoussoukro," is set in the Ivory Coast.
Here Naipaul reflects on his neutrality: "I was content to
be myself, to be what I had always been, a looker." Yet
Naipaul's main purpose to visit the place was to try and understand the people: "They too are trying to find order in the
world, looking for the centre."

D448. Mount, Ferdinand. "No Home for Mr. Biswas." Spectator
252 (May 5, 1984): 12-13.
Regards Naipaul's work as distinct both for its quality
and area of concern: with unsettled individuals and societies.
Commenting on his trajectory, notes that "his scorn withers
its victims without parching the surrounding landscape."
Sees in Finding the Centre a continuation of the relaxed tone
in his writing. Mount discerns in A Bend in the River--
that "glorious free swing" as he refers to it. In addition to
outlining the plot of the narratives, he offers an analytical
view of "The Crocodiles of Yamoussoukro." Concludes by
praising the beauty and clarity with which Naipaul begins his
autobiography.

D449. "Thanks Dad." The Economist 291 (May 5, 1984): 94.
Touches briefly on Naipaul's complaint that his background
hindered him from understanding D. H. Lawrence and Evelyn

Waugh, except with great difficulty, while at Oxford. Credits the tribute he pays to his parents amidst the influence which their difficulties had on his life. Notes that such a practice is "not all that common among creative writers." Regards the essay on the Ivory Coast as "a sustained piece of writing as fine as can be found anywhere in England today."

D450. Stevenson, Anne. "Heart of Darkness." Times Educational Supplement (June 1, 1984): 22.

A favorable review suggesting that Naipaul's success as a writer must be seen as a debt of gratitude to his father. Sees in "The Crocodiles of Yamoussoukro" a restatement of the central theme of "the superficiality of civilization," and its fragility in countries with darker and fiercer beliefs. Finds the book enlightening, and expresses thorough satisfaction with its conclusions, "the world is sand, life is sand."

D451. Taylor, Jeremy. "Book Week and New Writing." Sunday Guardian [Trinidad] (June 5, 1984).

Summarizes both essays fully. Recommends the semi-autobiographical piece to "all writers and serious readers." Detects a mellower Naipaul writing with some affection about the Ivory Coast.

D452. "Naipaul Recalls His Childhood in 'Prologue to an Autobiography.'" Trinidad Guardian (June 11, 1984): 25.

Consists of two essays. In the prologue Naipaul gives a "candid account of his own literary beginnings." Notes that he focuses on the Ivory Coast in the second essay with an unusual degree of sympathy and does he make any judgements.

D453. Burgess, Anthony. "Interior Excursions." Times Literary Supplement 4238 (June 22, 1984): 691-692.

Burgess outlines the content of "Prologue to an Autobiography" and its relationships to A House for Mr. Biswas as discussed in the introduction to the book. Commenting on "The Crocodiles of Yamoussoukro," Burgess mentions Naipaul's use of "the narrative technique selective reporting." Draws from this essay the moral of Africa's potential and capacity to engulf. Speculates that Naipaul's further ambition will be to produce his autobiography, a travel book or novel.

D454. French, William. "Echoes of Magic and Mystery in Naipaul's Search." Globe and Mail (July 5, 1984): E1.

The book consists of two essays. The first deals with the process of writing; the other discusses his impressions of the Ivory Coast. Mr. French sees "a subtle link between the two pieces that enlarge their meaning."

D455. J. T. "A Mellower Naipaul." Caribbean and West Indies Chronicle 99 (August/September 1984): 20-21.

The book consists of two essays. The first of these tells
of his father's early struggle, but more importantly of V. S.
Naipaul's own quest to become a writer. The other dwells on
a trip he made to the Ivory Coast. The reviewer notes a
sympathetic trait in this piece. Regards it as "a fine and
sensitive essay, which incidentally shows up the emotional
challenge beneath the glamour which good travel writing
and good foreign reporting involves."

D456.   Lyons, Gene. "In Search of a Voice." Newsweek 104 (Sep-
        tember 24, 1984): 82.

D457.   Lasdun, J. "Books and Writers." Encounter 63 (September/
        October 1984): 47-48.

D458.   Khan, Nisa. "A bit of Biography from Mr. Naipaul." Sun-
        day Guardian [Trinidad] (October 7, 1984): 7B.
        The first of two narratives recollects Naipaul's early
        years in Trinidad, his experiences as a freelance journalist
        in London, his quest in Venezuela to gather material for his
        stories, and more predominantly the tragic story of his father.
        Naipaul's impressions of his visit to the Ivory Coast are con-
        tained in the second narrative.

D459.   Gray, Paul. "Journeys." Time 124 (October 8, 1984): 57-
        58.
        Naipaul "restores to his non-fiction the considerable sym-
        pathy and understanding" for his characters, away from the
        invective of his previous book, Among the Believers. The
        first account discusses his early reminiscences as a budding
        writer, and the factors which influenced him to write this
        narrative. The other deals with his visit to the Ivory Coast
        where amidst the squalor, Naipaul unearths a well-established
        society.

D460.   Didion, Joan. "Discovery." New York Review of Books 31
        (October 11, 1984): 10, 12.
        Notes that both narratives in this book attempt, by differ-
        ent methods, to introduce the reader to the process of writ-
        ing. "Prologue to an Autobiography" points to the exact mo-
        ment when the impulse to write engulfs Naipaul. Traces the
        nine-year span between 1972 and 1981 during which he post-
        pones the work, and subsequently visits his mentor in Vene-
        zuela. "The Crocodiles of Yamoussoukro" Didion regards as
        "less off-hand but still general." Talks of his desire to visit
        any former French West African country. Focuses on Naipaul's
        advice to the literary traveller "to settle down for a finite
        period on unfamiliar ground and know that one must find the
        narrative." Reflects on Graham Greene's parallel experiences
        in writing Getting to Know the General, such as Naipaul por-
        trays in Finding the Centre.

D461. Snider, Norman. "A Writer Shows and Tells." Maclean's 97 (October 15, 1984): 69.

D462. Niven, Alastair. "Finding the Centre: Two Narratives." British Book News (November 1984): 699.
Offers a very incisive view of both author and book. Questions Naipaul's accuracy and the impartiality of his reportage; characterizes him as "the most impersonal and yet egocentric of writers." The first of two pieces traces the formative years of his literary career. The second essay, Niven believes, reinforces many of Naipaul's prejudices, false premises of racial superiority, and the well established view of his Third World insensitivity. Suggests that Naipaul's attempt to color the text with French words weakens the book, and presents an illusion of his perception and fastidiousness.

D463. Schoen, E. "Finding the Centre: Two Narratives." Mademoiselle 90 (November 1984): 86.

D464. Parini, Jay. "Thanks For the Memory." Horizon 27 (December 1984): 42.
Parini regards both essays as autobiographical. The first deals with Naipaul's early career. The second explores progress in the Ivory Coast, which Naipaul regards as the most forward West African country. Parini concludes that Western nations have not yet accepted the Third World nations on their own terms.

D465. Sachs, William L. "Finding the Centre: Two Narratives." Christian Century 101 (December 12, 1984): 1177.

D466. Brunnton, Rosanne. "Finding the Centre." Trinidad Guardian (March 3, 1985): 13.
The book consists of two narratives, each complements the other. The first traces the beginnings of Naipaul's writing career. Brunnton detects a different Naipaul; "no evidence of the trauma of the 'Middle Passage.'"

D467. "Finding the Centre: Two Narratives." Queen's Quarterly 92:2 (Summer 1985): 435-436.
The first essay, "Prologue to an Autobiography," has Seepersad Naipaul as the central character about whom V. S. Naipaul writes with warmth and feeling, rarely experienced in his other work. On Naipaul's visit to the Ivory Coast, the critic notes his discovery of a gloomy Africa behind the facade of economic and political progress. Records that Naipaul was unable to resist an expatriate European view that not only was Africa controlled by magicians, but that it could not survive if Europeans left it.

D468.   Dasenbrock, Reed Way. "Finding the Centre." World Lit-
        erature Today 59 (Winter 1985): 150-151.
            Believes Naipaul has reached the end of a phase of his
        writing career and "Prologue to an Autobiography," the first
        essay, "comes to make a new point of departure" from his
        work towards a more personal level. Further suggests that
        it helps to locate his stance, since many critics accuse him
        of aligning himself with the former colonial establishment.
        Dasenbrock thinks that "The Crocodiles of Yamoussoukro,"
        the second essay, reinforces Naipaul's position in a way that
        helps to refute this argument.

THE ENIGMA OF ARRIVAL:
A NOVEL IN FIVE SECTIONS (1987 EA)

D469.   Gray, Paul. "The Gift of a Second Life." Time 129 (March
        2, 1987): 75.
            Outlines the plot of the work which spans ten years. Sug-
        gests that the excitement the book generates emanates from
        tensions developed "when a sensitive grown-up finds himself
        living in a fantasy of his youth." Admires Naipaul's ability
        to give each little incident a sense of history.

D470.   Brien, Alan. "A Person of Refinement." New Statesman
        113 (March 13, 1987): 26-27.
            Considers the book essentially autobiographical, despite
        Naipaul's claim to the contrary. Questions many of his as-
        sumptions, citing the gardener's wife's "great delicate beauty"
        in relation to her standing, as one instance. Does not see
        many roles in the book, "little plot, few characters." Finds
        it repetitious, yet "exciting, informing and satisfying." Re-
        gards Naipaul's own development as a writer to be the most
        significant aspect of the book.

D471.   King, Francis. "The Clumsiness of a Great Writer." Spec-
        tator 258 (March 14, 1987): 37-38.
            Does not regard this book as essentially a work of fiction.
        He identifies Naipaul as the narrator throughout, and calls
        "The Journey" the least satisfactory section of the book.
        Focuses on Naipaul's detachment from the small community in
        Wiltshire, and further underlines this trait by his handling of
        the response to his female acquaintance from Earl's Court who
        writes to Naipaul. King feels "there is always something
        shocking in the self-protectiveness of writers." Credits the
        mastery of his style, but thinks the book is based on "scraps
        of information already given to the reader."

D472.   Koenig, R. "The Enigma of Arrival." New Yorker 20
        (March 16, 1987): 80.

D 473. Kermode, Frank. "In the Garden of the Oppressor." New York Times Book Review 92 (March 22, 1987): 11-12.
Regards the simplicity and lack of experiment in Naipaul's prose as ingredients which would preclude him from being called an "extraordinary writer." However, concludes at the end of the review that The Enigma of Arrival is not simple reading. Divides the book into three segments, and views it purely as addressing Naipaul's experience both as resident and writer in Wiltshire. Expresses surprise at Naipaul's attraction to it, which he treats with some detachment. Links Naipaul's affection for Wiltshire to the English sense of the place such as Thomas Hardy, E. M. Forster, and John Constable evoked here. Cautions that the consciousness of his own posture as a writer should not be interpreted as egotism.

D 474. Bayley, John. "Country Life; The Enigma of Arrival." New York Review of Books 34 (April 9, 1987): 3-4.
Draws a parallel between Naipaul's choice of the English countryside and Rosetta's fantasy in W. H. Auden's poem, "The Art of Anxiety." Admires Naipaul's technique in the book, set in the rural Wiltshire valley, of combining "the sense of innocence and wonder" with such clarity and intuition. Notes that out of it also evolves a vivid reflection of Naipaul's own makeup, as he focuses his attention on the lord of the manor. Bayley also touches on the issue of sex in Naipaul's work, suggesting "a rest from sex seems especially agreeable in the context of life and letters."

D 474A. Walcott, Derek. "The Garden Path." New Republic (April 13, 1987): 27-31.

D 475. Gussow, Mel. "The Enigma of V. S. Naipaul's Search for Himself in Writing." New York Times 136 (April 25, 1987): 16.
This review is centered on a conversation between Naipaul and Gussow. Gussow notes the second book to be written by Naipaul with an English setting, he calls a novel. Here Naipaul reflects on the reasons for calling The Enigma of Arrival a novel, even though it contains autobiographical elements. Naipaul, he says, defines it as his journey, "the writer's journey," dealing essentially with his writing. In the discussion, Naipaul also explains the problems in setting up the structure of the book, which he calls "the fictional scaffolding."

D 476. James, G. "The Enigma of Arrival." Maclean's 100 (May 18, 1987): 55.

D 477. Kemp, Peter. "Severed from Rootlessness." Times Literary Supplement 4401 (August 7, 1987): 838-839.
Suggests that Naipaul's urge to write has been an attempt to allay his own fear of "extinction." Explores the trends,

and identifies themes of location, sexuality, and post-colonial societies--all of which pervade his work. Thinks the book unclear about the landlord's "long retreat," and whose own physical condition underlines "the surprisingly high incidence of nervous illness" in rural parts of Wiltshire. Kemp sees travel as a vehicle to discover one's self as paradoxical in Naipaul's work, where everything is limited to the ambit of his own vision.

D478. Sontag, Susan. "Letter: V. S. Naipaul." Times Literary Supplement 4404 (August 28, 1987): 925.

A very forceful response on Naipaul's behalf to Peter Kemp's review of the book. She concedes there are some shortcomings by Naipaul in the treatment of marriage, the fate of former colonial countries, casual sex, and personal distress in his writings. There is repetition too, but such, Sontag maintains, is the mark of a "writer with a voice." Admits, however, that Kemp's criticisms of Naipaul could be summarized as the work of a "great writer with a tragic sense of the human condition and of contemporary history." She also believes that the book is judged as literature and by nonexistent standards for a writer at Naipaul's level.

D479. Kaseram, Romeo. "Fleeing from Decay into Desolation." Sunday Guardian [Trinidad] (September 13, 1987): 20.

Describes de Chirico's painting from which Naipaul's book derives its name as akin to "the uprooted experience." Kaseram vividly analyzes Naipaul's drift from the Caribbean "to escape the strangulating, decaying Caribbean past." He explores this theme of decay throughout Naipaul's work as Naipaul expresses it through the hyacinths and ivy bushes in A Bend in the River. Concludes that Naipaul has reached a plateau in his literary career.

APPENDIXES

1. LIST OF SOURCES CONSULTED

Abstracts of English Studies (Includes Commonwealth Literature
    since 1969).
American Book Publishing Record, 1960- .
Annual Bibliography of English Language and Literature, 1964- .

Bibliography of English Language and Literature.
Book Review Digest, 1955- .
Book Review Index, 1965- .
Books in Print, 1970- .
British Books in Print, 1971- .
British Humanities Index, 1962- .

Canadian Newspaper Index, 1977- .
Canadian Periodical Index, 1938- .
Canadiana, 1950- .
Carindex, 1977- .
Combined Retrospective Index to Book Reviews in Humanities Journals,
    1802-1977.
Commonwealth Caribbean National Bibliographies, 1975- .
Contemporary Literary Criticism, 1973/74- .
Current Book Review Citations, 1976- .

Dissertations Abstracts International, 1960- .
Dissertations in English and American Literature, supplement, 1969-
    1974.

English Studies in Canada.
Essay and General Literature Index, 1960- .

Hispanic American Periodicals Index, 1970- .
Humanities Index, 1974- .

Index to Bim, 1942-1973.
Index to Book Reviews in the Humanities, 1960- .
Index to Theses accepted for Higher Degrees in the Universities of
    Great Britain and Ireland, 1960- .
Index Translationum, 1955- .
International Bibliography of the Social Sciences, 1957/58- .

International Books in Print Cumulative Paperback Index, 1939-1957.
International Fiction Review.

Journal of Commonwealth Literature, 1965- (Annual Bibliography
   Section).

Library Journal Book Review, 1967- .

MLA International Bibliography (Trinidad & Tobago Literature section
   since 1981)- .

New York Times Index, 1955- .

Paperbound Books in Print, 1957- .

Readers Guide to Periodical Literature (Book Review Section started
   No. 36, 1976)- .

Short Story Index, 1950- .
Social Science and Humanities Index, 1965-1974.
Social Science Citation Index, 1969- .
Social Science Index, 1974- .
Studies in the Novel, 1969- .

Times Index, 1950- .
Times Literary Supplement Index, 1940-1980.

West Indian Social Science Index, 1963-1972.
World Literature Written in English, 1971- .

Year's Work in English Studies, 1960- .

2. UNIVERSITIES HOLDING COMMONWEALTH LITERATURE AND OFFERING COMMONWEALTH LITERATURE COURSES, AND LIBRARIES WITH COMMONWEALTH LITERATURE COLLECTIONS IN THE UNITED STATES, CANADA, EUROPE, AND THE WEST INDIES

(* Caribbean Content Courses and Collections)
(++ Caribbean Collections)

UNITED STATES

California

Los Angeles County Library
Afro-American Resource Center
240 West Compton B'lvd
Compton, CA 90222

University of California (UCLA)
Latin American Center
Los Angeles, CA 90024

University of California
Black Studies Unit
Santa Barbara, CA 93106

Connecticut

Yale University
New Haven, CT 06520

Florida

Florida International University
Miami, FL 33199

Historical Association of South
   Florida

Charlton W. Tebeau Library
101 Flagler Street
Miami, FL 33130

University of Florida
Latin American Collection
Miami, FL 32611

Kansas

Kansas State University
Farrell Library
Manhattan, KS 66506

Massachusetts

Pan-American University of New
   England
Shattuck Memorial Library
1051 Beacon Street
Brookline, MA 02146

University of Massachusetts/
   Amherst
Amherst, MA 01003

Wellesley College
Wellesley, MA 02181

New York

City University of New York
535 East 80th Street
New York, NY 10021

Cornell University
Africana Studies and Research
  Center Library
310 Triphammer Road
Ithaca, NY 14850

English-Speaking Union of the
  United States
16 East 69th Street
New York, NY 10021

Columbia University
Institute of Latin American and
  Iberian Studies
Morningside Heights
New York, NY 10027

New York Public Library
Schomburg Center for Research
  in Black Culture
515 Lenox Avenue
New York, NY 10037

New York University
70 Washington Square South
New York, NY 10012

Research Institute for the Study
  of Man Library
162 East 78th Street
New York, NY   10021

North Carolina

Duke University
Durham, NC 27706

Ohio

Ohio State University
616 Stinchcomb 7
Columbus, OH 43206

Pennsylvania

Pennsylvania State University
University Park, PA 16802

Temple University
Charles L. Blockson Afro-American
  Historical Collection
13th and Berks Streets
Philadelphia, PA 19122

University of Pittsburgh Libraries
171 Hillman Library
Dept. of Black Studies
Pittsburgh, PA 15260

Puerto Rico

Caribbean Center for Advanced
  Studies Library
Minillas Station
Box 41246
Santurce, Puerto Rico 00940

Caribbean Regional Library
University of Puerto Rico
Box 21927
San Juan, Puerto Rico 00931

University of Puerto Rico
General Library
Zenobia Y. Juan Ramon Jiminez
  Collection
Box C
San Juan, Puerto Rico 00931

Texas

University of Texas
Benson Latin American Collection
Austin, TX 78704

U.S. Virgin Islands

Caribbean Research Institute
College of the Virgin Islands
Charlotte Amalie

Dept. of Conservation and Cultural Affairs
Bureau of Libraries and Museums
Box 390
St. Thomas, Virgin Islands 00850

Washington

Howard University
Moorland-Spingarn Research
Center
500 Howard Place, NW
Washington, DC 20059

Johns Hopkins University
Libraries
Baltimore, MD 21218

Library of Congress
Hispanic Division
Thomas Jefferson Building
#239 E
Washington, DC 20540

Organization of American States
19th and Constitution Avenue
NW
Washington, DC 20006-4499

CANADA

Alberta

University of Alberta
Edmonton, Alberta T6G 2E5

University of Calgary*
2500 University Drive NW
Calgary, Alta. T2N 1N4

British Columbia

University of British Columbia*
2075 Wesbrook Mall
Vancouver, B.C., V6T 1W5

Simon Fraser University
Burnaby, B.C., V5A 1S6

University of Victoria
P.O. Box 1700
Victoria, B.C., V8W 2Y2

Manitoba

University of Manitoba
Winnipeg, Man., R3T 2N2

University of Winnipeg*
515 Portage Avenue
Winnipeg, Man., R3B 2E9

New Brunswick

Mount Allison University*
Sackville, N.B., E0A 3C0

University of New Brunswick*
P.O. Box 5050
St. John, N.B., E2L 4L5

Newfoundland

Memorial University of Newfoundland
P.O. Box 4200
St. John's, Nfld., A1C 5S7

Nova Scotia

Acadia University*
Wolfville, N.S. B0P 1XQ

University College of Cape
Breton
P.O. Box 5300
Sydney, Cape Breton, B1P 6L2

Dalhousie University
Halifax, N.S. B3H 3J5

Ontario

Carleton University*
Ottawa, Ont. K1S 5B6

Guelph University*
Guelph, Ont. N1G 2W1

McMaster University*
Hamilton, Ont. L8S 4L8

Queen's University*
Kingston, Ont. K7L 3N6

University of Waterloo*
Waterloo, Ont. N2L 3G1

Wilfrid Laurier University
Waterloo, Ont. N2L 3C5

York University*
4700 Keele Street
Downsview, Ont. M3J 1P3

Quebec

Bishop's University*
Lennoxville, Que. J1M 1Z7

Concordia University*
1455 de Maisonneuve Boulevard
West
Montreal, Que. H4B 1R6

McGill University
845 Sherbrooke Street
West Montreal, Que. H3A 2T5

Université du Québec à Trois-
Rivières
Trois-Rivières, Que. G9A 5H7

Saskatchewan

University of Saskatchewan
Saskatoon, Sask. S7N 0W0

UNITED KINGDOM

ENGLAND

Birmingham

University of Birmingham
P.O. Box 363
Edgbaston,
Birmingham B15 2TT

Boston Spa

British Library Lending Divi-
sion++
Boston Spa, Wetherby, West
Yorkshire LS 23 7BQ

Brighton

University of Sussex*
Sussex House
Falmer,
Brighton, Sussex BN1 9RH

Cambridge

University of Cambridge
Cambridge CB2 1TN

Canterbury

University of Kent at Canterbury*
Canterbury, Kent CT 2 7NZ

Colchester

University of Essex*
Wivenhoe Park
Colchester, Essex CO4 3SQ

Coventry

University of Warwick*
Gibbet Hill Road
Coventry CV4 7AL

Exeter

University of Exeter
The Queen's Drive
Exeter EX4 4QJ

Hull

University of Hull*
Kingston-upon-Hull HU6 7RX

Leeds

University of Leeds++
Leeds, Yorkshire LS2 9JT

Liverpool

University of Liverpool
P.O. Box 147
Liverpool L69 3BX

London

Arts Council Poetry Library
105 Piccadilly
London W1V 0AU

Australian Reference Library
Australian High Commission
Australia House
The Strand
London WC2B 4LA

British Library Reference Division
Great Russell Street
London WC1B 3DC

Canadian High Commission
    Library

Canada House
Trafalgar Square
London SW1Y 5BJ

Library & Resource Centre++
Commonwealth Institute
Kensington High Street
London W8 6NQ

India House Library
High Commission of India
Aldwych
London WC2B 4NA

India Office Library & Records
197 Blackfriars Road
London SE1 8NG

Institute of Race Relations Li-
    brary++
247 Pentonville Road
London N1

Lambeth Public Library++
Bibliographic Services
Carnegie Library
Herne Hill Road
London SE24

London Library
14 St. James's Square
London SW1Y 4LG

New Zealand High Commission
80, Haymarket
London SW1Y 4TO

Polytechnic of North London*
Holloway Road
London N7 8DB

Royal Commonwealth Society
18 Northumberland Avenue
London WC2N 5BJ

School of Oriental & African
    Studies
University of London
Malet Street
London WC1E 7HP

University College Library++
University of London
Gower Street
London WC1E 6BT

University of London Library
Senate House
Malet Street
London WC1E 7HU

West India Committee Library++
18 Grosvenor Street
London W1X 0HP

Westminster City Libraries++
Marylebone Road
London NW1 5PS

Manchester

Victoria University of Man-
chester
Oxford Road
Manchester M13 9PL

Newcastle upon Tyne

University of Newcastle-upon-
Tyne*
Queen Victoria Road
Newcastle upon Tyne NE1 7RI

Norwich

University of East Anglia
Norwich NR4 7TJ

Oxford

Bodleian Library++
University of Oxford
Wellington Square
Oxford OX1 2JD

Institute of Commonwealth
Studies++
University of Oxford

21 St. Giles
Oxford OX1 3LA

Sheffield

University of Sheffield*
Western Bank
Sheffield S10 2TN

SCOTLAND

Aberdeen

University of Aberdeen
Aberdeen AB9 1FX

Edinburgh

University of Edinburgh*
Old College
South Bridge
Edinburgh EH8 9YL

National Library of Scotland++
George IV Bridge
Edinburgh EH1 1EW

Stirling

University of Stirling*
Stirling FK9 4LA

WALES

Aberystwyth

National Library of Wales
Aberystwyth, Dyfed SY23 3BU

CONTINENTAL EUROPE

BELGIUM

Brussels (Bruxelles)

Bibliothèque Africaine*
7, Place Royale
B-1000 Brussels

Vrije Universiteit Brussel
Pleinlaan 2
ß-1050 Brussels

Liège

Université de l'état à Liège
7, Place du 20-Août
B-4000 Liège

DENMARK

Åarhus

Åarhus Universitet
NDR Ringgade
DK-8000 Åarhus C

Copenhagen (København)

Kongelige Bibliotek
Christians Brygge 8
DK-1219 Copenhagen

Odense

Biblioteket
Odense Universitet
Campusvej 55
DK-5230 Odense M

FRANCE

Besançon

Bibliothèque de l'Université
32, rue Megevand
F-25041 Besançon

Caen

Bibliothèque Universitaire
Esplanade de la Paix
F-14032 Caen

Dijon

Bibliothèque de la section d'an-
glais++
Université de Dijon
F-21000 Dijon

Lyons

Bibliothèque Interuniversitaire
43, Blvd. du 11 Novembre 1918
F-69622 Villeurbanne

Montpellier

Bibliothèque Interuniversitaire*
4, rue de l'Ecole Mage
F-34000 Montpellier

Paris

Bibliothèque Nationale
58, rue Richelieu
F-75084 Paris

British Council Library
9, rue de Constantine
F-75007 Paris

Toulouse

Bibliothèque Interuniversi-
    taire++
11, rue des Puits-Creuses
F-31070 Toulouse

GERMAN FEDERAL REPUBLIC

Bremen

Universität Bremen++
Bibliotheksstrasse 33
D-2800 Bremen

Cologne (Köln)

Universitäts- und Stadtbiblio-
    thek
Universitätsstrasse 33
D-5000 Cologne 41

Frankfurt on Main

Stadt- und Universitätsbiblio-
    thek++
Landstrasse 134-138
D-6000 Frankfurt a.M., Bocken-
    heimer

Giessen

Bibliothek der Justus Liebig-
    Universität Giessen
Otto-Behaghel-strasse 8
D-6300 Giessen

Göttingen

Niedersächsische Staats- und
    Universitätsbibliothek
Prinzenstrasse 1
Postfach 2932
D-2400 Göttingen

Hamburg

Universität Hamburg
Edmund-Siemers-Allee 1
D-2000 Hamburg 13

Mainz

Universitätsbibliothek
Saarstrasse 21
Postfach 4020
D-6500 Mainz

Munich (München)

Bayerische Staatsbibliothek
Ludwigstrasse 16
Postfach 34
D-8000 Munich

Münster

Universitätsbibliothek
Krummer Timpen 3-5
D-4400 Münster

Tübingen

Universitätsbibliothek
Wilhelmstrasse 32
D-7400 Tübingen

Wuppertal

Wuppertal Gesamthochschule
Gauss-Strasse 20
D-5600 Wuppertal 1

ITALY

Venice (Venezia)

Seminario d'Inglese

Università
Ca Foscari,
Venezia

Rådhusgatan 25-27
S-83180 Östersund

THE NETHERLANDS

SWITZERLAND

Utrecht

Centrum voor Caribische Studie*
Instituut voor Culturelle Antro-
pologie
Rijksuniversiteit te Utrecht
Heidelberglaan 2
POB 80.108
ND-3584 CS Utrecht

Fribourg

Université de Fribourg*
CH-1700 Fribourg

Winterthur

Staatbibliothek
Museumstrasse 52
CH-8401 Winterthur

POLAND

Warsaw (Warszowa)

Biblioteka Narodowa++
Hankiewicza 1
00-973 Warsaw

SPAIN

Zurich

Universität Zürich
Ramistrasse 71
CH-8006 Zürich
and: Winterthurstrasse 190
CH-8057 Zürich

Zentralbibliothek Zürich
Zahringerplatz 6
CH-8035 Zürich

Barcelona

Departamento de Inglés*
Facultad de Filología
Universidad de Barcelona
Plaza Universidad
Barcelona 08077

WEST INDIES

BARBADOS

SWEDEN

The University of The West
Indies*
Cave Hill Campus
Barbados

Östersund

Jämtlands läns bibliotek

Barbados Public Library++
Bridgetown
Barbados

GUYANA

University of Guyana*
Georgetown
Guyana

JAMAICA

The University of The West
    Indies*
Mona Campus
Kingston 7, Jamaica

West India Reference Library++
Institute of Jamaica
Kingston, Jamaica

TRINIDAD AND TOBAGO

The University of The West
    Indies*
St. Augustine Campus
Trinidad

Carnegie Free Library++
Harris Promenade
San Fernando, Trinidad

West India Reference Collec-
    tion++
Central Library of Trinidad &
    Tobago
81 Belmont Circular Road
Belmont, Trinidad

West Indian Library Division++
Trinidad Public Library
10 Belmont Circular Road
Port of Spain, Trinidad

3. V. S. NAIPAUL'S AWARDS AND PRIZES

1958: John Llewelyn Rhys Memorial Prize for Mystic Masseur (Vanguard).

John Llewelyn Rhys, a young Englishman killed on active service with the Royal Air Force in 1940, was awarded the Hawthornden Prize posthumously in 1942 for his book of short stories England Is My Village. As a fitting memorial to him, his widow, Jane Oliver, established this prize for a "memorable work" by a writer who is under thirty-five at the time of the book's publication and a citizen of any British Commonwealth territory. Entries must be received by the end of the year in which the titles are published. The prize is worth £500. The John Llewelyn Rhys Memorial Trust is now officially administered through the Woolwich Equitable Building Society.

1961: Somerset Maugham Awards for Miguel Street (Vanguard).

The Society of Authors, 84 Drayton Gardens, London SW10, England, administers these awards which were founded in 1946 by the late Somerset Maugham in order to encourage young writers to travel abroad. They are given to a promising author of a published work in the fields of poetry, criticism, biography, history, philosophy, belles-lettres, and travel. Dramatic works are not eligible. Candidates for the awards must be British subjects ordinarily residing in the United Kingdom and under the age of thirty-five. Works must be submitted to the Society of Authors by December 31 each year; awards are announced the following March. The books submitted may have been published in any previous year. The winner must use the prize of approximately £3,000/4,000 for traveling abroad in order to enrich his/her writing and experience.

1964: Hawthornden Prize for Mr. Stone and the Knights Companion (Deutsch).

The Hawthornden Prize, the oldest of the famous British literary prizes, was founded in 1919 by Miss Alice Warrender. It is now administered by the Hawthornden Trust, Lasswade, Midlothian, Scotland. It was formerly administered by the Society of Authors and is valued at £1,000. The award is presented annually to an English writer under forty-one years old for the best work of imaginative literature. It was last awarded in 1983. It is especially designed to encourage young authors, and the word "imaginative" is given a broad interpretation. Books do not have to be submitted for the prize; it is awarded without competition. A panel of judges chooses the winner.

1968: W. H. Smith & Son Literary Award for The Mimic Men (Macmillan).
The Annual Literary Award was started in 1959 to encourage and bring international esteem to authors in the British Commonwealth. It is given to an author whose book, written in English and published in the United Kingdom, makes the most significant contribution to literature published during the year under review. It is based on the decision of a three-judge panel. The value of this Award was worth £1,000 in 1959, and has been increased in value twice since 1968. In 1988 it was worth £10,000. There is no age limit and it covers a wide literary field.

1971: Booker Prize for Fiction for In a Free State (Deutsch).
Booker provides the funding for this award which has been administered by Book Trust since 1971. It was originally set up in 1968. This annual prize for fiction is awarded to the best novel published between January 1 and November 30 of the year in which the award is presented. A panel of judges in England makes the final selection. The prize is open to novels written in English by citizens of the Commonwealth. From its initial value of £5,000, the prize is now worth £15,000 and is Britain's best known literary award. Since 1981 the winner has enjoyed enormous press and television coverage.

1975: D.Litt. University of the West Indies, St. Augustine Campus.

1980: The Bennett Award. Sponsored by The Hudson Review.

1983: The Jerusalem Prize.
The Jerusalem International Book Fair, 22 Jaffa Street, Jerusalem 91000, Israel. This prize was first introduced by the Municipality of Jerusalem as part of the inauguration of the Jerusalem International Book Fair in 1963. It is awarded biennially at the opening of the Fair during the last week in April. Its purpose is to recognize the author who has made an outstanding contribution to world understanding and appreciation of freedom for the individual. The prize is worth $2,000 and is awarded with a citation.

1986: The T. S. Eliot Award. Sponsored by The Ingersoll Foundation.

4. A NOTE BY LAURENCE HALLEWELL ON COLLECTIONS OF COMMONWEALTH LITERATURE IN LIBRARIES OF THE CONTINENTAL UNITED STATES

There is understandably less interest in and even less awareness of the Commonwealth of Nations in the United States than in member countries such as Canada, the United Kingdom or the West Indies.
The only major American library to have pursued a vigorous policy of
acquiring material on the Commonwealth--Duke University Library at Durham, NC--down-graded its interest some years back. The bibliography
of the Caribbean members of the Commonwealth remains, however, of
potential concern to a wide range of library interests: English literature, Latin American and Caribbean area studies, Black studies,
Third World studies, Comparative literature studies.... But mostly
only potentially: anglophone West Indian literature tends very much
to "fall between the cracks" as no one's especial responsibility.

While West Indian writers are consciously included in English
literature selection at a few institutions such as Rutgers University
(New Brunswick, NJ) or the library of the English-speaking Union,
this seems a quite atypical attitude. By and large, English literature
selectors are apt to adopt, almost instinctively, a narrow Eurocentric
definition of what constitutes "English." Although one would have
thought that by now, in Naipaul's case, his long-established Wiltshire
residence would have given him as rightful an entry into the British
canon as that afforded Conrad for having settled in Stanford-le-Hope.

For most Black Studies collections, interest in the African
diaspora outside the United States is minimal for the 150 years since
Emancipation, especially for such élitist cultural manifestations as
belles-lettres. An outstanding exception is the Moorland-Springram
Research Center of Howard University in Washington, DC. There is
also Washington Public Library's Martin Luther King Memorial Library
of authors of African descent, worldwide, although that of course
would exclude West Indians of non-African descent, such as Naipaul
himself.

Most Latin American bibliographers accept the current State
Department definition of "Latin America" as including all countries
below the Rio Grande, but they too tend to ignore literature in

English, as they are usually beholden in their language and literature selection to university departments of Spanish and Portuguese. A notable exception here is the library of the University of Florida, Gainesville, whose Caribbean collection dates back to 1929. Although the original interest in this case too was almost wholly confined to the Latin Caribbean, systematic coverage was extended to the then British and Dutch territories at the beginning of the 1950s. This was done as Florida's obligation under the Farmington Plan, a federally supported program of cooperative acquisition. The Plan is now defunct, but Florida's enhanced acquisition policies have survived its demise. Several other universities in the state have strong Caribbean interests, but all but one seem to restrict themselves to the Hispanic countries. The exception is the William L. Bryant West Indies Collection at the University of Central Florida.

Yale University, which has long been strong in both Black studies and Latin American studies, stepped up its library coverage of the Caribbean in 1981. Since then its annual expenditure on the literature of the English- and Dutch-speaking countries of the region has been running at about $1,500.

Otherwise, when one investigates libraries with a reputation for strength in West Indian literature, one tends to find either that their program was effectively ended by the financial retrenchments of the 1970s, or that the actual budget is a merely nominal $500 per annum or so. One library currently spending three times as much asked not to be mentioned. It had only recently attained this level, and could not guarantee its continuance. The project derived from the Latin American bibliographer's personal interest, and she had so far failed to obtain more than lukewarm support from faculty.

Her opposite number at Cornell University expressed surprise when congratulated on the strength of the libray's holdings on the subject, explaining that there was no specific commitment or interest in the field: what was there had come as an incidental spin-off of his institution's pursuit of library adequacy in all areas of the humanities. The same could be said of a number of other major collections, including of course those of the Library of Congress and the New York Public Library.

It is easy nowadays to assess library holdings by looking up individual titles on such computerized union catalogs as OCLC (Online Computerized Library Catalog, of Dublin, OH) or RLIN (the Research Libraries' Information Network). The latter was consulted to discover the extent of Naipaul holdings among its members, which include most, although unfortunately not all, the country's major research libraries. The original edition of The Mystic Masseur seems to have been acquired by only six of these 600 or so libraries, that of Suffrage of Elvira by only four, and that of Miguel Street by none. Interest naturally increased as Naipaul became an established writer. RLIN libraries now own a total of 69 copies of Among the

Believers, 59 of The Enigma of Arrival, 54 of India, a Wounded Civilization, 52 of A House for Mr. Biswas, 44 of Guerrillas, 39 of The Loss of El Dorado, and 36 of The Return of Eva Perón, to mention only the most widely held titles. There would seem to be a distinct preference for the nonfictional works, implying that even Naipaul is bought more on a subject basis than as literature. This is well attested by the limited purchases of A Bend in the River. Although this novel appeared when Naipaul's reputation was already assured--four years after the New York Times Book Review acclaimed Guerrillas as "probably the best novel of 1975"--RLIN libraries report only seven copies between them. Apart from the Library of Congress and the New York Public Library the only other RLIN members consistently appearing as owners of all items mentioned above were Cornell, North Western, Stanford, and Yale university libraries.

Nor did there appear to be extensive holdings of criticism. New York Public was the only RLIN library to report a copy of Thieme's 1985 V. S. Naipaul, "The Mimic Men", and even Morris's Paradoxes of Order from an American university press was held by a mere 24 libraries.

Quite an unpleasant surprise was the high proportion of paperback editions among the copies reported. RLIN libraries possess altogether eight copies of three Naipaul titles in translation: The Mystic Masseur in German and Spanish, and A House for Mr. Biswas, and The Loss of El Dorado in Spanish.

NAME INDEX

TITLE INDEX